KU-280-503

The SALES-DRIVEN Company

Transforming Your Company - From the Mail Room to the Board Room - Into a Marketing Machine

Jack L. Matthews

IRWIN
Professional Publishing®
Burr Ridge, Illinois
New York, New York

© 1995, Jack L. Matthews

Originally published as *Sales Driven* ©1993

ALL RIGHTS RESERVED. No part of this publication may be reproduced, stored in a retrieval system, or transmitted, in any form or by any means, electronic, mechanical, photocopying, recording, or otherwise, without the prior written permission of the publisher and the author.

This publication is designed to provide accurate and authoritative information in regard to the subject matter covered. It is sold with the understanding that the author and the publisher are not engaged in rendering legal, accounting, or other professional service.

ISBN 1-55738-894-6

Printed in the United States of America

BB

1 2 3 4 5 6 7 8 9 0

This book is dedicated to my best friend . . .
Charlotte Matthews
. . . whom I love, like and respect.

Table of Contents

Table of Contents

Foreword

Of all the truths in marketing, there is only one universal: "Nothing really happens in this world unless a *sale* is made."

To survive, let alone thrive, in most businesses today, companies have to learn how to become truly "sales driven." More than ever, companies need to get *everyone* focused on the customer . . . understanding the customer's needs, how buying decisions are made, and what it takes to open as well as close the ultimate sale.

Most business professionals dream about achieving consistent, double-digit growth in annual earnings. They go on to imagine how easy it would be if only their sales force could be a stronger *selling force*. They may even fantasize what life could be like with double, triple, quadruple the number of sales representatives . . . or how wonderful it could be if more sales opportunities were created and more closings were achieved.

These, I submit, need not be business fantasies. Jack Matthews opens a very important door for us in *Sales Driven*. The book is a masterful blueprint for turning everyone—from the drawing board to the boardroom—into your sales force. It shows us precisely how every employee can contribute directly to sales . . . in effect, how to increase the sales power of a company without increasing the cost of sales.

You will find his simple insights eminently practical and well tested. This book will take you right through your customers' doors, into their heads, and all the way to their signing on the dotted line. Most importantly, it will give you the tools as well as the confidence to re-orient your whole business toward selling—above all else.

Nothing else can possibly matter in business unless the sale is made. *Sales Driven* ensures we never forget that.

Jeffrey K. McElnea
President
Einson Freeman, Inc.

Preface

Whether you are

◆ a white collar or a blue collar worker

◆ an entry level employee or the CEO

◆ selling to individuals or presenting to groups

◆ with a company that markets a product or a service

this book was written for you.

Much is being made of the world having evolved from a production to a marketing or sales-driven economy. The world is quickly becoming buyer-, rather than seller-, oriented.

However, not enough notice has been taken of the effect of that metamorphosis on day-to-day business operations and on the achievement of long-term business growth. The fact is, businesses that keep existing customers satisfied and win new customers every day are doing so because they focus their entire effort on producing and selling what their customers want, instead of merely pushing existing products through slick ads and promotions.

These top-performing companies are truly sales driven. They know that to be sales driven is no longer just a matter of educating and motivating the sales force or the marketing department. The entire company, from the copy room to the board room, must be focused on designing, producing and delivering products that customers want. These companies believe that customers' satisfaction begins in R&D, moves into production and manufacturing and carries over into the customer service function—just as much as they believe that their destiny lies in closing the next sale.

This involvement of the whole company in the sales effort has spawned a fiercely competitive climate. As a result, there is no such thing as a "nice secure business" anymore. There is no longer any room for a complacent "rest on our laurels" type of mentality. Every business today is a grow-or-die operation in quest of increasing profitability. This new, total, corporate commitment to sales performance is no longer just desirable—it is essential for survival.

Responsibility for your company's future can no longer be limited to management or the sales inner circle. Rather, it will depend on the sum contributions of every employee. You will benefit from opportunities to the extent of your ability to enlist every employee's commitment to increasing sales.

Realizing the readers of this book will range from a one-person sales force pitching by phone to a multi-national presentation team soliticing new business on a global basis, I have attempted to provide an all-inclusive, detailed approach that can be tailored to suit the needs of selling your particular product or service. Rather than guessing how many nuggets you can use, I have given you the mother lode.

Mine is a unique perspective because it offers revealing insights and examples from the toughest selling league of all—advertising agencies. Since ad agencies are paid to sell better than anyone else, they can also offer an untapped source of exceptionally imaginative approaches to upgrade the selling function into a corporate-wide commitment. I invite you to take advantage of a lifetime of lessons learned in the only industry that is in the business of selling. It is my utmost belief that this book is sure to provide you and your company with a competitive edge as you strive to be sales driven—whatever your business may be.

Section I

The Sales Driven Company: From the Drawing Board to the Board Room

The hardest part of turning your company into a selling machine isn't necessarily buying the idea yourself, or even selling others on this common sense approach to increasing sales revenue. The hardest part of any job is getting started. These first five chapters provide the foundation and springboard for getting underway.

1. Sales with an Attitude: Commitment and Dedication to the Program

2. Where to Begin a Successful Selling Program

3. Just These Ground Rules Are Enough

4. The Smarts for Picking Prospects

5. What Customers Now Expect—But Don't Tell You

Sales with an Attitude: Commitment and Dedication to the Program

◆ Perspective ◆ Management Dedication
◆ Impact of Production Manager ◆ Barriers to Sales
◆ Constructive Dissatisfaction ◆ Location
◆ Selection Rigged? ◆ How to Become No. One

Perspective

Success begins with commitment: dedication to an aggressive selling plan, consistently applied, not a sporadic quick-fix when an account is lost but an on-going activity accorded as much importance as customer service.

This amounts to your taking any initiative that will contribute to improving the corporate (and your) future. For openers, instead of relying on news of loose accounts, you need to make things happen. Decide on what customers you *want* to work with—based on desirability. For the record, a company's "desirability" isn't established by a gut feeling. Rather, it's the result of your calculating whether they would be satisfactorily profitable, offer appealing growth potential—plus be a compatible and fulfilling experience. Then take whatever action necessary to score. Remember, companies today are a grow-or-die business. If you're not gaining, you're losing.

Turning your company into the selling machine necessary today requires greater staff support for the line activity. You will especially need enthusiastic support from the top management and product development functions. This can only be achieved by their acceptance of how critical their mind-set is to sales results—and their willingness to come through as planned.

Management Dedication

There are two *functional* reasons why a company doesn't score in pitching new accounts: ineptness in selling strategy or offensive conduct. More insidious, though, is the matter of *attitude*, specifically of company principals who are no longer hungry enough. Their negative attitude is reflected in their reduced concern with growth and the minimal support they are willing to expend for this purpose. Their feeling is that they've paid their dues and are now entitled to a less frantic pace. This frame of mind isn't the result of age or burnout. Rather, having arrived, it is due to their loss of desire. Ironically, their personal success can stifle corporate success.

If any of you in top management have lost the drive to be more successful, then get out of the way. As normal attrition takes its toll, the company won't be able to afford to provide you with the comfortable income you've become accustomed to because complacency begets atrophy. And your employees will not tolerate this stagnation for long. They know they are not going to progress any more than the company does. So, sooner rather than later, they will opt for an organization still committed to growth.

Go back to the original appeal of your business: the excitement of winning. Instead of settling for holding your own, *rededicate yourself to the fulfillment of greater accomplishment.*

If you don't stay aggressive on solicitation activity, your competition will take not only your accounts, but also your employees. Due to your inertia, your company will no longer be considered a force to be reckoned with. And when this cavalier attitude becomes evident, the vultures won't circle for too long. Any company principal who no longer enjoys the hunt/kill function had better make room for someone who is turned on by this challenge. Otherwise, his or her last executive act will consist of presiding over its wake.

The Impact of the Production Manager

A successful new business program requires a *total* company commitment. For this to occur, management has to provide the necessary direction and inspiration. Every company has key employees who are responsible for product development/manufacturing. Among the various staff functions, there is one that can have significant influence on sales performance. But this person's capacity is seldom taken advantage of for selling purposes. I am referring to the individual

❝ If you don't stay aggressive ... your competition will take not only your accounts, but also your employees. ❞

in charge of producing your product or developing your service, the production manager. Despite pride of construction or authorship, she or he must realize that your ultimate corporate objective is to *sell, not own*, the result of their efforts. Is your production manager company- or function-oriented? One who considers himself or herself as an integral force in the entire company operation, or a prima donna who feels the selling end is a necessary evil, and anyway, it's not his or her job?

There is now enough evidence to conclude that there is a direct correlation between the production's outlook toward new business activity and the company's rate of scoring. If you have a production manager who is gung-ho in this respect, your company is blessed. Otherwise, you're carrying just a craftsperson—which isn't enough for today's company. If you involve the production manager, she or he will be gung ho.

However, applying his or her technical know-how to the selling function isn't solely the responsibility of the production manager. Constantly consider how to capitalize on the production manager's perspective (this could range from seeking further technical input for use as a sales tool to requesting being accompanied on a sales call to a major prospect).

Barriers to Sales

Who is your most important customer? It is not your biggest or most profitable customer. Your most important customer is your own company. If you lose that one, it is terminal. A company *is* its customers. This was often a fatal lesson to companies who thought their sole responsibility was servicing existing customers. I would often hear them blame their demise on the fact that they did not have time to go after additional business. The truth of the matter was that it just seemed like too much work. Other common excuses to rationalize their lethargy are

◆ "We'd sell more aggressively but don't want to risk antagonizing our customers." Let's put this misconception to rest. As long as customers continue to be satisfied with the amount and quality of attention received, they will be *pleased* with your new business success because it confirms the soundness of their judgment in having selected your company and in continuing to do business with it.

Even so, when you land a major account, some suspicious customer might needle you with, "Does this mean we'll get less service?" If appropriate, you might honestly reply, "Actually, you'll be getting *more* service. Because this new business will enable us to hire additional people who will serve as a source of further help and ideas for you. Also, we can now afford to add more functions and increase our computerization. So this growth will make us of greater value to you."

◆ "Soliciting the accounts of others is unethical." This, too, is a copout—ignoring reality: your account roster probably forms the new business list for your competitors. Therefore, you can expect some attrition for which you will have to compensate. Thus, the ethical question is not a matter of whether you should compete—only *how* you compete. If you sell, on a strictly positive and constructive basis—foregoing any devious behavior—then you will be perceived as ethical and have the respect of your prospects.

◆ "We are just too busy." This doesn't wash either because you establish your new business program and its application in advance. Then you only need to customize the strategy and materials for whomever the prospect. So don't lose out on a great opportunity because you lack the foresight to prepare for a successful future.

Therefore, while both of you should be playing this game—production and sales—the ball starts in your court. More sales, anyone?

In addition to using the ability and experience of other people in the company to support sales efforts, there are additional ways to give you that extra edge when out there hustling new business. So don't coast. Start by playing devil's advocate.

Constructive Dissatisfaction

A single idea is rarely responsible for closing a sale. Sure, you might luck out with an occasional miracle. But realistically, it is the application of *every* conceivable advantage that results in winning. To win bigger—and more consistently—takes an attitude of *constructive dissatisfaction* with your sales strategy and techniques. Then play: "Beat the Devil's Advocate." This can be easily accomplished by applying these two ultimate criteria:

◆ How can it be done better?

◆ What more can be done?

You know the *routine* components of the selling function. So do your competitors. The winners, though, are those who compound the basics by constantly assuming they can do better—and following through.

This includes not only having the tenacity to win—but making it happen by planning for it. Here is a classic example of how this was put into motion, and importantly, how the luxury of sensitivity wasn't allowed to be a deterrent.

An ambitious Minneapolis ad agency set its sights on a major blue-chip account, an advertiser much bigger than their size could justify. But the agency CEO told me, "I want this account so bad, I can taste it." When the account came loose, this David came in armed with a lot more than a sling. Their aim was good enough to get them into the finals. However, their opponent was really a Goliath. And despite our David's valiant efforts, the other was so much bigger, they were just too much to conquer.

So David didn't win. However, their CEO knew they weren't losers either. To his credit, he didn't go into a victorian decline and don sackcloth and ashes. Instead, he made up his mind that he wanted this account more than ever now. To accomplish this, he decided to stay in training for the next time around.

His plan consisted of instituting a monthly series of contacts. It would be a letter, a phone call or lunch. But there always had to be a reason for this, one that would be of value to the prospect.

It took a year for this persistence to pay off. Which is okay if, as is this case, the reward is commensurate with the investment. Out of the blue, our CEO received a phone call from this choice account asking, "No dog and pony show. Do you still want our business?"

The agency CEO told me he thought he'd blown it because in his surprise he blurted out, "But I thought you felt their creative work is so great." And this advertiser contact said, "It is." Our CEO then told me that this time he figured he'd really kissed it off because he followed with, "Then why do you want to leave?" The contact sighed and said, "Because we can no longer live with their arrogance."

There are actually two object lessons here. And both are applicable to any industry product or service.

First, while a customer expects the best performance available, they also *want* the very best relationship. Second, take a page from our CEO's book. I don't know if he thought of his follow-through as another step. He just never let up.

Location

When a person is assigned to a sales territory in other than a major metropolitan area, or in a less than highly desirable location, it is often assumed they are at a disadvantage. Some salespersons seem reconciled to this suspected handicap. I won't commiserate. Acknowledging location as a problem would do them a grave disservice because if there is a lack of achievement, location could then be used as a scapegoat—obscuring the real cause. Thus, they don't need sympathy, only perspective.

It is just this basic: Don't get hung up on not having an impressive address. Usually, all prospects care about is *what* you deliver, not from where.

Selection Rigged?

One of your first concerns in a competitive selling situation is whether the selection process is rigged. You're cynical. And justifiably so. Because too often, there is a hidden agenda. It is easy to develop a sour attitude which translates into less effort and impact in soliciting accounts. If you suspect that a given solicitation is a loaded beauty contest: skip it. Because if you suspect this isn't on the level, it will be reflected in the preparation of your support material and your presentation of it. And no one in a selling situation can afford to settle for optimum impact. It must be maximum.

Yet, there will be instances in which a questionable account is irresistible. It may be due to size, prestige or potential. It usually will be a judgment call. Do you have the stomach for the gamble? Can you justify the odds? Or would you be better off moving on to another prospect with whom you would have more of a fighting chance?

Whatever your decision, do it right—or not at all.

Be careful that you don't second guess yourself out of a desirable account. This lesson was learned the hardest way by an Arizona ad agency when the state instituted a lottery. This agency felt eminently qualified to handle the account but, as Governor Babbit was an Elder in the Church of the Latter Day Saints, they assumed it would be awarded to a Mormon-owned Agency.

They decided to spare themselves this solicitation ritual in which they felt they didn't have a prayer. How perceptive was this analysis of the situation? The lottery account went to a Jewish-owned Agency. So for God's sake—and yours—keep the faith.

66 Instead of cursing the darkness, light a candle.99

Instead of suspecting you are at a disadvantage because there is a possibility of the choice being predestined, shoot for the payoff. *Why couldn't the company with the inside track be yours?* What would it take? If it's too late to create bias in your favor this time, decide on what action to take to set up future prospects. This would be based on the dictates of each individual situation. This proacting will then give *you* the competitive edge. In going after an account, preparing your strategy should begin with becoming the rigger, rather than the riggee.

There isn't some arcane formula for becoming the rigger. Rather, it consists of doing what you have probably forgotten. Namely, select who you want to sell to, and consistently cultivate them. Take whatever action is necessary to score. This is in sharp contrast to operating on the basis of reacting to scuttlebutt regarding supposed opportunities—and being too late. Thus, get out in front and stay there—instead of trying to play catch-up.

How to Become Number One

The best example of how to become number one can be found in the ad agency business. Of the 12,000 in the United States (Source: U.S. Census 1988), Young & Rubicam is the largest. Their consistent success in landing new accounts is a constant source of amazement. Even greater is the curiosity as to *how* they do it. Significantly, their secret is every bit as appropriate and valuable to an individual selling at K-Mart as to a team selling box cars of grain to General Mills.

What's their secret? The secret is that there isn't any. In fact, Y & R would probably be proud to reveal why they are so tough to beat. They succeed simply *because they have such a compelling urge to succeed—matched by equally dedicated work.* Trite as it may seem, it is their New York Yankees/Notre Dame complex. Not only do they earnestly believe they can win, they are willing to get their hands dirty enough to make it happen.

Although much of the credit for Y & R's exceptional track record on new business was attributed to Ed Ney's and now Alex Kroll's personal charisma (the previous and present CEO), more significant is their having instilled a powerful *desire* to win in all their people, including the pride to be willing to pay the price.

This intense devotion to succeed is not due to a magical inspiration. Rather, it has been a cumulative effort. For instance, let's go back to when they were pitching on Kentucky Fried Chicken. As you may know, during the summer, Manhattan empties out on Friday at noon. And *all* those in the Agency business plan on beating the rush. As it happened, Y & R was coming down to the wire in wrapping up their presentation—with the only time left being on the Labor Day weekend. However, while you could have fired a cannon down deserted Madison Avenue, there were thirty-four staffers at the Y & R office over this long sacred weekend, putting the final touches on the KFC pitch. It's history: they made the necessary effort to win—and did.

As some frustrated agencies have put it, "How are you going to fight that kind of dedication?" Easy. Instead of cursing the darkness, light a candle. Motivation isn't some God-given gift awarded exclusively to Young & Rubicam. The only way you can compete against Y & R—or whomever—is to compound your ability and experience with an achievement/action-oriented attitude.

It's a wry gag that one of the ways for an agency to tell whether a client is in jeopardy is if Alex Kroll's name appears in the client's guest register. Formidable reputation needn't strike fear in an agency if it is as determined and psyched to succeed.

Sorry I couldn't divulge some esoteric answer for Y & R's winning ways. However, you now know the actual reason—and what it takes to combat it. It amounts to becoming a gung ho entity—with all employees realizing that their individual interests can best be served if the *total* company succeeds.

There is your gospel. Preach it. Live it. And you will outsell them all.

Having established the support you need that can provide you with a competitive edge, plus dealing with the considerations for enhancing your efforts, let's lay the groundwork for getting underway.

Where to Begin a Successful Selling Program

◆ Perspective ◆ Composition of the Selling Team
◆ Operate from a Marketing Plan
◆ Set a Goal For Growth
◆ Stature of the Selling Operation
◆ Create a Unique Selling Proposition
◆ Treatment of the Company Philosophy
◆ Document Advantages
◆ Increase and Maintain Intensity
◆ Generate Employee Involvement

Perspective

The sales operation begins with *attitude*. When a company gets the reputation of being hot, it's because their people made it happen. Their success is due to a compelling urge to succeed—matched by equally dedicated work.

The hot company's corporate attitude is that new business solicitation is an integral part of the company operation—with projects for prospects scheduled right along with those for customers. And neither new business solicitation nor customer service is performed at the expense of the other.

This operating strategy indicates greater respect for the selling function. There couldn't be a better time for you to exceed your sales quota because this achievement will now more likely be appreciated and rewarded.

Composition of the Selling Team

Who should be involved in your firm's selling operation? Members are usually selected arbitrarily—some deadwood may be chosen because of rank, while others whose contribution could be vital may be overlooked.

Actually, for a selling team to be most effective it should consist of *every employee* in your company to whatever extent feasible. Doing so provides the maximum source of talent and experience. Further, this action will make all employees more selling conscious—thereby increasing your potential for scoring. It is worth stirring up this reservoir because your major account lead may come from the unlikeliest source.

For example, an ad agency secretary had a blind date. During the evening, as they got to know each other, each identified their present job functions. Her date carried this mating dance a step further by revealing to her that he was switching jobs to become the ad director for Supermega Corporation. Since this potential romance didn't take precedence over her paycheck, our Mata Hari reported this development to her boss. The new Advertising Director was promptly contacted, congratulated on his upcoming position, and offered his own agency team to develop and execute Supermega's ad campaign.

The blind date was so amazed by the discovery of his forthcoming career move, that he agreed to a meeting prior to his actual move. As a result of this early contact, he was predisposed toward the soliciting agency because of their heads-up follow through, and he steered his business to them.

The moral of the story is that you should make it known to your enlisted personnel that they can be heroes as much as any officer. This strategy reinforces

---

❝ Your major account lead may come from the unlikeliest source.❞

---

that the objective is growth—no matter where it comes from. This growth could enable all the employees to fulfill their personal ambitions in ways they never would have considered before.

You may not have the wherewithal and authority to *institute a program encouraging involvement* by all employees. But you shouldn't have any shortage of initiative for submitting this plan to the powers that be. And you don't do it just for brownie points—any increase in sales can eventually benefit you.

To attract interest, send a bulletin to as many of your people as possible to inform them of

◆ The intention to become very aggressive in the new business area

◆ Their appointment to the new business team

◆ The opportunity for them to contribute to the success of the program

Your announcement shouldn't be a policy statement. Rather it should be brief, exciting—and motivating. Like this example.

"Want to make more money? Have more responsibility? Here's how. Our company's objective isn't survival. It's successful growth so we can all do better—corporately and personally.

"To accomplish this, we are going to be more than sales-conscious. We are going to become *sales driven*. Then we are going to compound this gung-ho attitude with our greatest asset: our people—including you.

"To increase impact on the marketplace, we are going to apply the combined abilities and experience of everyone. Thus, we want your ideas on how we can sell better corporately—and what you can do individually.

"It's this basic: as the company makes out, you do too. So for our sake—and yours—send your ideas to _____. And welcome to the (name of company) sales-driven team!"

Since they are now officially members of your selling team, and to maintain momentum, send them activity reports on a regular basis. These would include

◆ Progress made in solicitation efforts. (i.e., "Our persistence has paid off in lining up a full-scale presentation to the Acme Company on November 12.")

◆ News of wins or losses—with reasons if possible

◆ Notable contributions by anyone in respect to contact, ideas, information, planning, preparation, and presentation

A valuable by-product of this total company involvement is the impression conveyed that each employee, regardless of function, is vital to the company's sales performance.

Operate from a Marketing Plan

It is essential that you have a corporate marketing plan to provide organized direction for your solicitation activity. If your company doesn't have any such document, cover yourself with glory by proposing the plan furnished below. Even if one does exist, you would still look good by offering this input to possibly augment and strengthen it.

The following outline involves defining the four most important matters—by taking the action indicated.

This is purposely constituted so it can be implemented by any industry or business. Now it requires being fleshed out for application by your company. And only you can do that. Since getting started is the toughest part of any project, this outline provides the inspiration and means for getting underway.

1. *Where your Company stands*
    Analyze:
    Company image
    Financial status
    Customer stability
    Employee attitude
    Strengths/Weaknesses

2. *What you want to become*
    Decide on:
    Products and/or services to be offered
    Account type/size desired
    Growth rate
    Profit expected

3. *How this is to be accomplished*
    Identify problems/opportunities
    Formulate objectives/strategy tactics
    Determine future needs

4. *Who will be held accountable for results*
    Assign responsibilities to specific individuals
    Set completion dates
    Provide for periodic assessment and fine-tuning of progress
    Evaluate payout

Obviously, all four stages are necessary—in the order indicated. Of these, though, it is the second that can be your catalyst for action: *What you want to become.*

Are you familiar with Hesselbart & Mitten? It's not a vaudeville team. They are a very successful advertising agency. For many years, they were an art studio. Then one day, Bob Mitten decided to convert this operation into a full-service agency. However, Bob decided he only wanted to work on accounts in the Fortune 500. That was quite ambitious for yesterday's art studio.

But Bob was a shrewd head. He started out by going after the smallest division of each of these prestigious companies, those too modest for the heavy-hitter agencies to be bothered with. Then after knocking off these $100,000-300,000 accounts, he would move his foot farther into the door, and solicit the next larger divisions.

You may call this scavenging. Bob calls it highly profitable strategy. Because in 1989, H & M billed about $60,000,000—while headquartered in the megamarket of Fairlawn, Ohio. Bob Mitten gave much credit for this achievement to having established *who* he wanted to work with. This goal provided direction and incentive. And answering the question "Where do we start?" served as a springboard for action.

But, too often, a company will burn itself out in developing a marketing plan—and then not have enough ambition left to implement it. Companies sluff off for an unlimited number of reasons. As a result, they flounder through their selling operation in a manner considered inexcusable for others.

Whatever the excuses, the overriding incentive to apply the plan that has been developed is that it will provide you with a *competitive edge*. Specifically, the organization, accountability, and timing required will enable you to sell more successfully. The company that best applies this direction and discipline is the most likely to win.

So get off the dime. Cash in on your marketing plan. There are dollars to be made.

Set a Goal for Growth

Next, institute the payout phase of your marketing plan: the action necessary to consistently increase sales. This begins with a commitment to a specific goal—including provisions to make it happen.

What amount of growth is necessary—and realistic? A theory accepted by many companies over the years is that 50 percent of growth comes from existing accounts. So, it was assumed that new business activity would only have to produce the other half.

However, companies discovered in the last recession that customers can also account for 50 percent of a company's *loss*. So, this theory has been dumped. And although most companies are still as diligently attempting to grow customers, their new business program has since become a 100 percent effort—receiving the *full* attention it deserves.

In order to go the full nine yards, here is the best route to take. It is estimated that account attrition amounts to 15 percent annually. Shooting for this increase would mean no more than statistically breaking even. Not until you exceed this

" The new business water is cold only until you get into it. "

percentage will you achieve real growth. So tack on an additional modest 10 percent—thereby going for 25 percent.

Granted, sales quotas are assigned. However, achieving these results is not perceived as an impressive accomplishment. This is the performance expected of you. Only after exceeding this mandatory amount are you appreciated, and eligible for the recognition you deserve—beginning with compensation.

Here is how to be an over-achiever—which translates into being an over-earner. You can go beyond the goals established by scheduling an additional number of "missionary" sales calls. (Those accounts you want to go after, even though not sure of their inclination to buy.)

Because of the fierce competition among ad agencies, they often ask me, "How many new business presentations should we be making?" And I'll reply, "Whether competitive or missionary, one full scale pitch per month."

The usual reaction is, "Geez Jack, we got clients, too, ya know." It is assumed this is an unrealistic effort—and too tough a goal to shoot for. However, the new business water is cold only until you get into it.

When I follow up on these agencies six to nine months later, I'm told that the roughest part was getting started. They were then pleasantly surprised to discover that after hitting a rhythm of one presentation per month, conducting three in two months wasn't that much more effort.

Defining a full-scale presentation as whatever it takes to land the account, what amount of thrust and frequency applies to *your* operation? Establishing the number of sales calls per time period enables you to determine your destiny—and your success.

This consistent and increasing activity leads us to the secret for winning the business you want—faster. In the desire to discover the secret for landing accounts, a top ten agency compiled every conceivable factor involved in the soliciting new business, and fed them into a computer. This extensive input was then tabulated and analyzed, in what is acknowledged to be the most authoritative study ever made on the subject.

I can now reveal to you the conclusion produced by this scientific project: "The more presentations you make, the more new business you get." A lot of money was spent—but this agency felt it was worth it to confirm this truism.

Be willing to become more successful. Don't base your selling activity on how little you can get by with, but, on how much you want to accomplish.

Stature of the Selling Operation

This planning, however, won't be worth a damn unless you have the fire in your belly to aggressively apply it. Without an all-out commitment, you'll just be firing blanks.

In order to succeed, consider your company selling program a "customer." According it this stature, you will have no excuse for not giving it your best shot. As with any other account, its longevity will depend on your dedication to servicing it.

Get off to an up-beat start. Go out and celebrate your victory. You would sure celebrate if you landed an account the size of your company. Well, you did: your Company! Then start thinking in terms of your company as being the sum of its customers because it can only be as good a place to work as the number and caliber of accounts it attracts. *And you can affect this.* So bring in the business that will help make your company the type you want to stay with.

Create a Unique Selling Proposition

Brand equity begins with establishing an appealing image for your product or service—and then maintaining top-of-mind desire for it. This requires starting at square one: with your company. You need to create your own USP (Unique Selling Proposition), one that is distinctive, compelling, and memorable. Further, to be meaningful, it should contain a promise of benefit.

Companies procrastinate in developing their USP because of the assumption that it must consist of some awesome combination or words never before assembled. Since this improbable bolt from the blue doesn't occur, the company is at a disadvantage because of inadequate identity. Even worse, their amorphous impression can beget commodity status for their product or service. Namely, they take on the indistinguishable image of their company.

If your company doesn't have a grabber to distinguish itself, or if it uses a statement with the impact of pablum, propose some ideas that will represent your operation in the most dynamic manner. (This initiative will establish you as being a cut above the majority of employees who have a "That's not my job" attitude.)

You say slogans aren't your bag? You won't draw a blank if you try this for inspiration: If a prospect were to ask, "Why should I do business with your company?" and then walk away, what would you shout as he or she escapes? (Preferably it should be something ingratiating rather than an expletive.)

Another source of ideas is the areas of your company's achievement. The basis for your USP could be triggered by technological achievements, civic involvement and charitable activities, major improvements in operations, increased customer benefits, exciting new products or services, higher caliber of employees, etc.

However, don't mistake a catchy phrase for appeal. For instance, there is an agency in the southeast that has expended considerable money and effort promoting the concept "Our clients are better known than we are." When they said, "Dynamite, huh Jack?" my answer was, "That sounds like an excuse."

Compare this approach with that taken by Maclaren, one of the largest agencies in Canada. They simply state in all their promotional material, "Maclaren Advertising Works." And then they do an excellent job of relating this claim to the prospect's needs and the communication of the agency's message. As a prospect, which appeal would be likeliest to turn you on?

After offering your brainchild, recognize that for this type of matter, the wheels of corporate bureaucracy grind inexorably slowly. But if you have a claim begging to be heard, which can increase your sales effectiveness, don't stifle it until official blessings are received. Go ahead and put it to work so you start gaining from its impact now.

You represent those who execute managements plans—and know first-hand their effect. Thus, opinions from the field are especially welcome. Also, it is known that some of the best ideas come from where the action is.

So if you have a fresh sales approach that is as good as you think, test it in your area. If it proves particularly appealing, share the results with management so it can be applied elsewhere. They will respect your initiative, and might tangibly express their appreciation for your contribution.

Treatment of the Company Philosophy

Is it to your advantage to tout your company's philosophy? That depends on whether you use it as a working objective or as an ego trip. The purpose of a company philosophy is to officially set forth what you stand for—and to distinguish your firm from the others.

Unfortunately, the philosophy usually consists of a lengthy sermon, the triteness of which is exceeded only by its dullness. Even worse, prospects rarely take it seriously. Yet, a company should have a positioning statement, but not as a device for defensively competing against others with the usual string of clichés.

Instead, consider this selling strategy. Deny having any *generic* philosophy. Rather, communicate that you develop a new objective for each individual customer based on the action required to fulfill their specific needs. In contrast to an all-purpose panacea, customize your contribution to your customer. In this way, your philosophy becomes a tangible commitment, a philosophy the prospect will be more inclined to relate to and accept.

Document Your Advantages

All else notwithstanding, prospects want suppliers who can best satisfy their requirements for product or service quality, price, and availability. Because, to varying degrees, all these factors affect their profitability.

If you don't communicate why your operation is satisfactorily profitable, then what can they expect? Take the time to document your personnel and operational advantages. And keep this current as improvements occur. Then, when the situation calls for it, provide the prospect with the assurance desired—matching your success to their goals.

Increase and Maintain Intensity

There is a key, unwritten factor that strongly influences whether your sales efforts result in survival or success.

Here is what I've discovered: much selling activity occurs in fits and starts. This is due to slacking off, consciously or otherwise, after getting lucky for a while. Yet, there are salespeople with seemingly comparable resources and talent that regularly outsell them all. Why? Are they privy to some unavailable secret formula? Do they receive divine guidance? It is neither of these.

They are competing more effectively because of having a *higher level of intensity—consistently maintained*. Simply stated: they get "up" more for selling—and stay there. Learn from the winning athlete, the person who always stays in shape—who doesn't just train on a crash basis.

Conceptually, no argument here. Making it happen is another thing. With selling intensity being an attitudinal matter rather than a by-the-numbers procedure, it must begin with inspiration and direction from top management. Both by their buying into this discipline—and making their dedication to it obviously known.

To inculcate an optimum level of effort, on a regular basis, capitalize on the key component of intensity: *Initiative*. This would be undertaken by conducting a "What have you done for us lately?" program.

It would consist of requesting innovative ideas from your sales personnel on a steady basis. If an idea is worth using, the contributor would earn points for merchandise prizes. (Of course, their spouses would be sent the prize catalog so they could further turn up the heat.) And each month, there would be a cash award for the best selling idea received. With this approach, you're not counting on charming anyone into performing at the level desired. Rather, you're providing them cause and effect.

Then explore how this incentive to increase the potency of your sales thrust can be expanded to include *all* employees. By whatever means the others can enhance sales performance is a valuable plus. The inducement is that any improvement in sales indirectly accrues to them.

The clue to the success of this program is adequate duration. There are two methods by which interest and participation can be sustained. First, inform all concerned of the ideas implemented, and their effect, and compliment the contributor. Second, periodically notify them of the prizes won and by whom.

Exploit this opportunity.

Generate Employee Involvement

The companies that outsell the others all *do* have a secret weapon. It is the same one all the others have. However, the difference is they are the only ones who *use* it: involving *all* their people.

This is accomplished by making the entire organization more sales conscious. These gung-ho companies communicate how everyone can contribute—and individually benefit—from becoming involved.

Here is an event you can suggest that will stimulate employee participation. Institute a "What Have You Done for Both of Us Lately?" challenge. Promote this concept on a regular basis (i.e., signs, memos, flyers attached to paychecks—plus whatever offbeat approaches you can conceive.) Be sure to provide direction on *how* employees contribute (i.e., furnishing leads, originating promotional ideas, developing solicitation tactics, etc.)

Then, by all means, acknowledge the efforts of each, its value—and what will be done about it. Beyond this recognition, you may want to consider tangible rewards to promote participation. One angle could be to offer days off, the number being contingent on the value of the contribution.

This plan can establish both a corporate and an individual sales-oriented frame of mind that will compound each other. The result will be an up-front consciousness of the selling function as a *total* company operation.

And above all, this "What Have You Done For Both of Us Lately?" incentive offers the total organization the opportunity to be a vital part of—and benefit from—the success achieved. Finally, your initiating this idea establishes you as the first to demonstrate what *you* have done.

---

66 The companies that outsell them all do have a secret weapon ... they involve all their people. 99

The Ground Rules

◆ Perspective ◆ Accounts: Type
◆ Accounts: Size ◆ Accounts: Upgrading
◆ Speculative Proposals ◆ Compensation

Perspective

People in selling have a tendency to try to develop pat operating formulae. Then, no matter what the situation, they have an established modus operandi. This procedure is broadly accepted because it is based on empirical solutions. Sort of a "we've always done it that way" mentality. And its existence saves time and effort.

However, while an approach may have been appropriate under one set of circumstances, it won't necessarily be appropriate under another set. So sure, learn from experience. But don't let old approaches substitute for bringing to bear the most relevant strategy.

Nevertheless, from an overall selling standpoint, certain basics with universal application do exist. The following operating strategies, as distinguished from one-time ideas, can provide direction necessary for the success you desire.

Accounts: Type

Some companies will boast about being able to get all the new business they want. Then, as evidence of their prowess in this area, they will announce the number of accounts and employees they've added. And it's true. Their kill ratio has been very good among accounts that are volatile, time/labor intensive, and otherwise less than desirable to others. So much for quantity.

Admittedly, when a company is born, it has to chase down whatever business it can get to provide cash flow. But sooner rather than later, it has to grow up and go after the quality accounts. Quality accounts are businesses that

◆ you want to work with

◆ are satisfactorily profitable

◆ are marketing-oriented

◆ will reflect well on your company

◆ have good growth potential

◆ are interesting, fun, and exciting

◆ enhance your appeal to prospects

How do those on your customer roster stack up according to the above descriptions? A perfect ten is too much to hope for. But a general upgrading in their level of value wouldn't be. There are two means by which this can be accomplished:

◆ Set higher standards for the prospects solicited.

◆ As you attract more preferred accounts, weed out those you romanced for expedience.

It is not the number of accounts that matters but *who* they are. And it is not the volume of sales—but how *profitable*. Thus, if your company is at the stage where it's no longer necessary to pass the hat each month to pay the rent, it is time to progress from being a new business scavenger to a class act. Because you have now earned the right to work with customers who would be fulfilling—both professionally and financially.

❝ There is only one criterion for qualifying a prospect: profit.❞

Accounts: Size

It is understandable that companies will set a minimum size for accounts they will solicit or accept. This establishes a goal for quality—and rules out unrealistic or undesirable business. This policy is *not* valid, though, when the criterion is revenue, because the resulting figure could be a smokescreen for labor-or time-intensive accounts that could cause you to lose by winning. Namely, the ecstasy of victory will be quickly replaced by the agony of defeat if you can't make enough money from this customer. There is only one criterion for qualifying a prospect: *profit.*

You can get a reasonable indication of an account's viability by looking at the relationship of estimated income to projected workload, and expenses in servicing this customer. Although inexact, the use of these measurements is still more reliable than gross sales. Therefore, judge a prospect's potential according to its *worth*—not what it would spend. Then distinguish between gross and net income. The payoff isn't in what you're paid. It's in what you keep.

In this context, what do you do when approached by a company whose business is too small to handle? You never refuse per se. This company's management feels they are bestowing a great honor on your firm—and it is inconceivable to them that you wouldn't covet their account.

Backing off because it is economically unfeasible is not enough justification. It still nets down to your having rejected them. And after they have experienced this perceived humiliation, you're wiped out as far as this account is ever concerned. Then what can you do if their business increases to a size whereby they become desirable?

You can salvage a tacky situation with this type company for now— and if they enjoy significant growth in the future. Use the following strategy employed by Bob Bloom from the agency of the same name in Dallas. When offered an account whose billing is less than the established minimum, he tactfully informs the advertiser that his agency would not be appropriate for them—*at this time.* Then he promises to call back within one day with his recommendation of the three agencies that could best serve their interests (again, *at this time*) and whom to contact. Bob Bloom did the prospect a favor—and made a friend. And you can bet the ranch that if and when any of these advertisers become big enough, he will be there to harvest the seeds he planted.

Accounts: Upgrading

For both financial and possibly moral reasons, I am asked about the advisability of upgrading accounts. This concern particularly applies to going after larger accounts in industries whose character prevents suppliers from handling customers who are directly competitive. The first consideration is whether the prospect would be so much more *profitable,* and its *growth potential* that appealing, as to be worth the risk of losing your present smaller account.

If you can rationalize this gamble from a business standpoint (with no regrets), then it's a judgement call: immediate gain and opportunity versus the hopeful security of existing revenue.

Now let us deal with the matter of morality. Namely, the propriety of romancing a larger potential account at the expense of loyalty to an existing one. While respecting your intent to conduct your operation in a righteous manner, the final criterion needs to be *your Company's best interest.* Period. Sounds calloused, cynical? Try realistic. Because customers have all the characteristics of a dog—except loyalty. Therefore, whether you should try to parlay a smaller account into a larger one begins with your responsibility to your company, and ends with yourself. After these priorities are satisfied, you can be as dedicated to present customers as circumstances and income warrant.

Speculative Proposals

One of the most important judgement calls in selling is whether or not to gamble in preparing plans and materials as an inducement. Should your attitude be for or against this practice? Neither. Your position should be one of flexibility. Since it is controversial because of the time and expense involved, and the risk of your work being stolen, we had better first define "spec." It is *any* attempt to solicit an account. *Any* action whatsoever. And if you conclude this requires the use of spec, so be it.

Based on this sales-driven truism, let us take on the purists, those companies that righteously claim they never do spec. I have asked the management people responsible for this policy, "How about when you write and/or phone a prospect?" And I am told, "That's different. We're just showing interest." So I'll follow through with, "Then what about when you research them?" This time the answer is, "We are just showing that we care." Aw c'mon!

These companies feel justified—rather than hypocritical—in giving lip service to opposing spec, because spec samples aren't made, and models aren't built. Apparently, becoming a little bit pregnant is okay. As long as you don't deliver. The hard truth is that *every* company specs to *some* extent. It's just that there are those who won't admit it. Least of all, to themselves.

Having this perspective, we can now deal more realistically with this solicitation approach. Actually, the decision to incorporate spec in the sales pitch is a gray one—being a matter of degree. Yet, for some reason, companies feel compelled to take a black-or-white stand on the matter. But on what? The term "Spec Proposal" can range from a bare minimum of effort to a needlessly extravagant one. Thus, your interest can best be served by hearing out the prospect's terms. This enables you to base your judgment on a first-hand impression rather than assumption.

By smoking out the prospect's expectations, you can determine whether their presentation requisites are compatible or conflict with your method of operation. If acceptable, you can then conclude if the cost and effort involved can be justified. This positive approach will preclude taking your company out of contention for a desirable account because of having settled for rumor or gossip as to what it will take to land this account.

Therefore, instead of arbitrarily ruling out or plunging ahead, evaluate each opportunity on its own merit—then decide whether the game is worth the ante.

This isn't a matter of passing judgment on what degree of spec is right or

---

66 Customers have all the characteristics of a dog—except loyalty. 99

---

wrong—morally or financially. Rather, it is recognizing that prospects are increasingly using "shootouts" as a key consideration in their buying decisions. And like it or not, you will be increasingly expected to play the game.

So instead of resentfully *reacting* to this request when it's made, anticipate whether you want to initiate the effort to simply comply with it. If you conclude this prospect is worth going after, then your only approach consists of doing whatever it will take to win. By contrast, if going this full route is too steep a price to pay, forego it, because the most expensive presentation is a half-hearted one. Either way, whatever the prospect's requirements, *you* control the situation.

Compensation

Compensation is never given enough attention when pitching an account. It is often assumed that if you knock their socks off with your proposal, all else will fall into line. However, when soliciting new business, don't ever forget why. It is to produce *profitable* income as well as to produce a product or provide a service. On this basis, the hand plays itself. Either the compensation will enable you to realize the amount of dollar profit to which you are entitled, or you fold. Thus, there should be an ongoing conscious awareness of the compensation factor, from initial prospect contact to post-selling activity. How much you will be paid, by what method, and when?

Don't invest heavily in time and money in an attempt to impress, leaving the subject of payment as an afterthought. Because you may discover after all your effort and expense that the prospect is economically unfeasible. As vital as relationship is from a performance standpoint, if there isn't *financial* compatibility, it's academic.

This concern is especially appropriate now with compensation becoming an increasingly important influence in supplier selection. Granted, this isn't the only criterion. However, the financial consideration shouldn't come as a rude awakening—to either party, particularly once the prospect romance is progressing well.

In the final analysis, you are seeking to enter into a business arrangement that will satisfactorily reward your contribution to the account's success. There isn't anything crass about making your intentions known to the prospect. Because selling their product or service at a profit is their ultimate objective, too.

The Smarts for Picking Prospects

◆ Perspective ◆ Strategy ◆ Market
◆ Potential ◆ Account Conflict? ◆ Rifle Shot
◆ Buckshot Approach ◆ Account Vulnerability
◆ Overlooked Business ◆ Gilt Edge Contacts ◆ Customers

Perspective

Akey failing in prospecting is the appalling waste of time spent chasing rainbows. I'm often asked, "Do you have any magic for going after new accounts?" In solicitation activity, the only magic is what *you* make happen. This takes commitment to an aggressive plan, consistently applied. I'm going to give you the rabbit. But, you'll still have to pull it out of the hat.

But first, let's get this straight. An individual tactic such as your company's advertising campaign, direct mail, "old boy" contacts, your country club membership, civic involvement, or an occasional speech is *not* a new business program. Each tactic is worthwhile and contributes to the effect. But the results depend on action taken by others. Instead, *you* need to take control. Because you—not fate—should determine your sales results. This chapter will concentrate on the direction necessary for this purpose.

Strategy

I keep hearing this good news/bad news scenario: "I have an unusually high rate of scoring—however, I don't get up to bat often enough." It is often assumed there must be a secret solution to this problem, one that others who land accounts more frequently have discovered.

Upon delving into the matter, I found the reason these under-achievers are unable to come up to bat more often. They tell me, "It's because I don't hear about enough available business." This passive approach abdicates their selling responsibility to fate. Effort based on prospect susceptibility (i.e., assuming them vulnerable to being had) is restrictive and least productive. Instead, you need to originate contacts with prospects *you* want at the rate and quantity you desire. (A valuable by-product of being proactive is that information on available prospects will materialize.)

Next comes opening doors. There isn't any secret angle for getting in. The proved means consists of establishing and applying a planned series of efforts, ranging from initial contact (letter/phone call) to follow-through. You—rather than events—should determine results. This requires your taking the initiative—not waiting for prospects to emerge. Because by the time they hang out the welcome sign, it's for those they have already developed a preference for.

To whatever extent practical, you can solicit whomever you want—if you are willing to commit yourself to making it happen. Your more successful competitors have dedicated themselves to controlling their destiny—and are achieving what you are hoping for.

Market

The geographic area in which a company can prospect for business is influenced by economic feasibility. And the smaller the operation, the more restricted its activity. As a result, companies will carve out a region consisting of a few counties or states, and assume this to be the extent of their market. But this severely restricts their opportunity to the confines of the boundaries arbitrarily established. Also, this strategy obscures *who* their market actually is.

For perspective, your market is not geographic. It is those accounts to whom your operation and expertise is especially appealing. There are countless cases of suppliers serving customers who are 1,000—even 2,000—miles away because they convinced these accounts that they couldn't get a better product (service) or more dedication anywhere else.

Yet sellers often limit their potential by assuming that servicing a distant customer would be unaffordable. Not necessarily. In many industries, if a prospect is

66 Your strategy … is to subtly create constructive dissatisfaction.99

sold on you, they will negotiate a compensation arrangement that will enable you to realize a satisfactory profit. Your value is exportable.

So don't hamper your sales growth by mistaking geography for market. You're not going after land. Your objective is getting customers.

Potential

When attempting to determine the feasibility of going after a desirable prospect, don't assume that *any* account is unattainable. Regardless of how good a job their present supplier(s) may seem to be doing, customers will always have a nagging concern about whether they are getting the best product or service and treatment available.

So, exploit this uncertainty which exists in the mind of every company. Because they can never be *really* sure.

How? First, let's start with the premise that any account will *eventually* move. So its not a matter of if—only when.

Having established that the opportunity exists, let's move on to the concept of your taking control. This consists of your classifying your prospects into two categories:

1. There are those you are presently concentrating on that offer a reasonable possibility of closing before too long. These constitute your primary objective. The ones you will persist in bringing to fruition.

2. In addition, there are the prospects you salivate for. But seemingly they are locked in. Thus, for prospects who are especially desirable, plan on cultivating them over an extended period. Your strategy, of course, is to subtly create constructive dissatisfaction. Then when the time comes for change, you won't be the fair weather friend, but rather, the one who wanted their business all along.

This one-two punch gives your sales efforts dimension. In particular, it adds a future to your present.

Account Conflict?

Sometimes, those in industries offering customers category or geographic exclusivity arbitrarily assume that a prospect they are interested in would be competitive to an existing account, and thus write them off. Don't.

Rather than second-guessing, sound out your customer. First, it is probably impressive to them that a related account also wants you. Second, contrary to your assumption, they may not perceive your opportunity as being a direct conflict. Even if they do, though, the worst thing that can happen is that they will object to your accepting the new account.

You will, of course, graciously acquiesce, but the point will have been made. Namely, a firm they consider too dangerous to be in the same shop believes your operation is preferable to any other. So capitalize on being wanted. It makes you more appreciated by those who have you.

Rifle Shot

Your opening round is the rifle-shot approach—a magnum load. Start out with your best shot: the category of account or occupation in which you are a proved authority. (Which industry? What function?) Having earned a reputation for expertise in that field, you are a natural for any related account—wherever it is located. These are your *likeliest* prospects, the ones you should get. And you surely haven't exhausted this source of your greatest potential.

Next, your follow-through shot should be aimed at the void that exists in your account roster: the type of account you particularly want, in an appropriate field you have not yet exploited.

Then, for both the established and new categories, select the five most desirable, viable accounts. (Using the applicable standards I provide you in Chapter 7. Then, go all out—taking whatever action necessary to score, based on what you flushed out in your pre-presentation meeting.

With this approach *you* are deciding on your direction. And results are based on your initiative—not some external surprise. Advertising, direct mail, "old boy" contacts, country club memberships, civic work, speeches, etc. can then be used to specifically support your plan and increase its potency.

The sales pros consistently tell me that this concentrated, full court press is the most successful strategy for landing new accounts. Among other things, your efforts will be better organized and you will be more persistent.

Granted, there are those of you who are assigned a specific list of prospects. Most of your company's salespeople will restrict themselves to this prescribed list. But those among you with an entrepreneurial attitude can employ the "rifle-shot" approach to augment what's expected of you. The results you produce with this voluntary effort will establish you as the employee always worth taking good care of.

Buckshot Approach

Another means to increase your sales possibilities beyond the accounts assigned to you is the buckshot approach. With this approach, you target prospects with whom you *might* get lucky. In this case, you are playing the law of averages, the first law of which is the more sales calls you make, the more business you get. Capitalizing on this potential is what makes the difference between an implementer and an innovator.

But first, let's dispel the misconception that exists at some companies that the source of new business is essentially loose business. With all due respect to the value of ferreting out accounts that are planning to add or change suppliers, this is only the tip of the new business iceberg. The mass of your potential lies submerged.

Yet, you can take advantage of this much broader selling opportunity through systematic missionary work (i.e., going after the accounts you want, even though unaware of their receptivity). Here is how this strategy can be applied most productively:

1. Identify all feasible prospects.

2. Qualify them according to as many of the fifteen criteria furnished in chapter seven as possible.

3. After compiling your hit list, itemize the prospects according to their short- and long-range potential:

   ◆ Short range are those prospects you can offer a reason so compelling as to induce change soon.

   ◆ The others are ones so desirable as to be worth cultivating over an extended period.

4. Organize each list according to priority of action.

Of course, you will continue to keep your ear to the ground. But while doing so, get your hands dirty. In this way, you can control your destiny by making things happen.

Account Vulnerability

Beyond the combined effect of this rifle/buckshot strategy, there is a variety of other opportunities just waiting to be exploited because one supplier's poison can be another's meat. Due to circumstances, it is always open season on *some* accounts. They are susceptible when any of the following situations occur:

◆ Change in Buying Authority

**❝ The whole world may be your oyster.
But you still have to find out
where the pearls are.❞**

Whenever a personnel change is made in this function, it is a foregone conclusion that suppliers are placed at risk. Instead of being considered a source of stability during this transition, suppliers often come under scrutiny as being another means for shaping up operations.

Thus, when a new buyer is employed by the prospect, contact her and offer to complete the fresh start by providing her with her own team. This assurance of loyalty when coming into a new position can be a very appealing inducement.

◆ Significant Drop in Sales or Profits

This causes the type of prospect uneasiness that you can capitalize on. Whatever measures for improvement you can provide will at least earn an audience—and maybe enough gratitude to earn you their business. (i.e., why your product or service can contribute to bettering their operation.) This could take the form of providing a price advantage, a technological advance or a unique marketing tactic.

◆ Radical Change in the Economy or Their Market

This condition often causes a company to reexamine their entire marketing operation. And if the concern is deep enough, this could also include a reevaluation of their suppliers. Be alert to these circumstances because your timing, and fresh approach, could be propitious.

Once aware of these opportunities, there is no excuse for not taking advantage of them. Institute a system for keeping informed of prospect developments which cause them to become susceptible to adding or changing suppliers. This simply involves having an inside person at your office start the day with business pages of the newspapers in your sales territory and appropriate trade publications. He can use a red magic marker to circle news of prospect losses in sales or profits and management changes, then turn tear sheets over to you for action. And every prospect cited becomes a likelier sale.

Overlooked Business

The whole world may be your oyster. But you still have to find out where the pearls are, and decide which ones you want and are able to get. Competitors, like you, have preferences about who they solicit. The larger your competitors, the more discerning they become, particularly in respect to concentrating on the most prestigious accounts and creaming off the more appealing portions of the business of these blue-chip companies.

However, despite the selective selling by the heavy hitters, this could still leave a lot of excellent opportunities. Maybe the passed over business is not as glamorous—but it could be more profitable. Further, these remaining portions can provide an entré to lure the balance of the account in the hands of others.

This potential occurred to Ed Nowak of Spencer Bennett Nowak. They had been plodding along for years with only incidental growth. Being success-oriented, he concluded that there were many valuable assignments being jobbed out by larger advertisers, work that the heavy-hitter agencies consider too menial.

To exploit this potential, this agency compiled a list of accounts having seven-figure or more media budgets—and only one agency. Then they developed a presentation to explain why the prospect should have a second agency, a back-up agency. How well have they done? They found, as did Ed MacMahon and Art Carney, that being second banana can still be gratifying. After the agency's first nine years of existence, they plateaued at $5,000,000 in billing. In the two and one-half years after instituting this plan, they grew to $15,000,000.

You can probably think of a number of prospects to whom this strategy can be applied, those you didn't pitch because someone else had already scored with them. Yet, an end-run could make you a high-paid player in their game, too.

Now that you have the idea, how are you going to apply it? You're limited only by the extent of your ambition—and the desirability of the business that exists.

Gilt Edge Contacts

Here is how to get a crack at the leaders in business and industry in your area. You can rub shoulders with the top executives of the most important companies with whom you would not otherwise associate.

This strategy is based on a worthwhile lesson learned by an agency that got stuck with a lemon—and made lemonade. Most of you can benefit from this experience.

This involves two agency types who left their employer to set up their own shop—accompanied by that agency's largest account. On the strength of the client's commitment, these budding entrepreneurs entered into a long-term rental lease and purchased office furniture and equipment. Although the client's word was solid, what they hadn't anticipated was the fury of the incumbent agency's president. When he found out about this fast shuffle, he threatened to sue for piracy.

Attorneys for the two defectors advised them not to get into the ring because the fight was fixed. First, they were outclassed, since they couldn't begin to match the existing agency in funds for the legal expenses. Second, the laws in their state tend to favor the injured party in this circumstance. Since there was obviously no sense in trying to take on Goliath without a slingshot, the new operation decided to forego the disputed client. And it now looked like they were going to go belly-up before issuing their first insertion order.

Fortunately, they weren't in the usual under-capitalized position and had some financial staying power. This provided them with a grace period but not enough time to chase rainbows. Since their new business funds had to be productive reasonably soon they had to skip as many stages in the prospecting process as possible. This required getting directly to the decision-makers—in an ingratiating environment, one in which they would be exposed to the agency's great work and could be receptive to it.

Coincidentally, the boards and committees of the various civic and charitable organizations are populated by many prominent executives in the production and service industries. These movers and shakers are dedicated to their pet projects—and have an affinity toward those who contribute well to these causes.

It occurred to this fledgling agency that the institutions mentioned would offer an excellent means for showcasing their talents to those with whom their efforts would realize the fastest payout. So they attempted to become the volunteer agency for as many of them as possible. They went after every operation, ranging from the zoo to the symphony to the United Fund. And for good measure, their hit list also included the museum, the local Lung Association, the S.P.C.A., etc.

The city leaders bought this altruism. And the agency began to knock off one after another of these organizations. As planned, this strategy served a wonderful dual purpose. It enabled them to hobnob with the heavy hitter influentials—and provided high visibility for the agency's work.

Yes, Sharp Hartwig in Seattle succeeded. In fact, new accounts began materializing much faster than they had hoped for. And you can bet the ranch that this agency hasn't forgotten the source of these valuable prospects—and aren't letting go in maintaining these relationships and pursuing others.

This strategy that worked so well for an ad agency can also be very productive for you. And you can surely be resourceful enough to wangle your way onto one or more of these boards. Doing so is worth whatever effort it takes because at their meetings, you become a peer of people who can do you a tremendous amount of good.

Customers

But your likeliest opportunity for getting more business is *growing customers*. You have developed a plan for soliciting prospects. But what organized effort are you making to generate further business from all of your customers?

Existing accounts are your most probable source of additional sales. You know their needs, what will appeal to them, who the decision-maker is—and have already proved your worth. Since you don't have to start from scratch, existing customers are also your most economical targets for prospecting.

With all this going for you, you should have a documented plan of action for getting additional business from them. Considering your customers as prospect's, here is how to make it happen:

◆ Identify the exact business desired and the routine for handling it.

◆ Flush out their needs and prepare a rationale as to why you can best satisfy them.

◆ Determine the selling approach likeliest to appeal to them.

◆ Develop a detailed procedure for implementing your plan and set timing for each phase.

◆ Assign responsibilities to specific individuals—and then hold them accountable for fulfillment.

◆ Set dates by which results should be produced.

◆ Evaluate results and decide on whatever fine-tuning and follow-through is needed.

Now, implement this program for growing customers as aggressively as if it were an all-out prospect effort. Because at the very least, even if this activity doesn't produce immediate results, it could serve as a deterrent to customers cutting or canceling purchases.

❝ Being second banana can still be gratifying. ❞

Remember, a prospect's stipulations may not be their only concerns. They also want the assurance that your company's support services will back up their primary requirements most effectively.

Faster Payout

Prospects also want the fastest payout for their money and efforts. So, to be considered, you need to demonstrate that you understand and appreciate this expectation—and are especially qualified to fulfill it.

As necessary as the standard five-year marketing plan is, economic circumstances have caused U.S. business to live on a quarter-by-quarter basis. Thus, selling according to what your product or service will eventually do for the prospect won't cut it. They want to know how fast buying from you will produce results. And the sooner the better.

Therefore, your understanding of the conditions under which they are being forced to operate need be immediately conveyed. Then register how this purchase will be a sales catalyst—and possibly how quickly.

Exceptional Adaptability

Because of rapidly changing economic conditions, and the accompanying uncertainty, companies expect exceptional adaptability from their suppliers. So, position your firm as a can-do operation—that is geared more to functioning on a crash basis when necessary. Capitalize on having this *flexibility*, and not being restricted by any industry practice of requiring set lead times for whatever the contingency. Rather, you have the capacity and willingness to promptly respond to the unexpected.

It is possible that the prospect you're pitching believes that their present supplier is so rigidly systematized that trying to deal with any exception to the rule through them would be extremely frustrating. Such a prospect would be receptive to any reference to your being able to turn on a dime.

Strong Internal Leadership

A prospect is sensitive to, and highly respects, strong internal leadership of suppliers because *it assures them* of the authority and decisiveness necessary to fulfill their needs. Strong leadership, then, should be amply evident in your solicitation activity.

Comment on your top management's hands-on involvement and intimate knowledge of operations. And for further effect, mention the name of a contributor to your proposal, and the name of the person whose approval was required. (If you can carry it off, implying that you have somewhat of a pipeline can't hurt.)

Involvement by Top Management

Prospects understandably assume that the supplier's top management is its ultimate talent. Thus, they expect that if they award you their business, your principals will give it reasonable attention. But be careful not to promise an unrealistic share of management contact time as bait. Most prospects are fairly calloused to this transparent ruse. Besides, it could prove disastrous.

There is an agency president in Chicago who is such a spellbinder that he is frequently interrupted during his portion of the presentation by the prospect asking, "If we were to award your agency our business, what percent of your time could we hope for?" He has his reply rehearsed to a gnat's eyelash.

First, he closes his eyes to give the impression he is thinking. Then, he places his hands in a pious position to symbolize the truth of his reply. And finally, after a suspenseful pause, he authoritatively states, "49 percent." (Obviously, promising one-half or more could be unbelievable since the CEO also has an agency to run.)

The agency scored quite well for about a year—until these new clients began to meet each other and discovered he had allocated 336 percent of his time. After that, at the first indication of friction, these clients had no compunction about leaving because they had been deceived in the presentation.

Constant personal contact isn't expected. What the prospect really wants is the assurance that your management will have a direct interest in their account. This concern can be satisfied by pointedly revealing that your management will be involved with their account *to whatever extent necessary.* Don't trap yourself by promising a fixed percentage of management time or a specific number of hours. Represent their involvement as being based on *need.*

Nevertheless, to the prospect who has read "The Art of Negotiating" by Gerard Nierenberg, this explanation may not suffice. For instance, how about when they are smitten with one of your key people and zap you with "We'll give you our business on the condition that we get 50 percent of Bruce's time," but your firm's workload makes fulfilling this request impossible, and they deserve only 10 percent.

Acquiescing and making a promise that can't be kept could backfire. Instead, here is how a heavyweight who was fast on his feet dealt with this situation. He countered with, "Don't restrict me to 50 percent. There may be circumstances when I'll want to devote more time to your account. Let *me* determine how I can be of most value to you." The prospect bought it; the supplier landed the account—and didn't risk deceit.

Acknowledgment of Their Growing Sophistication

Increasingly, buyers believe they are equal to those they do business with. Thus, it would be a shrewd move to make a point of acknowledging their growing sophistication—and taking it into account in your relationship.

Receptivity to Their Contribution and Willingness to Listen

Today's buyer wants the opportunity to contribute—with the seller being receptive to and respecting their ideas. Therefore, cite recognition of this desire and your willingness to operate on this basis.

Prospects especially want suppliers who will hear them out—so their expectations will have a better chance of being fulfilled. Assure them that you use your senses in proportion to their number: you have two ears and one mouth.

You've gone on record regarding your dedication to listen. It takes two requirements in order to deliver: desire and know-how. Listening, as opposed to just hearing, must begin with the *want* to do so. Your best incentive is that in a selling situation, you can't afford not to.

As to *how* to listen more effectively, there are numerous tips for accomplishing this. The best advice is that espoused by the Minneapolis Institute of Learning. They found that people use only 25 percent of their ability to listen. However, this can be increased to 75 percent if you listen with the intent of asking a question afterwards about what has been said. This is an easy discipline that offers a valuable reward. Apply it and your recall will enable covering all bases—thereby being home safe.

Belief in Field Work

The prospect's ultimate concern is where the action is: where their sales can be made. So you need to come across as more than an order taker. To whatever extent appropriate, register your earnest belief in getting involved out there—and

❝ Use your senses in proportion to their number: you have two ears and one mouth.❞

your willingness to get your hands dirty with them—flushing out what is happening, what can be improved—and recommending how. And cite that this doesn't mean a sporadic trip, but planned, periodic field work. In fact, as evidence of your sincerity, provide the prospect with a procedure and timetable for this purpose. (It is unlikely that any competitor of yours will lay it on the line this way.)

Summary

While these nine prospect desires may seem obvious, many suppliers soliciting business are not fulfilling them. You can distinguish your company by pointedly registering what prospects want confirmed, since most suppliers take for granted that the prospect knows this. But they don't. And they want to hear them.

Section II

The Prospect Mating Game

The developments occurring in this economic climate are making thorough planning even more necessary. To varying degrees, this has affected all industries. Your company has probably experienced most of the following situations:

◆ Leaner operating practices

◆ Tighter financial control

◆ Strategic reduction of inventory

◆ Increased price negotiations

◆ Application of "everyday low prices" concept

◆ Seeking alternate marketing options (i.e., database marketing)

Planning begins with a company taking maximum advantage of its most valuable asset: *its people*. Like you. A vital part of this procedure is rewarding the overachievers. This begins with the obvious inducements: raises and promotions. Then there is the incentive of a more appealing territory or desirable prospects. Finally, although maybe not appearing in the employee handbook, there is the opportunity for preferential treatment and perks.

It is academic that a person is hired for a specific purpose and that they are likely to be more productive if they are furnished with a job description. Yet management assumes each employee is aware that his or her responsibility also includes representing their company in the most appealing manner, both at work and away from it.

It can't be emphasized strongly enough that promoting the company isn't just the responsibility of those specifically employed to perform this function. It has to become *everyone's* job—to whatever extent possible.

Consequently, it is incumbent on management via oral and written communication to periodically register to their people the value of being a constant ambassador for the company—and to suggest the means for doing so. And from your standpoint, of the sales representative, whatever ideas you can generate to further promote the company will make you that much more valuable—which can pay off in respect to compensation and upward mobility.

The most successful companies are those whose planning includes applying the greatest totality of selling effort. This must begin internally with management creating the employee interest and desire to compound the actual selling activity.

Then they capitalize on every form of communication.

◆ *Advertising*: To persuade their target market to buy.

◆ *Sales Promotion*: To stimulate purchases at the store level.

◆ *Direct Marketing*: To attract immediate response from your likeliest prospects.

◆ *Public Relations*: To conjure the most favorable awareness and image for your brand.

◆ *Trade Promotion*: To elicit their cooperation in featuring your product.

◆ *Training and Motivation Programs for the Sales Force*: To inspire them to perform over their heads.

◆ *Employee Bulletins and Newsletters*: To encourage them to become sales-driven.

It takes this integrated marketing activity, plus internal synergism, to turn your company into the marketing machine necessary to thrive today.

The next four chapters provide the organization and direction for your solicitation strategy.

6. How Prospects Judge Salespeople

7. Smoke Out Desirable Prospects So You Don't Get Burned

8. Twelve Sources of Leads You Can Exploit

9. Appeals and Tactics for Getting Appointments

6

How Prospects Judge Salespeople

◆ Perspective
◆ The Necessary Impression
◆ The Four Sought-After Attributes

Perspective

From a performance standpoint, of course prospects want the highest quality product or service at the most economical price. Regarding your interaction, they expect

◆ an open relationship

◆ planned communications

◆ involvement by your management

◆ reasonable familiarity with their company, industry, and market

◆ accountability for your company's performance

In order to convince a prospect of your ability to deliver in the above areas though, you need demonstrate having the personal characteristics they believe it takes. While seldom mentioned, prospects have key expectations of the individu-

45

❝ Today's customer wants someone who can start fires—not just put them out.❞

als they deal with. We had better examine the necessary traits set forth in this chapter. Because they need to be consciously applied to satisfy prospects' desires.

The Necessary Impression

A prospect will piously declare their total objectivity when considering a supplier. They will claim their judgment is based entirely on the content of the proposal. However, if your company is a service business (and to a lesser degree, if a product is involved), *their impression of you is the deciding factor.*

What turns them on or off? This can best be answered by the key question they ask each other after meeting you: "Is he (she) our kind of people?"

Thus, your first consideration is not *what* you sell, but to *whom.* So it is imperative that you know each prospect—and direct your appeal accordingly.

Here's why. An agency president recently asked me in because he was fed up with always being a bridesmaid on new business presentations. He said, "I want to start throwing the bouquet—instead of settling for trying to catch it." He then continued with, "And I'm confident we must have a damn good pitch because we never come in worse than second." (Have you ever heard of coming in third?)

At this point, he gave me the script for a recent presentation to a retail chain, and asked me to take a look at it and tell him where they had gone wrong. I didn't have to get past the Table of Contents to discover why they blew it. It began with

   a.   Modular Marketing

   b.   Critical Marketing Path

And it kept getting heavier and more esoteric.

This approach may have been great for an M.B.A. Brand Manager at P & G. But the selection team was composed of store managers who were looking for shirtsleeve ideas and solutions, not scholarly profundities. So even if the content was brilliant, it was doomed to failure because it was inappropriate to the audience. Thus, so was the agency.

Actually, there is nothing wrong with a "by the books" pitch—if the three R's are applicable. And for a new business presentation—which includes any prospect contact made—the three R's are the following:

- The prospect should be able to favorably *relate* to you.

- Its content must be *relevant* to their interests and needs.

- And the *results* promised must be believable—and better than they could get elsewhere.

So do your homework, and you'll graduate with honors—and the account.

The Four Sought-After Attributes

Even with your efforts directly targeted, though, their effect depends on the vitality you exhibit. The following four attributes indicate to the prospect the kind of person you are.

1. *Leadership.* Although loathe to admit it, customers want *leadership. It maybe discreetly exercised in the guise of direction, but nevertheless, leadership.*

The ad VP of a major insurance company told me, "We have a controlled relationship with our agency. We dictate to them precisely what's expected. Then they either comply or they're fired."

He then went on to say, "In fact, we just got a new agency." So I asked, "How come?" And he looked me right in the eye and said, "Because the old one never provided any leadership."

The crux of the matter is that no customer wants to get caught playing catch-up regarding their industry or market. They are looking for a supplier who realizes its responsibility exceeds benefitting itself. They are especially eager to find one that will anticipate conditions and can recommend any necessary adjustments in course.

In addition, there is another key reason for their greater expectations of you. Since they, too, are operating with far fewer personnel, you are expected to compensate for the information and ideas previously furnished by ex-staff members.

2. *Decision-Oriented.* A customer also wants to deal with someone who is decision-oriented, the type of person who, upon making the sale, has the drive to follow through without having to be spoon fed on how to serve them.

3. *Initiative.* Another characteristic highly regarded is *initiative.* Sounds like 101A? I hear this word repeated too often in industry to take it for granted.

Customers know they can get implementers anywhere. But they want someone to challenge them to more productive, profitable activity. Today's customer wants someone who can start fires—not just put them out.

4. *Innovation.* Still another desired attribute that crops up frequently is innovation. They want more innovation then imitation.

Your customers are becoming concerned with the growing buyer belief that there is insignificant difference between brands. They're equally concerned with the inroads being made by private labels and generic products.

Thus, customers are increasingly anxious for your company's uniqueness, freshness—across the board. With all due respect for your individual contributions, they want to know what others at your company can offer. *All* are expected to contribute, thereby compounding your value. Therefore, your company's other functions and people should be promoted as being as dynamic as you are.

These four words are particularly meaningful to prospects—and they are impressed according to the degree of your evidence of these attributes. Thus, the combination of your capacity for leadership, being decision-oriented, plus dedication to initiative and innovation, could be stressed as the basis of your operation.

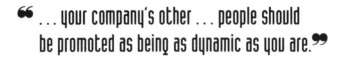

❝ … your company's other … people should be promoted as being as dynamic as you are.❞

Smoke Out Desirable Prospects So You Don't Get Burned

◆ Perspective ◆ Opportunity ◆ Quantity ◆ Type
◆ The Fifteen Standards for Qualifying Customers
◆ Is It Worth the Time and Effort?
◆ Transom (Unsolicited) Business

Perspective

The total selling program, conducted as diligently as is necessary to win, is a laborious process. There's no magic, no miracles, just a thorough, all-out effort to prevent coming in second again.

One of the most critical functions in the process consists of evaluating prospects for solicitation. The purpose is to explore, without spending much time or money, whether a prospect would be a viable customer.

This chapter includes the necessary standards for evaluating prospects. It is well worth applying as many of these standards as possible because even though you can't pick your relatives, you *can* pick your prospects.

❝ Without consistent follow-through, prospects are only suspects. ❞

Opportunity

Your prospect list can consist of whatever customers you want—for which your product or service is reasonably appropriate. Then, rumors to the contrary, go after them. (These rumors were probably started and perpetuated by your competitors anyway.)

It is assumed that certain accounts are locked in—and thereby unapproachable. But the most indelible impression made upon me in working with various manufacturers and services is that no supplier owns any customer. So the matter of *least* concern to you is an account's vulnerability. A supposedly satisfied customer may be surreptitiously planning an evaluation of its suppliers.

Quantity

Don't consider any aspect of soliciting business as being too basic, even if it is as basic as "How many prospects should I have?" Your operation can only amount to the sum of its parts.

For perspective, let's define *prospect*. It is an account you will actively pursue. Without consistent follow-through, prospects are only suspects. Prospects can be categorized as *competitive*—those which have indicated being receptive to buying, or *missionary*—accounts you want to go after even though you don't know if they are willing to buy. In either case, they represent your potential for growth beyond the additional business that can be generated from your customers. With this understanding, let's answer the following question: How many prospects? You should have as many as you are willing to go the full route in soliciting their business—ranging from introductory letter to post-presentation activity. And each should be worth the time and effort you have to take to score.

Obviously, the specific number of prospects would depend on your company's size and character—and your individual capacity. Don't base your decision on how much time you have left after all your customers have been taken care of. Challenge yourself. Establish a number that can produce significant growth—not just replace what is lost by attrition.

Type

Are your selling accomplishments causing you to lose by winning? You can become smugly satisfied with your performance because of scoring so well, blithely equating conquest with success. You are only right if the only criterion for achievement is the number of accounts landed. But are these the accounts you really *want*? Be as self-serving in selecting potential customers as they are in choosing suppliers.

If aggressive enough, you can always pick up transient and slow-pay dogs. Or dull, stagnant accounts. (The former are unaffordable and won't last long. As for the others, you wish they would leave and take their drudgery with them). Somewhat better are one-time sales to more desirable companies. However, your objective is a long-term relationship. This is the difference between a prospect being a buyer or a becoming a customer.

It seems that if a prospect will buy—and pay—they qualify. But selling, like life, isn't that simple. There is a variety of factors that determine the appeal of an account, reduce risk—and make this portion of your life more palatable.

Instead of being a collector for the sake of numbers, convert your operation into one that you can *enjoy*—both financially and professionally. It doesn't cost any more to go after desirable business than to pursue drudgery. Customers don't want a mediocre supplier. Why should you settle for that type of account?

Since prospects establish specific criteria for selecting suppliers, it is just as appropriate for you to develop standards for qualifying them. Listed below are the fifteen I consider essential. (If you can think of any more, I would appreciate hearing about them.)

The Fifteen Standards for Qualifying Customers

1. *Profitability.* If the dollars aren't satisfactory, nothing else can make up for the shortfall. Therefore, don't be lulled by intermediate words such as *sales* or *income.* All that matters is the amount of profit you come away with.

2. *Excitement.* Having passed *the first* hurdle, the second most important consideration is whether you could get *excited* over working with this account.

   Excitement will enable you to cope with all the aggravation and frustration inherent with any customer. If there isn't the ecstasy to offset the agony, this will be a brief encounter of the worst kind.

3. *Compatible Relationship.* If the prospect is sufficiently appealing, then the potential for a *compatible relationship* needs to be determined. Are they *your* kind of people? Could you live with them? Would they make you

❝ An obnoxious prospect will become an obnoxious customer.❞

look good? If the prospect doesn't bring these three traits to the altar, you won't change them after the wedding.

Even if the dollars seem right, if the chemistry isn't there, you can't afford what would soon become an ex-customer. So, without being paranoid, you need to be sensitive to a prospect's conduct. It is the clue to the type of account they would be. Do they treat you like a potential partner or like a peddler? Are they cooperative or combative? And re-member—at this stage, they are on their good behavior.

Regardless of how far you've progressed with a prospect—and how much time, effort, and money you've invested—if necessary, bite the bullet while you can still spit it out. Where do you draw the line? *You should never have to take abuse from a prospect.*

For example, here are two recent experiences of abuse during a presen-tation. In one case, the prospect person in charge kept moving his fore-finger in a circular motion—giving the presenters the speed-up signal. In the other, the prospect person in charge repeatedly interrupted with the dare, "C'mon, tell me something I don't know." In both instances, the rudeness had a devastating effect on the presenters.

I was asked by each agency what they should have done under the circumstances. There is only one answer. At the onset of this adversarial behavior, they should have packed up their tents and left. An obnoxious prospect will become an obnoxious customer. If you persist, you're a masochist. Besides, this type doesn't deserve you.

Yet, despite the critical nature of compatibility, there are people in sales who, for economic or competitive reasons, have a "sales at any price" attitude. But, the purpose of solicitation is to satisfy more than the "hunt/kill" challenge. Rather, its ultimate intent is to acquire profitable accounts—with whom there can be a harmonious relationship.

4. *Expectations.* How do their *expectations* of a supplier compare with what you believe to be reasonable?

    Actually, for whatever time or work requested that they are contractu-ally entitled to, if they are willing to compensate you accordingly, they qualify. (Of course, this presumes the prospect measures up based on the previous three requisites.)

5. *Reason for Change.* If the prospect is planning to change suppliers, flush out the reason. Then objectively consider whether you buy it, or have the gut feeling of becoming their next victim. Better satisfy yourself with their integrity now—rather than ending up as another one of their capricious changes.

6. *Legitimate Search.* You will also want to be sure that the prospect is conducting a *legitimate search* as opposed to using this event as a device to get a batch of ideas—cheap—or as a means to scare the hell out of their present supplier. It's bad enough being had by customers. You shouldn't have to be taken by prospects, too.

7. *Marketing Problems and Opportunities.* What about the prospect's *marketing problems and opportunities*? Would you be associated with a winner? Or one you could help become a winner? A supplier is considered only as good as their contribution to the success of their customers. If, for whatever the reason, you can't become a hero, back off. If the product is an Edsel, or there isn't a viable market for it, the last thing you need is to be associated with a failure.

8. *Dynamics.* In addition, how about the *dynamics* of this prospect? Are they aggressively introducing new products? Or stagnating with those at the tail end of their life cycle? Go with the company that thrives on the same stimulation as you do.

9–12. *Advertising/Sales Ratio, Attitude toward Marketing, Potential for Growth, Credit History.* Basic as it may seem, don't overlook appraising the prospect's *advertising/sales ratio, attitude toward marketing, potential for growth,* and *credit history.* (If appropriate, pull a credit check.) Any of these factors could provide you with a valuable insight to the character and status of this prospect—and strongly influence whether this should be a go or no-go proposition.

13. *Special Requests.* If the prospect requests a speculative proposal (involving a write-up and examples beyond standard practice), you need to ask yourself some questions. Is the request reasonable? Are they worth the expense? Although a price tag can't be put on the ideas and information in the proposal, there are circumstances under which you shouldn't have to eat the entire cost either (unless you want to retain ownership.) If their intentions are honorable, your contribution should be an investment with sufficient possibility for payout, not dues required to play the game.

14. *"Musical Suppliers."* Unfortunately, there will always be a hard core of companies that will impetuously dump a supplier as soon as any diffi-

culty occurs. They use this device as a panacea to cover for whatever is wrong with themselves.

Little can be done about this breed, but for solicitation purposes you should know who they are. Thus, prior to spending any time or money on a prospect, check the duration of their previous supplier affiliations. And if you find their tenure to be unstable, recognize that being associated with this type of account would be a crapshoot. If, however, one comes along that seems irresistible, only become involved if they can be profitable from the first day.

15. *Think Bigger and Bolder.* Finally, *think bigger and bolder*—for three critical reasons. First, it can cost just as much in time to go after a used car dealer as in trying to get your foot in the door at General Motors. So why not invest the same effort in greater, surer potential.

Second, the larger account is likely to be more profitable. Since their people are usually more knowledgeable, there is less need to educate them prior to presenting your proposal. So selling time can be reduced to a minimum—which translates into more economical use of your time.

And third, it has been found that, in general, the larger the account, the greater the longevity. By contrast, it has also been learned that the smaller the account, the likelier it is to overreact to difficulty, often naively assuming that changing suppliers will provide the solution.

There you have it. The fifteen means for judging a prospect. Be discriminating. Concentrate on those with as much as possible going for you. It costs much less to lose a prospect than it costs to lose a customer. Further, those prescreened according to as many of the criteria provided will stay longer. And you will have a happier, more profitable relationship.

Is It Worth the Time and Effort?

When you get the opportunity to pitch an account of acceptable size, you may jump at the chance—without first determining whether it is the best use of your time and effort. If the presentation requires going all out, this total immersion may preclude doing the same for other prospects during this preparation period. But other prospects may be substantially bigger—yet entail only the same amount of work.

So don't take yourself out of contention for a much more valuable account by settling for a bird in the hand—unless you've flushed out the rest of the bush first.

Transom (Unsolicited) Business

Sometimes, though, this evaluation system gets thrown out of whack—when a prospect contacts *you* offering their account. This is such a wonderfully flattering experience that your objectivity may vanish. There is much to be said for being wanted, but in this warm glow, little thought may be given to the prospect's desirability—and you may succumb to their initiative.

But they might be unprofitable, dull, incompatible, unreasonable, fickle, a loser, lethargic, cheap, stagnant, unrealistic, slow to pay, adversarial, and/or too small. Even worse, your company may have to staff up to service this dog, and then be faced with the heartache of having to cut back.

Here is how to spare yourself this possible trauma. When approached by a potential customer representing an effortless conquest, ask this sobering question: *Would I have contacted them?*

If not, don't get carried away by having your ego massaged. However, if you find you would have contacted them, the affiliation is far likelier to be a successful one.

❝ It costs much less to lose a prospect than it costs to lose a customer.❞

Twelve Sources of Leads You Can Exploit

◆ Perspective ◆ Employees ◆ Company CEO
◆ Customers ◆ Customer Board Members
◆ Customers' Suppliers ◆ Questionnaire or RFP
◆ Corporate Advertising ◆ Business Services ◆ Competitors
◆ "Hot" Salespersons ◆ Trade Shows
◆ Job Applicants ◆ Summary

Perspective

There is a variety of sources of leads. But they are usually unused or misused due to misconceptions regarding their worth. Such being the case, in this chapter I will present you with twelve opportunities. How many of these are you taking advantage of?

To varying degrees, these are not conventional sources of leads. If you slough any off as being too remote, you may also slough off income. By restricting yourself to those that are traditional, you are setting a limit on how much you can earn. So dare to shoot for more than the obvious.

Employees

Start with your most logical source of leads, those having the greatest stake in your company: your employees. They offer two mutually valuable opportunities.

Here is a plan you can propose to your company that will provide a continuous source of sales potential, a share of which can accrue to you—along with management appreciation of your contribution.

First, bulletin all employees, informing them that their possibility for raises and promotions depends on company growth. Then ask them to furnish the names of anyone they know who could be worth soliciting. This could be a friend, relative, or neighbor who might be able to influence their company's decision to purchase your product or service.

To encourage employee cooperation, inform them that they don't have to do anything but supply the names. And they can remain anonymous if they choose to. Employees should be surveyed for names on a regular, semi-annual basis.

Some of you may assume you can't use this idea because your company is too large. But LINTAS/New York has been conducting this survey for years—and they have 451 employees in that office! I am told they get more leads than they can possibly follow up. What more compelling appeal could there be than raises and promotions? Apparently, this survey is one of the many things they are doing right which has contributed to such a successful new business record.

Second, have every one of your people submit the name of a single prospect (appropriate to your operation) that they want your company to acquire more than any other. These names should be placed at the top of your new business list. Doing so allows you to channel your efforts towards prospects who turn your people on—rather than grinding away at uninspiring but assumedly more vulnerable accounts. And it will also encourage your employees to volunteer additional leads.

From a personal standpoint, this strategy produces a worthwhile bonus: working with desirable customers. With the heavier demands made upon you for increased sales results, if you aren't enjoying yourself selling, you might just as well go back to mud wrestling.

Company CEO

The most valuable antenna for sales leads is often the least used: the head of your company. Human nature being what it is, employees with leads would prefer to divulge them to the CEO. But the CEO is often unavailable. Yet, if your CEO isn't exploiting his or her position to attract leads, your company is being done an injustice. Maintaining a high profile for receptivity will encourage both employees and outsiders to volunteer such information.

If you are the CEO, make it known that anyone with a legitimate new business tip has automatic entree to your office. To most people, this is a powerful incentive because it enables them to ingratiate themselves with the most important person in the company.

Ideally, communicate this request to your people in an imaginative manner. For instance, send them a simulated engraved invitation. This makes it official. And the sense of humor conveyed by this device should generate good response because it indicates you would be easy to meet with.

Customers

Of course, evidence of customer satisfaction is the most impressive tactic for attracting leads. You can't ask customers to take any initiative on your behalf. If you do, they might feel as though they are being used. But you can request their endorsement. In doing so, you imply you would welcome being tipped off to any leads—and that you appreciate their recommendations.

Customer Board Members

The best sales lead is a matchmaker. Like this one.

Unless any of your customers are a one-man band, they probably have some sort of board of directors. And it is possible that some of its members sit on additional boards. Seemingly, they should have a favorable attitude toward your company. And they could be quite influential on your behalf.

Therefore, identify your customer board members—along with the other corporations with whom they are involved. The simplest way to find out who they are is from their annual report—which is available to anyone. And with a little ingenuity you can flush out their other connections. Then decide which of these accounts would be appropriate and desirable prospects for you.

Next, check internally to find out who has an inside track to someone at this company who is in a position to set up a meeting for you with whatever board members you desire. Your objective is to gain entree to the person(s) at this board member's other affiliations with the authority to buy your product or service. If this board member will pave the way, it enables going in with the blessings of someone very important to this company.

❝ Start with your most logical source of leads ... your employees.❞

Seems unrealistically ambitious? No way. If a board member will see you, it won't be for the purpose of rejection. So you will at least have an audience. And as a salesperson, you're on your way.

Capitalize on this pre-conditioned source of clout—earned by the positive impression made in doing business with them. Entering on a red carpet sure beats the usual bed of coals.

Customers' Suppliers

Apropos of your customers being a springboard for additional business, find out who all of their suppliers are. Although this strategy precludes approaching any competitors, there will be enough other kissin' cousins who, with some stretch of the imagination, could be valuable prospects for you. Inasmuch as a mutual interest exists, there is a bona fide reason to see you. And you are going in with the implied endorsement of a shared customer.

Obviously, your thrust is based on the logic of serving both, and why this arrangement would strengthen this other supplier's relationship with your shared customer.

This action should be taken for each new account landed—thereby compounding your new business opportunities.

Questionnaire or RFP

A questionnaire or RFP (Request For Proposal) from a possible customer should receive priority attention. How you handle this challenge will be a door-opener or door-closer.

I'm aware that these inquiries are usually sent to those in a staff capacity—rather than people in a line capacity such as yourself. However, the source of this inquiry may be in your territory—possibly giving you a special insight. Or your particular experience could be valuable for furnishing the answers needed. So if you get wind of one of these forms that you could help fill out, consider how you could best contribute.

The questionnaire or RFP is the prospect's screening process. Besides obtaining the information desired, this tactic saves them from many time-consuming pitches. From your standpoint, the caliber and pertinence of questions provides a valuable insight into the character of the prospect and whether they would be desirable as a customer.

Some of these exploratory surveys are mailed because it is assumed this is a procedure that must be observed. As a result, a generic form is sent to a ridiculously long list of potential suppliers. Or this procedure might be used by the person conducting the search to impress associates and protect their flanks. Or even worse, it may be a device to legitimatize a hidden agenda (i.e., already predisposed toward selecting a preferred supplier).

Because a questionnaire can range from a considerable amount of work to a cover-up, critically appraise each. For instance, ascertain whether this is a canned form or one specifically prepared for this project. Is it intelligently conceived from which a rational decision could be made? Do you have a gut feel that they are on the level—or does this seem to be a routine they are observing, but won't abide by? And finally, while it's flattering receiving one of these RFPs, objectively ask yourselves, "Do we really want this account?" Then take off the rose-colored glasses and decide whether you can justify the effort and risk.

If you conclude that the odds are acceptable—and this company is on the level—here is how to win in the questionnaire game. For openers, if you deem it worth participating in what may be a charade, you need to begin by distinguishing your operation from the multitude of competitors. This applies equally to the following factors.

Concept

Your reply is the first impression of your company. It must be business-like—but must not come across as a legal document. Rather, your straightforward answers should be packaged with a flair: visually as well as verbally intriguing.

Appearance

This is the first indication of your vitality. I am not advocating pop-out inserts or die-cut pages. However, your visual treatment should be highly conducive to being read. Specifically, the format should be so attractive that you would want to take personal credit for it.

Then, as evidence of its importance, insert these pages in an impressive binder, one that is conducive to being opened. And this, too, should serve as a vehicle to demonstrate your vitality.

Content

At this stage of the project, your contact will have neither the time nor inclination to sweat out a thesis. Don't try to impress them by the pound. To encourage them to read your reply, be brief. To encourage a favorable reaction, be clear.

It is important to comply precisely with their directions. Answer *every* question. Your replies should deal directly and fully with what they want to know—not what you prefer to promote.

For instance, if they inquire as to what extent you company can perform various functions, don't come back with, "We are a full-service operation." This answer appears to duck the issue, and could be seen as a smoke screen for inadequacy or unavailability of this function.

❝ Entering on a red carpet sure beats the usual bed of coals. ❞

Remember: if any license is taken, or if there is any omission or evasion, you become suspect, providing the prospect with the reason for eliminating you.

However, while playing the game, there is still a selling opportunity available. After having completed this exercise, strictly adhering to the ground rules, add a brief statement at the end explaining why your company should be selected. As this is the final shot, if it is compelling enough, the prospect will be likelier to retain what you most want them to know.

Yet, even with this disciplined approach going for you, you are still one of too many suppliers who have responded. Now go the payout step further. When returning their questionnaire, include one of your own—seeking the input needed to customize a presentation for them. (If they cooperate, you have a live one.)

This action separates your company from the others in the cattle call, conveys professionalism and initiative—and registers that your presentation will be based on their needs, not your wants. This strategy can provide the competitive edge that will enable you to make the cut at this stage.

The questionnaire you receive is a means of weeding out candidates so the sender can concentrate on a manageable group for consideration. Granted, you can't *win* them all. But you sure ought to at least qualify.

Corporate Advertising

If your company conducts an aggressive advertising campaign, will it produce leads for you? Of itself (unless it contains a coupon requesting a response), don't hold your breath.

Regardless of how brilliant it is, it can only create a favorable environment for subsequent *direct* selling effort. It doesn't have any tangible value—unless merchandised. Sound familiar? When this campaign is announced at the sales meeting, it is touted as establishing buyer acceptance for you. Ostensibly, the nice warm feeling generated will motivate the sales force to produce over their heads.

However, after the mass euphoria wears off, you have to individually apply the general direction given. Namely, convert the overall strategy furnished into greatest local impact. This includes using evidence of your company's advertising to communicate to prospects how this will be of value to them. The implementers will save their jobs. The innovators will ensure them—and make more money.

The difference lies in *how* you capitalize on the advertising—beyond the standard instructions you receive. Realistically, its function is to create desire for your product or service—not for you. So, it is up to you to harness its appeal to serve your own purposes.

Ideally, your company's campaign is distinctive and memorable. So there should be at least familiarity going for you. Determine what grabber exists in the message that will grease the skids for you. What opener does it inspire? How can it help you close? This corporate investment will pay off for you individually only to the extent that you cash in on it.

Business Services

Being in a selling capacity, you can't afford to overlook a single opportunity. One source that is seldom taken advantage of is the services your company retains: legal, accounting, and insurance. It is very possible these sources also do business with potential customers of yours, and could be influential on your behalf.

Get clearance from whomever necessary at your company to contact the person at these firms who handles your account. In this case, since you are the buyer rather than the seller, you are entitled to ask your representative at these firms to apply whatever clout in your interest at these prospects.

Then, periodically (after having paid one of their invoices), check with them to find out to whom you've been recommended. Because people do what you *inspect*—not what you expect.

Competitors

Here's a twist. How about your competitors: other salespersons who pitch the same prospects? On occasion, they are approached by, or tipped off to, susceptible accounts with whom they would have a customer conflict or are undesirable to them for other reasons.

Develop a reciprocal arrangement with a key group of your peers so that when such a situation arises, they suggest you as an alternative or at least inform you of the availability of this account. Obviously, the incentive for them to cooperate is your willingness to do likewise.

For this plan to be meaningful, take it beyond the hollow gesture stage. To get underway, select those in your area who, by virtue of their company's specialty or size, are not head-to-head competitors. Then arrange to demonstrate your basic sales approach for them—and for them to reciprocate. Now each can knowledgeably and confidently recommend the other when appropriate.

Then multiply this source by going beyond it. Make this handshake offer to other competitors who could be a threat with whom you have a close personal contact. Since there may be instances in which you might come up against them, obviously you will have to be more circumspect about what you reveal. However, it is worth negotiating this agreement for the insider advantage it can provide.

In fact, to cover all bases, the person who heads up the new business operation for a major New York agency has a plan for having lunch with his counterparts at other shops. These back-scratching sessions are scheduled with maximum frequency. While no one is giving the store away, he has found he can thrive on the free samples collected.

This strategy of one hand washing another could clue you in on accounts in a buying mode and techniques for selling them that you might not hear about otherwise.

"Hot" Salespersons

People in sales get in the rut of thinking of new business leads in terms of obvious sources. And they all wind up tilling the same worked-out fields.

Go beyond the routine into a relatively untapped area. An area that on the surface seems so improbable, few exploit it: "hot" salespersons.

Having achieved the reputation of being "hot," it is assumed their accounts are untouchable. However, sometimes a closer study of their track record reveals that while they are scoring so well, a significant amount of this business falls through the cracks afterwards. There are several reasons for this revolving door effect:

◆ Success can beget complacency. These men and women are lulled into believing their reputation will make their accounts safe from predators. Then they become careless. And their customers become vulnerable.

◆ A hot new business streak can also cause arrogance. This results in illusions of omnipotence. And the salesperson lapses into sloppy account handling—whereby their customers can be had.

◆ Then there are the salespersons experiencing explosive rather than controlled results. And they begin to unravel before knowing what hit them.

◆ Finally, there are the cases in which going after the prospect becomes more fulfilling than servicing them as a customer. When customers discover this, they quickly revert to being prospects—for someone else.

So just because some men and women have been scoring heavily on landing new business, that does not mean they are correspondingly "hot" in holding on to accounts. Actually, some effort may have been diverted from the follow-through function—with their customer roster becoming susceptible to others offering greater dedication.

Thus, regardless of how formidable those showboat salespersons may seem, their preoccupation with conquest could enable you to lure their disenchanted customers before their susceptibility becomes evident to their current suppliers.

Trade Shows

You have targeted a specific industry or occupation to be cultivated (one in which you are a proved authority, another for diversification). Now comes the laborious task of contacting each prospect individually.

But what if one or more key executives from most of these companies regularly congregate in the same building for the same several days? They do—at their industry's annual trade show.

Sure, you know that. Because when you have a customer exhibiting at this type of event, you try to get over there and roam around for a while, and of course, dutifully put in an appearance at their space. Then, in addition, if you should happen to run into a prospect, that would be a welcome bonus.

For solicitation purposes though, instead of this being a casual occasion from which something might accidentally occur, exploit this opportunity via a planned course of action. Compared to the usual time-consuming series of letters and follow-up phone calls attempting to make contact, prospects attending these events are like ducks in a shooting gallery. Establish a procedure for intentional contact that would establish

◆ What individuals you want to reach

◆ How your approach would be conducted in this environment

◆ What you want to accomplish at this time

Granted, those you want to contact are there for another purpose, one very important to them. And your interfering would be resented, *unless you are perceived as being worth meeting.*

Here is how you can gain this stature. Offer to deliver a report to this event on a matter currently critical to this industry or occupation. The report would consist of vital research or case histories that would result in solutions of value to them. If your offer is accepted, you achieve somewhat of a celebrity status. Further, the acceptance amounts to endorsement by the sponsoring organization—acknowledging you as an authority in their field.

The usual reaction to this idea is: "Super idea—but it is out of my league." But working a trade show takes an angle this bold in order to produce. The opportunity is so great that it is worth trying to play over your head. Because you will then become a seller rather than just a visitor.

Despite this inducement, you may conclude this action would be personally impractical. Even so, don't write off this opportunity. If at all possible, find someone else in your company to capitalize on it. Because at least, you'll be able to benefit by association.

Job Applicants

Here is an opportunity that is seldom taken advantage of—but can result in landing your next major account. Arrange with your personnel department, or whomever does the hiring at your company, to exploit job applicants. In the interview, they may be able to reveal account vulnerability—and divulge the strategy necessary to sell these live prospects.

It is necessary to flush out why this person left their employer—or wants to do so. Is an account shaky? Is the company? The latter would indicate the receptivity of existing customers to change.

Of course you'll have to take whatever the applicant says with a grain of salt. Is this person bitter? How privy is he or she to what is really going on? Interpretation is required, but it is worth the effort. Because even if it is a matter of finding the rare pearl in an oyster, the reward can justify the dive.

The value of this tactic was confirmed by Jim Stein. He was Executive Creative Director at Campbell Mithun in Minneapolis when I was conducting a New Business seminar there. Jim mentioned that he manages to spend some time with whomever comes in to apply for a job in copy or art. (This is no minor feat considering there are 460 people employed in this office.) "Admittedly," he said, "Nine out of ten are a pain in the neck. But from that tenth one, I get something. And it pays off."

So a practice should be made of probing those looking for a job—especially in sales. Then periodically check with those performing this function to find out what is being learned that could benefit you.

Summary

We have now dealt with planning your new business program, developing prospects, and exploiting leads. Critical to the success of these functions is setting timing for each phase. Because goals without due dates are just wishes.

Appeals and Tactics for Getting Appointments

◆ Perspective ◆ Advertising Medium ◆ Level of Contact
◆ The Letter: Content and Appearance ◆ Getting Through
◆ Telephone Techniques ◆ Inducements ◆ Persistence
◆ Extent of Follow-Through ◆ Rejection
◆ Unexpected Contact ◆ Gimmicks ◆ How Innovative?

Perspective

Some companies keep a low profile in the new business arena so customers won't suspect this activity will cause them to receive less attention. Other companies claim they don't have to bother soliciting new business because their outstanding products will produce so much transom business. And the parade passes both of them by because there is a direct correlation between solicitation activity and prospect interest—they equate such effort with success.

Companies are discovering that when it becomes known they are aggressive in selling, prospects begin to contact them. If companies slack off, though, prospects will as well. Becoming more active also offers a valuable by-product: it makes it likelier that you will find out about accounts that are receptive to buying.

Advertising Medium

Once a company decides to become more aggressive in going after additional business, they want immediate results. This objective starts with taking the action necessary to generate leads. To begin with, lengthy meetings are held to determine what medium would be most productive. (i.e., trade publications, newspapers, radio, billboards, etc.) However, after the medium is selected, the creative concept is developed and the schedule is run, there is a rude awakening: *nothing happened.* Such brilliant copy—yet no response. Why would there be? As far as prospects are concerned, if you want their business, you have to *come after it.* But you can't feasibly find out who saw your ad or heard your lead-seeking commercial. Thus, you're stymied.

Sure, the advertising created favorable awareness. But your objective is to get appointments at prospects with buyers. And the only way this can be accomplished is via one-to-one contact, namely *direct mail* to targeted individuals whom you have qualified as prospects.

Your follow-through activity can now be gotten underway. Specifically, phone calls to set up meetings. Persistent in practice—and with compelling reason why it would be to their advantage to clear time for you.

While impersonal media can develop a positive image for your company, they don't actually *sell* for you. In the final analysis, only you can do that through direct contact. Since you are the *ultimate* direct contact, you deserve all possible help. Admittedly, it may be totally impractical for you, as an individual, to conduct a direct mail program. However, if your company isn't providing this support, they are only at fault if your request for it is refused.

Submit a proposal as to why this door-opener is needed. To increase management receptivity:

◆ Itemize your problems and opportunities

◆ Set forth the objectives for the mailing(s)

◆ Suggest the procedure for implementation

◆ Identify the audience to be reached

◆ Pay it off with the results that can be expected

Then, as a clincher, furnish a draft of the letter along with samples of any enclosures (later in this chapter, see Letter: Content and Appearance). Now all management has to do is execute and pay for it.

In the event preparing the above proposal seems like more than you can handle, try this scenario. You've determined that this mailing could significantly contribute to improving your sales performance. Management approves this project—if *you* execute it. The odds are that somehow you'd figure out how to come through.

Are you reluctant to do so because this isn't your area of expertise? Don't sell yourself short. Who would know better what support you need? You're only lacking if you fail to check periodically on the fulfillment of this project.

Level of Contact

I am often asked, "At what level should you start an initial contact?" I respect that there are those of you whose contact is dictated by prospect operating procedure. However, for the majority of you who are not restricted to a designated buyer, and who can take some license in your approach, the following strategy has proved effective.

A person in sales will usually start with a contact perceived as being at their peer level because they are more comfortable with this person and can better relate to him. However, if this lower echelon person is feeling sorry for himself that day, and refuses to set up an appointment, you've effectively been ruled out for that prospect. Then your only alternative is pulling an end run. And he will cut you up if you try it.

Instead, start with the person your research indicates is the decision-maker. Maybe it is one of their vice presidents. If you luck out and she'll hold still— great. You've landed on Boardwalk. While it is likelier that she won't see you, it is quite possible that she will buck you to the appropriate buyer.

Now you have acceptance. Send the VP a thank-you note, with a copy to the buyer, confirming that you will follow through *per the VP's request*. Of course her subordinate will see you. Now it's a matter of convincing the buyer of why it would be to *his advantage* to explore the value of your product or service. Thus, your initial contact should be where the power lies—rather than with whom you feel more confident. Go for the gold. It is your likeliest way to get into the game.

Your approach is limited only by its appeal. Fallon McElligott, a hot ad agency in Minneapolis, attributes a significant amount of its new business success to their level of prospect contact: the CEO. The agency selects a short list of desired blue-chip accounts. Then, under the guise of being a major investor, they contact approximately ten financial firms, Merrill Lynch, Shearson-Lehman, etc., regarding the advisability of buying this prospect's stock. This survey also includes inquiries as to growth potential ROI, etc.

❝ If there is anything said ... that would require any thought, either simplify it or omit it.❞

Upon completion of this research, a letter is sent to the prospect's CEO, informing him of the confidential financial study just conducted on his company, listing the prestigious security analysts contacted, and the series of critical questions asked. The letter concludes by mentioning that the agency will phone in two weeks for an appointment to reveal these vital findings. Obviously this offer is irresistible. So you can bet the CEO's first act is to get on the phone to the agency and insist, "How about today at 2:00?"

This strategy enables Fallon McElligott to cut through all the bureaucratic layers of management and get directly to the person in charge of decision making. Then, if sufficiently impressed, the CEO has the authority to at least institute an agency review.

Thus, you too can start off at as high a level as you wish—if your reason for contact is intriguing enough—and get action sooner, because of leading from strength.

The Letter: Content and Appearance

Every attempt to get an appointment should be initiated by letter. (This would only be disregarded if the account is ridiculously small or your contact is illiterate. In either case, you probably wouldn't want them anyway). This implies the importance of your contacting them and makes you a known quantity. If you don't identify yourself in advance, in your follow-through phone call you'll be "Charlie who?"

Bear in mind your initial letter to a prospect is the equivalent of an introductory ad for a new product, both visually and in terms of content. So apply the same standards.

Considerable thought and effort is given to oral skills and selling techniques. And there is a variety of training firms specializing in this field who are retained to improve speaker delivery. Yet, there is nowhere near as much concern for your *written* communication, although it is even more important because it is your *first* contact with the prospect.

Are your solicitation and follow-through letters as appealing as your presenters have been programmed to be? Are these mailings as personable and disciplined? From what I have seen in my cross-pollinating among advertisers and 396 agencies: probably not. Vocally, you want to be so appealing as to attract and hold attention, and to be effective enough to persuade. These accomplishments depend on your appearance, the interest level you create, and your command of the language.

Well then, shouldn't these same objectives and requirements be applied to your written approach? You're just using a different medium for the same purpose: to convince the prospect that your product or service is best for them.

To convert your verbal impact into writing, here are the ground rules for your letter:

◆ To encourage its being read, be brief. Write it telegraphically—as if you were paying for it by the word. And, according to a study by the Direct Marketing Association, no paragraph should be more than four lines long.

◆ The opening statement should contain a promise of benefit.

◆ Then, pay it off with your plans for follow-through contact.

And finally, from no less an authority than Bob Stone, retired CEO of Stone & Adler, (who is probably the ultimate maven on direct response activity): "If there is anything said in the letter that would require any thought, either simplify it or omit it."

To apply these ground rules most effectively, considering what's at stake, forego any false pride. Don't hesitate to get the reaction of anyone you admire as being very articulate. How well is its content expressed? Any suggestions for improvement? It is also important to determine how its visual effect can be enhanced. Asking for feedback does not cast doubt on your ability. Rather, it is evidence of your professionalism.

One more key suggestion: Break the mold. Nowhere is it required that your letter look like all the others—routine and unimaginative. Instead, have the courage to be distinctive, especially if it enables giving greater emphasis to the selling points. The sample letter on the next page is one of the techniques I use in soliciting agencies.

There are conclusive reasons why you should pave the way with a letter. First, cold turkey phone calls smack of canvassing. And second, if you fail to create interest first, it is too easy for a prospect to brush you off. So use the letter/phone sequence of contact. It makes the difference between being a professional and being a peddler.

Getting Through

Your phone call is intended for your contact. Usually, however, that isn't who receives it. Rather, it is routed through the secretary or assistant, who becomes

❝ A secretary, like anyone else, thrives on recognition.❞

July 27, 1989

Mr. Hall Adams, Jr.
Chairman & Chief Executive Officer
Leo Burnett Company, Inc.
35 West Wacker Drive
Chicago, IL 60601

Dear Cap:

Q. What will your Agency gain by scheduling my shirt-sleeve session on New
   Business?

A. THE INSIGHT AS TO ACTUAL ADVERTISER REACTION TO AGENCY
   SOLICITATION—AND WHAT AGENCIES ARE DISCOVERING SUC-
   CEEDS OR FAILS.

Q. Why does this session prove so valuable?

A. IT REVEALS THE TESTED IDEAS AND SOLUTIONS THAT CAN
   TRIGGER YOUR WINNING THE BUSINESS YOU WANT.

Q. How can you keep pace with your competition?

A. SCHEDULE THIS SESSION, CUSTOMIZED FOR YOUR AGENCY, AS
   HAVE 395 OTHERS (OVER TWO-THIRDS OF WHOM HAVE INVITED
   ME BACK).

Q. How much for this payout investment?

A. THIS EIGHT-HOUR SESSION, HELD AT YOUR OFFICE TO BENEFIT AS
   MANY OF YOUR STAFF AS DESIRED, IS A FLAT $_____ (PLUS
   EXPENSES).

Q. What more will your Agency gain from these "street smarts" on what
   works or doesn't?

A. THESE WILL SAVE YOUR STAFF CONSIDERABLE TIME AND EF-
   FORT—AND MAKE THE DIFFERENCE BETWEEN WINNING OR COM-
   ING IN SECOND.

Q. **Since there is always the time to become more successful,** how soon can
   you take advantage of this opportunity?

A. _____

Cordially,

Jack L. Matthews

P.S.

Q. Do these Agencies having scheduled this New Business session actually
   find my input so rewarding?

A. SEE ATTACHED TRANSOM LETTER.

JLM:cam
Attachment

your *primary* contact. Only after his or her screening will you be cleared for conversation. Getting through this filter doesn't require several dozen long-stem American Beauty roses or tickets to the big game. Instead, here is how to emotionally and safely ingratiate yourself.

A secretary, like anyone else, thrives on recognition. Therefore, your *first* phone call should be to the receptionist, or the Personnel Department if necessary, to find out the secretary's full name. Then call back so you can address her or him accordingly.

This gives the impression that you have so much respect for the importance of the secretarial function that it was worth the effort to learn her or his name in advance. Whatever you do, *do not* start out on a first-name basis with the assistant. As a result of this deference, the secretary will be a conduit rather than an obstacle to communicate with the contact you're seeking.

Telephone Techniques

Since the telephone can be your selling friend or foe, here is what you need to know regarding the content and conduct of your phone conversation. (And if you are afflicted with phoneaphobia, this will help you pick up the 10,000 pound phone.) Regardless of how intriguing the written contact is, if the personal approach isn't correspondingly appealing, you will run out your string with that prospect.

To begin with, your phone call should start *before* you dial. You need to identify in advance a reason why the prospect should listen to you, rather than hoping that something occurs to you after she answers.

Now for your opener. Is there some irresistible grabber? Don't strain yourself. Buyers have heard most of the hackneyed nifties before. Instead, how about starting with something as logical as *why* you are calling her? This approach makes you acceptable because you are not wasting your prospect's time. Then, having opened by levelling with the prospect, skip the weather forecast and tired jokes. Your reason for contact should be intriguing enough so that you don't have to resort to small talk. Instead, stay on target by explaining why their company would benefit from meeting with you. Then set a date.

Granted, the prospect may have reservations about seeing you, and might offer some resistance. You will want to overcome any objections convincingly and unemotionally. In evaluating your rebuttal, apply this criterion: Would you put it in writing? Could you afford to have it on record?

Then, be easy to talk to. Obviously interested and receptive. Certainly not confrontational. Above all though, hear him or her out.

Yet, don't let the conversation drag. End it on a high note. It is especially important to leave the impression that it was worth his or her time because your input was so interesting, vital and useful.

Be prepared for the possibility that your contact may be a delightful person but have a lousy phone personality. So, listen to *what* is said—not how; your concern should be with the message, not its delivery.

In this initial phone conversation, you will probably be asked one of the two following questions. How you field it will determine whether or not there will be any further contact.

◆ Don't get caught off base by the most common question they ask. That is, "Why do you want to see us?" Well, why *do* you want to see them? Your answer should certainly be more imaginative than, "Because we want your business."

◆ If they snap, "Why the hell should we see you?", most often salespersons will counter with, "Because you owe it to yourself to know more about us." They don't owe themselves anything of the sort.

A buyer is held accountable for the specifications established (i.e., product characteristics, price, availability, etc.). Therefore, in reply to either question, tell them what they most want to hear. No mind games. Nothing cutesy. Get right to the point with: "Our product (service) can best satisfy your requirements."

If they ask, "How?" their inquiry provides the reason for the appointment. You answer, "This will be determined by the ten questions I need to ask you." Putting it more bluntly, there was the reason given by J. Walter Thompson to Schlitz as to why they should be selected: "Because our agency can help you sell more damn beer than any other."

That clinched it. With that response, they cut through all the competitive clutter—and reached the prospect's jugular.

Inducements

As the acknowledged authority on selling, Red Motley said, "Nothing happens until a sale is made." In your case, nothing can take place unless you set up an introductory meeting. However, a prospect will hardly ever see you just because you want to. Running leaner and meaner, they now need to be given a compelling reason to justify clearing the time.

Here are your eight tickets for admission. Any one of these can get you in:

◆ Research on their company, industry, market and or product, hitherto unavailable (If you conduct the research, of course it's been unavailable.)

◆ A new marketing insight of particular value to your contact

◆ An unusual industry development that he or she might not be aware of

◆ An idea for a new product—or the repositioning of an existing one

◆ If the prospect is planning to change or add suppliers, offer the input and direction for conducting a search and selection. Even if they presume they have all the information needed, they will be curious enough about what you may have to set a date

◆ An exceptional occurrence at your company that would be relevant to their interests and needs

◆ A choice bit of information about their competition. That's irresistible.

Yet, despite the appeal of any of these inducements, there will be some prospects who will flat out refuse to see you. But if you hate to accept defeat because this would be a marvelous account to have, play your trump card: "I have an idea for your industry that is so great, some company in it is going to use it. And because of my respect for your operation, I would like to give you first crack at it." (If you're good enough to solicit this account, you should be able to come up with this great idea.) It is highly unlikely that a prospect could turn down this offer. But if they are still obstinate, take it to any of their competitors who will want to see a good thing when they know it.

Whatever your approach, though, it had better be amply intriguing.

Persistence

Prospects have only as much potential as the extent to which you pursue them. The importance of perseverance in follow-through activity can't be stressed enough.

Get this. Prospects frequently express surprise at how easily suppliers give up on soliciting them. Apparently, there is a substantial amount of business going begging by default. There are several causes for blowing these opportunities.

No Guts

It takes a killer instinct to go after new business. The successful pitch requires attack—not just scouting. Any approach less than this amounts only to motion—not action, and no results!

False Pride

Here is a typical example. An agency had a very encouraging reaction to its pitch, so encouraging they thought they had scored. But they were informed they had been rejected because they were considered too small.

The agency president was devastated by this apparent injustice. I asked if he had countered with the fact that the company wasn't buying numbers, but people, and that his team had convincingly demonstrated their talent and experience. His reply was, "I'm not going to grovel."

He lost perspective. There aren't any principles compromised by offering a logical rebuttal to a sales objection. The only shame is allowing temperament to overrule judgment—thereby succumbing to an obstacle instead of conquering it.

So don't get in the new business pool unless you intend to swim the entire length. Because the deep end is a helluva place to quit.

Lack of Confidence

We all get underway enthusiastically on a desirable prospect. But if the response isn't enthusiastic or fast enough, some of you assume you're out of your league.

That's not the problem. The problem is you become discouraged too easily.

Regardless of how awesome a prospect may seem, a concerted effort might ultimately pay off. This was proved in a novel manner by *Cosmopolitan* magazine.

It occurred to them that many exceptionally beautiful women are married to extremely homely men. Because of its editorial value, a survey was taken to find out why. The usual answer was startlingly simple: "He kept on asking me." Sure makes the point, doesn't it?

I'm often asked what the right amount of contact is, how often, and for how long, before you antagonize the prospect. You can follow through to whatever extent you desire—as long as the contact is of value to the prospect. There must be a worthwhile reason for every letter, phone call, and meeting; any such communication should provide useful information. In this way, you won't wear out your welcome.

Don't be like the person who created 6-UP. Nothing happened, so he developed 8-UP. Again, nothing. So he gave up on it. Instead, establish a system for *follow-up* based on frequency and appeal.

Extent of Follow-Through

In attempting to make contact, and being unable to do so, there is a point beyond which you're beating your head against the wall and need to use your efforts more productively elsewhere. To what extent should you persevere before it becomes useless? Experience has proved the following series of attempts to be the optimum number:

1. Send an introductory letter.

2. Follow up with a phone call one week later.

66 It takes a killer instinct to go after new business. 99

NOTE: Whenever leaving a message, in addition to your name and phone number, include an intriguing one-liner as an inducement to return your call.

3. If your call is not accepted or returned, phone again after one more week.

4. If you draw another blank, write this person an empathetic letter acknowledging their burden of being on a fast track—and explain why they would benefit from responding to you.

5. A week later, if there is still no response, give it one last shot by phone.

If this action proves futile, move on to another prospect who will have either more courtesy or curiosity. If these five attempts in five weeks don't stir this person, you're not going to get lucky. Instead, redirect your energies to a more deserving (and profitable) prospect.

Rejection

When, despite irresistible inducements and your dazzling charm, a prospect still refuses to see you—then, even though his or her behavior is totally irrational—it hurts.

You're in good company. For most people involved in selling, the toughest aspect is dealing with rejection when contact is made. Yet you can cope with this disappointment by realizing these two facts:

1. In solicitation activity, rejection is the norm. It is not necessarily a reflection of your performance. Rather, it is a routine part of the prospect mating game.

2. There is hardly ever anything personal in the rejection. It is the proposal that is being rejected—not you.

So you needn't suffer a wounded psyche. Instead, recognize that a certain amount of failure comes with the territory. However, when acceptance does occur, how sweet it is!

Unexpected Contact

A sales call is usually thought of as a structured event conducted in an office or conference room. But how about when unexpected contact is made with a prospect? It might be on an airplane, at a cocktail party, or on a golf course. You know: *the ambush pitch*. You don't have any of your selling materials—just opportunity, and maybe only a few moments to take advantage of it.

Are you prepared with a succinct statement, compelling enough to convince the prospect to explore this matter further? You only need a few sentences summarizing why your product or service is especially desirable, but don't count on being able to react well when the opportunity arises. Rather, literally develop your "impromptu" statement.

To assist you in accomplishing this, suggest to your management that they poll a random sample of employees on why they believe your company and its products or services are preferable—in 25 words or less. This will provide a fresh interpretation of your strengths—and can inspire you to capitalize effectively on them.

It will also be interesting to see how the composite judgment of your co-workers compares with the corporate party line. This comparison might produce the germ of an idea that could increase the potency of the impression your company wants to convey.

Importantly, this will also furnish a valuable insight as to how they perceive your operation—and reveal any necessary upgrading in perceptions.

By applying the above disciplines, you will all be speaking out of the same mouth—saying what you want said. Doing so will compound the impact of your selling activity.

And where did this appealing idea come from? The person on the way to becoming the fair-haired boy or girl at your company: You.

Gimmicks

I'd like to offer a few words of caution regarding solicitation activity. Don't let your eagerness to score obscure good sense, like by mistaking desperate devices for aggressiveness.

Here is an example. Not long ago, a Chicago agency president phoned me and asked, "How about doing lunch with me and my Exec VP. We have a great idea for a new business program and want to bounce if off you." I said, "Sure"—figuring I'd learn something.

He opened by mentioning he was quite bitter with his account executives because of their lack of initiative in the new business area. He went on to say, "Then I got introspective and it occurred to me that maybe it's because I didn't give them the necessary inspiration and direction. Well, now I'm going to do exactly that."

He then described his plan: Have each Account Executive conduct a blitz telephone campaign, calling five prospects a day, 25 a week, for four weeks—a total of 100 prospects.

I told him, "I've heard that before." And he countered with, "But these will be structured calls." He explained they would all use the same tactic, opening with, "Hey, we just got the confidential news that you're going to change agencies!" His rationale was that even if 99 out of 100 denied it, there could be the coincidence of the 100th saying, "How did you find out? This was just decided yesterday at 4:00 PM."

But is it worth it? I told him, "Look, to 99 out of 100 prospects, you come across as the agency that doesn't know what it is talking about. And the next time you contact them, they will suspect you of trying to trick them again."

This president hasn't asked me back. Actually he couldn't. He isn't there anymore.

If you feel the need for a new angle to jolt prospects, start with a totally uninhibited thought process. Your tactic should exploit the prospect's imagination rather than confirm the obvious. Then role-play, being the prospect. Would the concept strike them as hokey? Or worse, offend? Or, in their place, would you grab on to the idea?

How Innovative?

There are probably as many devices for door-openers as you have prospects. So, the question becomes, how creative can you get in solicitation activity? You can get as innovative as you wish—as long as you never demean yourself or your company. If you do, that's not creative. That's dumb.

Like promising them a real dog-and-pony show and coming in with a real dog and pony. A Boston agency tried this tactic. The prospect had just installed new carpeting. They never got past the reception room.

> **❝ Your tactic should exploit the prospect's imagination rather than confirm the obvious.❞**

Section III

Getting Your Hands Dirty

Now you're ready to make things happen, to find out what it takes to get in, what you need to know in order to sell, and then to develop an irresistible presentation.

Ostensibly, it is the buyer's responsibility to purchase the products and services that will best satisfy his company's needs. Actually though, consciously or otherwise, this person's objective is to buy whatever will make him look good, namely, function in a manner that can improve his security and opportunity.

So, while appealing to buyers' corporate dedication, recognize that they aren't working there as a labor of love. Rather, their ultimate motive (like yours) is self-serving. So before you can sell the prospect on what your product or service can do for her company, this person first needs to be convinced of how the purchase will serve her personal goals.

The following four chapters will reveal how to put into effect this phase of your operation.

The Pre-Presentation Meeting: Flushing Out the Information on Wants and Buying Strategy

Perspective

What is the *most* important requirement for landing a new account? Without a doubt, it is holding a pre-presentation meeting with the prospect. Whether the pitch is competitive or missionary, this action is essential to winning.

It is incomprehensible to a prospect that you could put on a presentation without getting any reading from them first. If you don't, you're thought of as a one-shot canvasser.

Function/Purpose

The *function* of the pre-presentation meeting is to obtain the information necessary to determine if and how to develop a presentation for this prospect. If you conclude they would be a desirable account, then the *purpose* of this meeting is to convince the prospect that it would be worth their time to receive a full-scale presentation from you—and to schedule a date.

You aren't trying to land the account at this point—only the opportunity for doing so. You want to insure the circumstances in which you can give them your best shot.

Who Should Attend?

Who should attend this pre-presentation meeting? It's been found preferable to have your company represented by *two* people from different disciplines at a pre-presentation meeting. This precludes the risk of error from relying on the interpretation of a single individual. Their combined perspectives can be more valuable.

1. An individual from management who would be ultimately responsible for their account—one who could take action on their behalf without having to get permission

2. Someone (preferably you) who is sufficiently knowledgeable about the prospect and circumstances to conduct a probing interview. This needs to be the person who can establish a quick comfort level because of familiarity with their trade talk and industry developments.

From the prospect, try to get as many of those involved in the buying decision as possible to attend.

Strategy for Conduct at the Meeting

Prospects often claim that suppliers waste this meeting. It is used as a general warmup session, instead of to obtain the information necessary to develop the most appropriate presentation.

The pre-presentation meeting is not a selling opportunity in the usual sense. Rather, you have the opportunity to impress them with the soundness of your questions. So don't ask them for published information, but for information unobtainable elsewhere. You want to find out their expectations of a supplier—not statistics. Also, if you ask for published information, they will resent doing what they consider to be your job.

I am going to give you the ten factors plus one that you will need to ask about the prospect's buying policies and attitudes in order to put on a presentation. You needn't be reluctant to ask any of these questions because they all pertain to your company's performance and relationship. It will be evident to the prospect that you aren't seeking any proprietary information, only that necessary to determine whether this could be a mutually satisfactory arrangement.

Send the prospect a list of these ten factors prior to the meeting. It will enable them to provide better prepared, more reliable answers. It will also protect your contact from being embarrassed by any inquiry for which he or she doesn't have an immediate reply.

1. What do they need this product (service) to do? What do they want the supplier of this product (service) to do?

2. Why are they changing suppliers?

3. What are their short- and long-term objectives?

4. What characteristic of your product (service) impresses them? Do they need this particular characteristic?

5. Will they require speculative material? If so, what type?

6. What is their method of compensation?

7. Who will be at the presentation meeting?

8. Who is the main decision-maker?

9. What is the client's attitude, experience?

10. What is their ultimate deciding factor?

Plus 1. Is this prospect right for you?

At the meeting, *you* initiate the questioning. Even if prospects refuse to supply all the information you want, they will still respect your professionalism. How-

---

66 Your job doesn't end when a sale is made. 99

---

ever, it is unlikely they won't cooperate. In fact, prospects often express surprise and disappointment at how few questions suppliers ask of them.

They *want* to talk about their business—and the supplier's involvement. And they are particularly impressed by those with the smarts to seek their input in both respects. While they're talking, be alert to their use of any inside buzz words or expressions in their responses. You can use this language later, in the presentation, which enables you to come across as their kind of people.

What Do They Need This Product (Service) to Do?

To develop a selling approach likeliest to be successful, you must base it on what the prospect perceives as their needs—not what you assume they should be. Remember: it is not a matter of what you have to sell. Rather, it is what they want to buy.

Therefore, your first question to the prospect has to be, "Have you defined what you need from this product (service) along with the involvement expected of the supplier, and the reasons why?"

Their answers will clue you in on whether you want the account. And if you do, the answers provide the insight into what approach will most appeal to them. Even though it is likely that the prospect has formally set forth product or service specifications, it is improbable that they have also identified the supplier attributes they want. They aren't about to admit it. But they will be grateful to you for providing this professional direction. And you will be recalled as the one who has already been of value to them.

You can informally inquire as to what they consider their present suppliers' three greatest strengths, those most admired and respected. Then *wait* for a reply. No matter how long it takes. In all likelihood, their answer will consist of what they *hope* to receive from a supplier—but aren't necessarily getting. This desire can then be exploited in your presentation: capitalizing on the incumbent's inadequacies—and featuring your dedication to fully satisfying their expectations of a supplier.

In fact, while you have them thinking, assist them by confiding the six strengths that should be sought in a supplier. Coincidentally, these also happen to be *your* six strengths (or five or seven). Then, of course, in your presentation you refer to these strengths, capitalizing on the knowledge you previously instilled in them.

Note: When soliciting an account, any reference to the incumbent should always be as their "present" supplier. This registers the transient nature of this relationship. If the prospect picks up on this tactic, you can reply that, "No supplier owns any customer." They can only be wonderfully impressed by this attitude.

Why Are They Changing Suppliers?

In the case of a prospect who is planning to change suppliers, find out *why*. Don't settle for rumor or gossip. What actually happened can be learned directly from the prospect if you convey that your intent is constructive, and will enable you to develop a more appropriate presentation. They will be inclined to cooperate in revealing this background because they will want to reduce the risk of the problem reoccurring.

An advertiser recently told me of their experience with agencies before settling upon their present one. When their budget became big enough to warrant retaining an agency, it was decided they needed the most creative shop obtainable. After an extensive agency search, they were satisfied that the one selected best met this qualification.

However, several months later, they discovered that the billing was terribly fouled up. As this advertiser put it, "It looked like the agency operated out of a cigar box." A few months later, having had enough of this casual bookkeeping, they fired them. Then this advertiser decided maybe it would be better to settle for one not quite as creative—but more businesslike. This compromise didn't work either.

The third time around, they notified the candidates of the primary requisite for agency selection: the one with the most efficient billing department. Then they parenthetically mentioned, "And if we get some good creative with it, this would be a welcome bonus." This example drives home the point that the prospect's *reason* for changing suppliers becomes the basis for your selling strategy.

And there is another moral to this story: while the desirability of your product or service can be instrumental in landing an account, it is too much to expect its appeal alone to *keep* the account for you. Thus, your job doesn't end when a sale is made. If keeping this business is in your best interest, it is essential that you ride herd on the performance of your support functions to make sure they don't undermine what you accomplished.

What Are the Prospect's Short- and Long-Term Objectives?

Next, ask the prospect to provide a general indication of their short- and long-term objectives. Then, as evidence of your desire to get to the heart of their needs, ask what they consider to be their most critical marketing problem. You will come across as wanting to make a more significant contribution—beyond the sphere of the specific purchase. Because you have the vision to see the big picture while others calling on them may restrict themselves to the confines of their narrow interests, you make it evident that you are a valuable person to do business with.

Whatever information they furnish will help you decide which of your successes to present—case histories that could be related directly to the prospect's interests and that would indicate how the prospect could specifically benefit from your experience and ability.

Note: In some industries, there are circumstances in which your arrangements with a customer prevent you from doing business with certain of their competitors. So when one of these accounts is lost, this selling strategy becomes especially applicable and potent for use among those previously forbidden prospects. With them now being fair game, you can detail chapter and verse the value of your hands-on experience and proved performance.

What Characteristic Impresses the Prospect?

Usually there is a certain product characteristic or service function that the buyer is especially impressed by, or for which they feel a particular need (price, style, durability, maintenance). Determine this interest in advance so you can emphasize it in your presentation. How do you find out? *Ask them.*

Here is tangible proof of why this question is so necessary. Not long ago a major beer account conducted an agency review. Upon narrowing down to two finalists, the Senior VP at the brewery in charge of the search mentioned to me, "It's going to be interesting to see how literally both of them take the pre-presentation input I furnished." He went on to explain, "I told each of them that what I want of my new agency is *creative leadership.* I want to be taken by the hand through the creative process." Then he had come down heavily with the admonition, "Don't tell me how well you buy media. I'll tell *you* what media to buy. And if I need research, I know where to get it."

Being curious as to how the finalists would deal with this autocratic direction, I followed through after the presentations were made. The Senior VP told me that Agency "A," which prided themselves on their marketing capacity, featured how shrewdly they select and buy media, and the profundity of their research service. He said the presentation was outstanding. He then capped off his reaction with, "But I couldn't care less."

By contrast, Agency "B" came in and told the brewery team what they wanted to hear about: Creative. And they won the account. This does not mean this is all they presented. The ground rules, though, did set forth the amount of emphasis and sequence for this subject.

Thus, Agency "B" opened with creative—and gave it the attention expected. Next, they followed with how capably their research operation would serve creative. Then they continued with how their media function would provide the best environment for the creative message. And the same related technique was used for the other services worth covering.

This approach enabled Agency "B" to present whatever strengths and appeals they desired because the total presentation was creative oriented. By playing with the stacked deck dealt them, Agency "B" won.

Take a page from this experience. Flush out the buying requirements, in order of importance, for each prospect. Then cater to that preference.

Will They Require Speculative Material?

If a prospect requests speculative material, find out precisely what they mean by this. There can be a substantial variation between your interpretation of what they want and what they actually want. From their clarification, you can then decide on the appropriate effort and expense, avoiding extravagance and unnecessary work.

Sometimes, upon sharp-penciling their request, you will conclude that the expense cannot be justified. Suppliers are discovering, though, that they can present the prospect with a typed list of what the out-of-pocket expenses would be—*and offer to split it with them.* On occasion, the prospect will say, "Okay, that's fair enough." Thus, sometimes spec can be affordable. Further, this prospect involvement and ensuing familiarity with your operation can set the stage for their investing in your services thereafter.

If, however, they refuse to split the expense, you have an indication of how sincere they are—and what kind of a customer they would be. Incidentally, if the prospect throws up to you that the other suppliers soliciting their business are willing to prepare spec material for nothing, you can matter-of-factly observe, "Well, they ought to know what their work is worth."

What Is Their Method of Compensation?

The most critical development in selling is that you can now expect much more negotiation on price and terms of payment than in the past. The line has been broken on any industry uniformity. Thus, the financial factor has become an even more important criterion in product or service purchase.

Understandably, buyers are strongly opinioned regarding supplier compensation, so espousing a contrary method can be a deadly blunder. This especially applies to suppliers who use some hokey concession as a selling device, for exam-

66 The more the prospect talks, the more appealing we become. 99

ple, offering bait like, "Have we got a deal for you"—without first having checked out how the prospect would feel about it. Besides, this tactic gives the impression that your product or service isn't worth what you charge for it. Anyway, most prospects are aware that there is no such thing as a free lunch.

Fee negotiation comes down to this: it is bad enough to be conned into an arrangement in which some of your income is taken from you. It is even worse giving it away. Method of compensation is the *first* thing you should learn about a prospect. It is essential that you find out the prospect's present method of supplier payment—and, as important, their attitude toward it. (They may harbor some unexpressed resentment which can be brought to the surface.)

This is the time—*in advance*—to find out whether a satisfactory profit can be made. If so, they are your kind of people. However, if you conclude that their terms are unacceptable, you can save the time, effort and expense of developing a presentation which could cause you to lose by winning.

A tactic currently being used by one of the nation's largest retail chains in a midwestern state illustrates the importance of this advance knowledge. The retailer has been contacting local ad agencies and informing them, "We have been watching your progress and are quite impressed with your performance. In fact, we would even welcome a presentation from you."

Being romanced by this mammoth retailer caused the agencies that were approached to salivate. Believing they had an inside track, they spent a bundle on the pitch (comprehensive layouts, videotaped commercials—the full nine yards). The scenario would conclude with the agency being told, "You have confirmed the soundness of our judgment. Thus, we hereby award you our account for this state." Then came the catch. "Now, because of the vast prestige of being associated with us, and the tremendous potential it offers, undoubtedly you'll be amenable to working for five percent" (one-third of traditional compensation).

Thus far, none of the agencies have touched the offer. But they were out a substantial amount of time and money. Why didn't they check out the financial arrangement beforehand? This is inexcusable—unless they can afford to run their agency as a hobby.

Sometimes the question is raised, "But what if they won't tell you?" Then pack up and move on. You wouldn't take a job without knowing the salary.

Who Will Be at the Presentation Meeting?

Although suppliers are diligent in becoming knowledgeable about customers' markets, you seldom bother to adequately explore your prospect audiences. A little digging here could unearth the secret for winning the account.

To begin with, if more than a designated buyer is involved, find out how many will be in attendance, who they are, along with the function each performs. And if possible, learn their pecking order.

Then obtain one usable fact about each member of the buying team. (With the proliferation of "Who's Who" books, you can probably find one or more of them without much difficulty.) This could be a reference to their academic, armed forces, or career background, especially any honors or awards received. Interjecting this insight, when appropriate, in presentation is ingratiating and can be used to encourage their participation. Having this additional familiarity will provide another means for involving them. Without involvement, a presentation is just a recitation.

As one agency head observed, "The more the prospect talks, the more appealing we become." This background will also enable you to relate to the buying team and present to them as acquaintances rather than strangers. Significantly, even if you are selling only on a one-to-one basis, the same principles of knowing and involving this individual apply.

Who Is Main Decision-Maker?

Among those who influence purchases, obviously one has more authority than the others. (The buyer may be responsible for *recommending* the supplier to be chosen. But who *approves?*) Find out who the decision-maker is—and how to appeal to him or her.

It is likely that the individual at the prospect who would provide the pre-presentation input would be the buyer—or somebody at that peer level in the pecking order. You can't brazenly ask him *who* the decision-maker will be in supplier selection. It might not be him. And being reluctant to admit this, it is possible he will give you misleading information.

So, instead of confronting him head on, ask *how* the decision will be made. If you're asked what you mean, you can guide him toward the desired answer by asking, "By committee or an individual?" Then if the buyer hedges with, "Committee," you can target more tightly by inquiring who would exert the most influence among them. By this process of elimination, you should be able to deduce where the power lies.

If you have any doubt regarding the validity of the decision-maker identified, and want confirmation, here is an informal—but effective—means for doing so.

At the presentation, note the person to whom they direct most conversation, and, correspondingly, the person who is doing the most listening. If this is the same person, that's the decision-maker.

Next, flush out her career background so you can *speak her language.*

◆ If the decision-maker came up through production, compare the disciplines applied to your product or service with their quality control.

◆ A decision-maker with financial background will spark to any reference to ROI (return on investment).

◆ And if the decision-maker's career began in sales, mention how your product or service will eventually contribute to increasing their sales. (Will it improve quality, reduce cost, lessen maintenance?)

Here is an example of an agency whose homework really paid off. They found out that the decision-maker at the prospect company was the Executive VP and that he came up through sales. But he had a total aversion to advertising—even though they had a media budget of over $2,000,000.

Knowing this, the agency figured it would take a performance-oriented presentation to score. Thus, they came armed with speculative ad layouts and taped commercials. The agency's strategy was to come across as being as sales-driven as the Executive VP decision-maker. So they opened by featuring, in his vernacular, the "sales support" proposed for newspaper. When their presenter moved on to the next layout, the Executive VP interrupted by asking, "What's that suppose to be: advertising for magazines?" And he was told, "No, we recommend that you concentrate with 'sales support' only for this medium. Now if we can dim the lights. . . ." And the Executive VP said, "Here comes the ads for television, right?" This time the presenter replied, "On the contrary. We suggest the exclusive use of 'sales support' here."

Sounds contrived? This agency landed the account. Because they came across as being *his kind of people.* No principles were compromised. They just spoke his language.

But don't overlook the possible power behind the power. Sometimes the source of approval in supplier selection isn't the decision-maker. A $9,000,000 agency just learned this the hard way. They spent $50,000 on a new business pitch for a loose $3,000,000 account because the agency president had such a close personal relationship with his counterpart at the advertiser. The agency was further encouraged to dig so deeply into the till because the prospect's president had confided to them his expectations of his new agency—in regard to personnel, operations and creative approach. Having this confidential insight, the agency assumed they had it made.

Then the prospect's president delegated responsibility for the agency search to his VP of advertising—with instructions that his friend's shop be included. However, this responsibility also included establishing judging criteria—which turned out to be significantly different from the specifications of his president. According to the revised ground rules, a different agency proved preferable. The ad VP's documented justification of his choice prevailed—and the favorite son candidate was defeated.

The explanation given by the ex-prospect's president to his agency buddy provided a retrospective reminder of corporate life. Namely, if the president were to overrule his subordinate's decision, it would strip this person of his authority and stature internally—and seriously weaken his hand in dealing with the new agency. And the head man wasn't about to cause these problems.

Thus, when it came down to deciding between backing his ad director and accommodating an agency friend, the wired-in agency was short circuited. The upshot is that the agency with the supposed clout was lulled into a false sense of security by having mistaken authority for action.

So, of course, cultivate whoever will "officially" okay the choice of supplier but don't overlook convincing those who will supply the reasons for the recommendation made.

What Is the Client's Attitude, Experience?

    A. Awareness of Prospect Attitude

    B. Sensitivity to Smoking

    C. Account for Sophistication Factor

Awareness of Prospect Attitude

While it is admittedly difficult, try to smoke out the attitude of prospective clients. Are they secure enough to be constructively company oriented? Or would they resort to being strictly self-serving?

If the latter is the case, prepare for closer-than-usual scrutiny. In particular, guard against being cut up by someone who may try to look good at your expense. Brace yourself. It happens.

Sensitivity to Smoking

Find out if there is any objection to smoking at the meeting. If it offends anyone, this is a handicap you don't need. So play if safe; there are agencies with heavy smokers who have a policy of total abstinence while at the presentation.

Account for the Sophistication Factor

There is one more matter that is seldom considered—but well should be. It can directly influence the thrust of your pitch. What is the experience of those who consider suppliers? If they have participated extensively in this function, they will be more proposal oriented. If not, their reaction to you (and anyone else from your company) will dominate. It's the difference between being either affected by substance or personality.

Thus, determine the amount of exposure your contact (and that of others who may be involved) has had in choosing suppliers. Then adapt your appeal accordingly.

Remember: your presentation has to be customized not only for the prospect corporately, but also for any individual's degree of sophistication. Then with the content and conduct of your presentation tailored to be most appropriate, the prospect will more easily relate and be more receptive to your sales message.

What Is the Ultimate Deciding Factor?

Thus far, I have furnished nine of the ten factors that you need to know to score. The tenth is the most important. Ask what the deciding factor in product (service) purchase will be. Then offer direction, asking the prospect: "Beyond all the judging criteria established, if you were allowed only one ultimate consideration, what would it be?" For instance, do they feel strongest about

◆ Price and terms of payment?

◆ Speed and quality of service?

◆ Proof of performance?

◆ Supplier management involvement?

This list will help them jell their thinking. And their answer will become the key thrust of your presentation and the catalyst for a prompt decision.

Is the Prospect Right for You?

And now for the *plus one* that I referred to. The ten factors I have detailed will provide you with the necessary input on the prospect's needs and buying strategy. This will help you prove why your operation is best for them. *But are they right for you?*

Sure, you want to make the sale. But is it worth the price? Would their payment be commensurate with their demands of you? Finding out afterwards that they are unaffordable can be brutally expensive.

Ask the prospect: "What makes you a desirable customer?" Besides the unique insight this will furnish, it will also indicate what kind of people they are. If you are comfortable with their response, you can get underway positively—without reservation.

The Introductory "Leaver"

Leave the prospect with a brief description of your operation, customers, and support personnel who would be assigned if you are awarded the account. How many of your competitors go this extra mile? Hardly any.

Also include the six strengths (yours) that should be sought in a supplier. However, this written description shouldn't steal any of your forthcoming thunder. It should pave the way for, not compete with, your forthcoming presentation. Finally, even though the cover of this "leaver" may be a stock item, the package must give the impression of having been developed especially for them.

This wrap-up paves the way for the presentation by enabling you to devote more time to the prospect.

The Confirming Letter

Upon returning to your office, promptly send the prospect a letter confirming the input they furnished. This will reduce the risk of any misunderstandings.

It will also provide advance indication of your thoroughness. This tactic can be quite impressive because customers often accuse suppliers of doing a shoddy job of communicating with them. By comparison, you have followed through before even having the account.

Refusal to Furnish Information

Granted, sometimes a prospect planning to change suppliers will refuse to furnish this necessary background information. Ostensibly, this is because they do not want to bias the thinking of any candidate or to give any an advantage.

If this resistance occurs, counter with the fact that your objective is to develop the most appropriate presentation, one that will be most meaningful and pertinent to them—thereby making the most productive use of their time. On this basis, they might relent.

66 You can't sell a product or service without knowing what the buyer wants.99

If, however, this rationale doesn't work, ask for a 15-minute question-and-answer phone call that will enable you to customize a presentation. If you can't get cooperation in this respect either, ask if you can *send* your list of ten questions. The response could then be furnished by mail or in a subsequent phone call—whichever means is most convenient for the prospect.

Then if the prospect still refuses, let this one go. Shooting from the hip is tough enough. And without ammunition, you could die at the presentation. Instead, move on to another prospect—one with whom you would at least have a fighting chance.

It nets down to this: *If you can't get any pre-presentation input, you can't put on a presentation.* Because you can't sell a product or service without knowing what the buyer wants.

This experience should be followed by a brief report on the appeal of the prospect to the person(s) who would further the activity, if any. All else notwithstanding, the report should assess the following five key matters:

1. Prospect profitability to your company

2. Expectations of your company

3. The human equation: compatibility

4. The presentation strategy necessary to win

5. Should the prospect be pursued or passed over?

Note: Even if the size of the account doesn't warrant this thoroughness, it is still worth your applying a modified version of this procedure. This could be as easy as sending staggered mailings to this secondary echelon of prospects, requesting answers to the ten questions enclosed. Their inducement to cooperate would be that it will enable you to customize a presentation for them—thereby making the most productive use of their time. This approach enables either kissing or killing the prospective account without having spent much time or money on the prospect.

If the prospect is sufficiently desirable, you can use the information and impressions you received to provide direction on how to further pursue them—and to determine if anyone else from your company should be included in this activity. If your reaction is negative, though, keep moving until you hit a prospect you believe is worth going all out for—both in effort and expense.

You can move confidently in soliciting those accounts deemed worthwhile because of having flushed out their buying policies and attitudes. But that is only half the equation. The same diligent assessment need be applied to your company. This will enable determining why the fit is right—and develop the rationale to convince the prospect of why your product or service is especially desirable. The following chapter will provide the direction for performing this introspection.

The Nuts-and-Bolts for Preparing a Winning Pitch

◆ Perspective ◆ Prepare to Win
◆ Take Stock of Your Company's Operation and Image ◆ Controls
◆ Factbook/Sources ◆ Research
◆ Presentation: Visuals ◆ Presentation: Content
◆ Presentation: Value ◆ Spec Proposal Strategy
◆ Three Land Mines ◆ Rehearsal
◆ Selling Team No-Shows ◆ The Presentation Agenda
◆ Prospect Objections ◆ Extent of Preparation

Perspective

I realize that my readers may range from a one-person sales force pitching by phone to a presentation team soliciting on a global basis. Under these circumstances, how can the content for developing selling strategy and materials be made pertinent for each individual?

To fulfill this need, I've erred on the side of providing too much for preparation purposes. Rather than guessing at how many nuggets you can use, I am giving you the mother lode. Then you can mine it to whatever extent relevant to your situation and ambition.

Prepare to Win

To acquire new business, it takes more than the will to win. It also takes the will to *prepare* to win. Because the same quality of effort required to keep accounts is what it takes to land new ones. Despite this fact, development of the presentation is your most disorganized activity. This is because circumstances require it to be sandwiched in between routine sales activity and customer service. And it is usually conducted on a crash basis.

Take Stock of Your Company's Operation and Image

Corporate Name

To enable planning from strength, analyze your company in as calculating a manner as if it were a customer's operation. Then implement your findings to create a more successful selling program.

Let's start with the first factor by which prospects are influenced: your company's name.

How well is it known? Are you one company, invisible, with anonymity for all? What impression does it convey? Authoritative studies have proved there is a direct correlation between awareness of a company and the respect for it. Therefore, your company name should be a selling point for you—not a secret.

Be they right or wrong, prospects have preconceived notions about many suppliers. And if their attitude towards your company ranges from apathy to contempt, it is unlikely you'll get a day in court regardless of how fascinating your approach.

This fact was driven home—painfully—to a supposedly dynamic agency new business man. (The "Bird Dog" in this industry, brought in to generate billing on a "produce-or-out" basis.) They were scoring so well that he actually believed he was solely responsible for its success. As a result, he confronted the agency pres-

> ❝ ... success is ... highly marketable to prospects because they want to be associated with a winner.❞

ident with the ultimatum that he be made president—and have his name put on the door.

I'll spare you the details, but his desk was cleaned out for him. He did relocate—a number of times. However, he couldn't catch fire again anywhere. I ran into him after several subsequent tours of duty. Always curious regarding how a rainmaker fares afterwards, I inquired as to how he was getting along. In a burst of frustration (and rare humility), he said, "I never realized how the agency name opened doors for me."

How well are you capitalizing on *your* corporate name? It already has years, maybe decades, of acceptance. When you associate yourself with all the good will built, some of it will come to you.

Further, whatever your company's advertising, promotion, and/or public relations activities, it is creating a favorable attitude toward you. This pre-selling on your behalf is one of your most valuable sales tools. So benefit by making your own and your corporate name synonymous.

Corporate/Personal Image

What's the word on the street about your company? Prospects planning to change suppliers usually base their judgment on some vague impressions they've often received, nothing more authentic than rumors or gossip.

Yet they develop definite opinions. Of particular significance is the basis for the prospects' assumptions. These are formed according to not only *what* your company does—but *how* they do it.

What's your company's image? A follower? An implementer? Or is it regarded as having courage and charisma?

Unfortunately, even with stuffing the suggestion box, there is little you as an individual can do to directly affect your corporate image. And although it influences your reputation, ultimately it is your performance that determines your income, position, and tenure.

So let's begin by improving *your* image—and hope it becomes contagious throughout your company. Begin by landing two new big accounts. This makes you "hot"—and it is assumed you must be doing an outstanding job. Not only does this success make you a role model within your company, this success is also highly marketable to prospects because they want to be associated with a winner.

In the interim, level with yourself regarding your corporate and personal character of operation. Before trying to tell someone else how you can handle their business, physician heal thyself. The following two-step treatment can provide the cure:

1. From a corporate standpoint, find out from whomever necessary in your organization how the company is perceived. Then, in your solici-

tation activity, capitalize on your company's strengths and compensate for its weaknesses.

2. As for your personal approach, get introspective. Objectively identify your appealing characteristics, and, those that might offend. And here too, adapt accordingly.

The sum of this insight, applied to your conduct, will substantially increase the possibility of your attracting the business you want.

Controls

Although somehow the various components of the presentation seem to come together, they do so despite the above conditions. In retrospect, it is often discovered there were oversights which lessened the presentation's effectiveness. For optimum impact, it is necessary to begin with the basics by applying the following controls: traffic, checklist, and timetables. You know what these are—but seldom use them. Put these disciplines to work for you—and minimize the frantic factor. No matter to what extent others in your company contribute to the development of your sales presentations, the result is your responsibility. For your protection, set up a written procedure to which you will hold yourself accountable. Here is what is needed so that nothing is left to chance.

Traffic

Establish a plan to keep tab and coordinate every phase of the presentation. Essentially this amounts to the following:

◆ Preparing what you have to say: selling strategy

◆ Providing for how you want to say it: written and visual aids

◆ Collecting the items needed for use in presentation: samples, display material, props, etc.

◆ Assigning responsibilities for the work to be performed

◆ Setting completion date.

However, any plan is only as good as the extent to which you personally check on the assignments being performed. Because people do only what you *inspect*; not what you expect.

All responsibilities, materials and devices involved should be itemized with procedures established for compliance with assignments made.

66 More ideas come from information than inspiration.99

Timetable

As part of the process of developing your strategy for presentation, be sure to decide how much time each subject will be allotted—rather than having presenters compete for time at the presentation.

Also, because of the interdependence of the components, completion dates must be strictly observed. This will prevent any "Oh my God" oversights and useless fault-finding.

There are enough ways for fouling up without depending on a presentation that was haphazardly pulled together. Remember: victory doesn't begin across the desk or at a podium. It starts with all the activity it took to get there.

Factbook/Sources

The development of new business presentations is becoming too sophisticated to start with a hunch. Rather, you need to begin by assembling a prospect data base. Prepare a factbook containing all data of consequence on the prospect's company, industry, and market. This will provide you with the insight you need—and serve as evidence at the presentation of the professionalism that can be expected if you are awarded the account. (Bring the factbook with you and use it as a prop.)

The following sources can furnish you with practically all the information you will need:

◆ Begin with the prospect. (Check on whether they have a PR department.) Get a copy of their annual report and any promotional material they've published. Obviously, this is what they want you to know.

◆ Your next most valuable source is their trade association—a key function of which is compiling all possible market data.

◆ If your company subscribes to a computerized information service, explore every means by which it can assist you.

◆ If the prospect is listed on a stock exchange, get a spec sheet on them from your stockbroker. This will supply you with worthwhile financial information.

◆ Also, if appropriate, pull a Dunn & Bradstreet. (But take it with a grain of salt.)

◆ Make use of your public library—which has developed an extensive information retrieval system.

◆ Finally, if your company belongs to an industry association, by all means take advantage of your membership to receive whatever information and support it can provide.

Remember, when soliciting new business, it's not only *who* you know, it's also *what* you should know.

Research

Admittedly, not many of you can authorize conducting independent research—focus interviews or group dynamics sessions—with people representative of the prospect's market. However, if they are especially desirable, it could be worth recommending to your management that this action be taken.

The revelations produced by those companies that have conducted focus groups, and the plans it inspired, have resulted in a much higher rate of closing. Because *more ideas come from information than inspiration.*

For example, advertisers have informed me of instances in which they had no intention of changing agencies. But the information furnished in presentation was so valuable, and the action proposed so worthwhile, they couldn't resist switching to take advantage of it. Couldn't this inducement be as appealing in your field?

Besides the necessary familiarity these techniques provide, they offer a valuable incentive for prospects to move—now. This potency warrants considering its appropriateness for any major solicitation. Because at the very least, this research is a great door opener.

Focus groups can identify the prospect's *needs.* Your pre-presentation efforts will flush out their *wants.* Now go for the final payout step: in addition to whatever field research you perform, arrange to spend some time traveling with their field personnel. Then, in presentation, your name-dropping of their people on the front line can be very impressive. (For elaboration and results, see Chapter 22.)

While your competitors may come across as having done their homework, you will give the impression you have written the book for them.

Finally, after conducting whatever quantitative and qualitative methods for researching the prospect, there is also some cloak and dagger work that can produce worthwhile results. With all the information accumulated, the following approach might reveal how the prospect *actually* operates and what kind of people they *really* are.

This tactic is dicey. But if your information is reliable, its value can transcend all the prospect's pronouncements and numbers.

Here it is. If the prospect has decided to switch, get a reading on them from their previous supplier. Understandably, the worth of their horse's mouth input will depend on the conditions under which the severance occurred.

If the supplier ended this relationship without any recrimination, they will probably be objective in that reported to you. But if the supplier was dropped, for whatever reason, they are bound to be bitter to some extent. And any information they give you will be biased accordingly.

Yet, it is worth exploring this source. Being sensitive to whatever the circumstances, you can interpret their response and determine its degree of validity. Then cautiously decide how to apply what you've learned to your selling activity.

Presentation: Visuals

Having done your homework, your next objective is to develop a presentation that will prove why your product or service can best fulfill the prospect's requirements. And you have such a great opportunity to distinguish your operation from the others.

Your prospects claim most supplier pitches are stereotyped—characterized by a dull sameness, or, they also claim, a same dullness. In particular, this complaint refers to the use of visuals.

It's easy to minimize the importance of the physical appearance of your presentation. Because that's not the business you're in. But the prospect's first reaction to your slides, poster cards, and/or flip charts is: "Is this indicative of their work? Is it the caliber we want?" They feel the visual effect of your presentation is the first and possibly most important clue to your creativity—evidence of your capacity to innovate with respect to product or service development.

Consequently, you need to provide the most appealing visual communication of your message possible. Accomplishing this requires applying the following hard-nosed discipline.

If any circumstances prevent you from preparing materials that would do your message justice, don't go through with it. Because regardless how dynamic your message is, you will be platforming your proposal with an inferior depiction of it. Having placed yourself at this disadvantage, you will seriously lessen your chance of success.

And adding insult to injury, the prospect could trash your operation to peers at other companies as the one that came in with the sloppy visuals.

Presentation: Content

As to the content of your proposal, prospects are expecting it to be more sophisticated than in the past. You can't count on last year's approach anymore: touting your product or service's advantages—and trying to overwhelm them with pluses by the pound.

Prospects now want you to explain any claims you make in terms of benefits to them. For instance:

◆ Any product or service feature covered should be followed by an explanation of the competitive edge it will deliver.

◆ Mention of your corporate activity to create acceptance for your product or service should set forth why this will support the prospect's purchase.

◆ If you offer a price break, explain how it will improve their profit picture.

This is the kind of contributory selling prospects now want. How compatible are your intentions with their desires? If you fail to present yourself in this way, prospects will conclude you're out of date—and out of contention.

Presentation: Value

You're a finalist for a very desirable account. The prospect assumes that any of those qualifying from this esteemed group would be *acceptable*. Now, who would be *preferable*?

A key objective in presentation is to distinguish your operation from the others, and to make yourself memorable.

Thus, a prime requisite for accomplishing this is the *value* of the presentation to the prospect. Sure, you will concentrate on communicating why your product or service best fulfills the prospect's requirements. But will there be anything in its content that they could benefit from—now? Did they *learn* anything? Build some gems of information into your pitch that the prospect can use. Then, when they apply one of them, they will recall you—and be grateful to you—for having made them look good. And their appreciation is bound to provide you with a competitive edge. So while promising a better future, deliver now.

Spec Proposal Strategy

When a prospect changing suppliers requires a competitive shootout from the finalists, these finalists face a tough decision about strategy:

◆ Should they develop the approach they believe to be in the prospect's best interest?

◆ Or should they develop the approach they assume is likeliest to land the account?

When you're in this position, bet on *your* convictions. If you try to second-guess *their* desires, you could wind up shooting yourself in the foot. Further, there is the risk of the prospect being able to sense that your work was created to sell them—rather than their market. Go with the concept on which you would spend your own money. You will be more convincing in presentation, and more able to field questions with authority. Even if you lose, what you have developed will be so dynamic, it could be highly appealing to another prospect in the same field, particularly one more perceptive.

Three Land Mines

The difference between salespeople and order-takers is their desire to become more knowledgeable about a prospect's company, industry, and market, and their initiative in contributing to a buyer's success. This distinction is reflected in their income: comfort versus survival.

I assume you are reading this book because of being, or wanting to be, in the first category. The type who thrives on achievement—and will take whatever ethical action necessary to make it happen. Such being the case, you need to be aware of three land mines as you plan your sales approach: *statistics, jargon,* and *marketing.*

Conveying a knowledge of the prospect's company, industry, or market can be a valuable tactic because your experience in these areas forms the basis for their

> ❝ The difference between salespeople and order-takers is their desire to become knowledgeable.❞

confidence in your operation. Consequently, you need to make sure you know what you're talking about, particularly in these three areas:

1. Statistics

Obviously, the prospect is intimately familiar with their numbers. So, any error you make in this area will cause them to view the rest of your presentation with suspicion. Be especially careful when referring to statistics they regularly live with.

For example, when you started developing your presentation for them two months ago, you found that their share of the market was 18.6 percent. To show your familiarity with their operation, you mention this statistic in your presentation. But this figure has since dropped to 12.4 percent. And it is inconceivable to them that you could be wrong about so critical a matter.

If you are going to quote any numbers, verify them just before leaving for the presentation. And mention your source—to provide authority and attribute responsibility.

2. Jargon

Be adequately familiar with your prospect's trade talk. Any incorrect use indicates you don't know their business.

A prime example of the importance of using the appropriate language is the case of the ad agency that learned that the president of a very large account had become disenchanted with them—but not enough to let the word out on the street. Fortunately, the agency had a third-party contact who was able to arrange for a presentation to the president. They figured that he would be very receptive. And since there wasn't any competition, they figuratively went all out with a full-blown dog and pony show.

The account was a wine company. Actually, they make very cheap wine. In fact, research found that the primary location of consumption is on curbs.

As a result, the agency came up with an intriguing creative concept. This consisted of depicting the wine being imbibed in the most posh surroundings. And it featured uncharacteristically beautiful people—always in formal attire.

However, one-third of the way through the presentation, the president of the wine company interrupted and said, "Pack up. All you've demonstrated is an ignorance of our business."

What I didn't tell you was the headline for the ads—which was very appropriate to the graphics: "The Rich Wine." If anyone at the agency would have taken a few moments and checked with editorial at the local beverage journal, they would have learned that in this industry, the word "rich" means "fattening." No advertiser is going to switch to an agency that couldn't bother to do such basic homework.

3. Marketing

If it is appropriate for your operation to tout strategy, then first find out how they operate. For instance, a couple of summers ago, the Michigan Apple Commission soured on its present agency—and made it known that they could be had—throwing it open to anyone who was warm. One of the agencies based their presentation on an approach for investing the prospect's budget in the shrewdest, most economical manner.

Not surprisingly, the commission's antenna vibrated at this opportunity. After having peaked their interest, the agency revealed that this would be accomplished by concentrating the total expenditure in the State of Michigan.

The commission chairman said, "My God, how can you recommend that when 80 percent of our crop is shipped out of state?" Well, before anyone from the agency could throw themselves on the grenade, the chairman announced, "Next."

Any error—be it statistical, in respect to trade talk, or regarding marketing—can blow the credibility of your entire presentation. So make judicious use of your smarts to impress. Because you can't be too careful when venturing into the area of expertise.

Rehearsal

The selling situation may consist of you pitching to an individual. Or it might involve a team of your people presenting to a buying committee. Either way, how you rehearse for this opportunity can be the determining factor in whether the sale is made or lost.

If it's a one-to-one scenario, you are in no way relieved of the responsibility of practicing your pitch. To be effective—and mildly confident—the rule of thumb is: deliver it *out loud* six times. If a prospect isn't worth this preparation, you shouldn't have been cultivating them in the first place. Rather, concentrate on those who deserve a winning effort.

In the case of a selling/buying team encounter, the matter is more complex. Because of the critical nature of this function, let's take it from the top: catastrophe insurance, simulated combat, and technique.

Catastrophe Insurance

The largest single cause of presentation failure is a lack of adequate rehearsal. Yet a variety of excuses are used to avoid rehearsing. The list is usually headed by "No time." As a result, the rehearsal consists of whatever can be held in the elevator on the way down to the meeting.

However, the time factor isn't the *real* reason for sloughing off on a complete run-through. It is often more deep-rooted than that. The fact is, it is awfully tough

66 There are three requisites for a successful presentation. The first is rehearse, the second is rehearse, and the third is rehearse. 99

to perform in front of your coworkers. Your palms will never be sweatier than in this environment. However, after having survived this ordeal, you can go into the actual presentation with the confidence this baptism of fire will provide, and the knowledge that the worst is behind you.

Simulated Combat

If the conduct of this dry run is just a recitation, though, it fails to take into account the make-or-break factor in presentation; prospect participation. Regardless of how polished your delivery, your audience can devastate you with a zinger. Thus, a key function of the rehearsal is have these zingers thrown at you by your colleagues. Being cut up in rehearsal can be merciful and useful compared to the prospect's version of the Spanish Inquisition.

I know of an agency that keeps an ongoing list of bizarre prospect questions and comments that have occurred in previous presentations. It is then used to prepare their team for actual combat. (This procedure will also prevent your rehearsal from degenerating into a free-for-all, and will preclude any of your participants from taking this grilling personally.) I am told that after these maneuvers, even green troops behave like seasoned veterans in battle.

You can't afford any presenters who are thin skinned. Granted, this simulated combat can be a traumatic experience. But being forearmed will protect them against any low blows by members of the buying committee. And better your people should learn to deal with getting shot at in your office than in the prospects'.

Technique

Bear in mind that the prospect is quick to discover and lose respect for fouled-up timing, repetition among speakers, missing props, etc. Therefore, a dress rehearsal is necessary. This would include individual speaker participation, operation of A-V equipment, use of props, and display of material. This kind of rehearsal will help produce a synergistic team effect—which is certainly more impressive than a series of individual efforts.

Remember that the purpose of a rehearsal is to plan and evaluate the content and delivery of a presentation. However, it can be only as productive as the rehearsal technique employed. Here is what it takes to achieve the results desired. This strategy is based on my being contacted recently by a very frustrated head of the new business operation at a hungry agency. It seems as though they were doing everything necessary. As a result, they had no difficulty getting up to bat. But they usually struck out. He concluded that the problem had to be with the presentation. Yet, this was baffling to him, too, because they were so diligent about rehearsing.

Since the planning of the presentation was so thorough, the content so relevant, and the materials so impressive, it occurred to me that the culprit might be the *approach* to their rehearsal. This director of new business development took strong exception to my assumption, stating, "That can't be it. I personally rehearse each presenter. Individually and privately."

I then asked if all the components were pulled together for a complete dry run—simulating the actual presentation. He replied that wasn't necessary because each knew his or her part so well. And he finished with, "Besides, it prevents anyone from being embarrassed by criticism."

This confirmed my hunch. The agency didn't lose in presentation. They had already blown it by their method of rehearsal, for these reasons:

◆ Their practice session does not reflect how the presentation will be conducted. Thus, they will be winging it in a situation in which there isn't any room for error.

◆ The agency's approach consists of a series of individual efforts. This forfeits the synergism produced by a team effect.

◆ The impression left on the prospect is that of a canned pitch. And this is one of the worst indictments by a prospect.

This agency lost sight of the purpose of rehearsal. *Its function is to stage a winning presentation.* Not parade a series of reciters. Your preparation needs to literally be a *dress rehearsal.* Anything short of this thoroughness is the extent to which you handicap yourself. And no one selling can afford to concede any advantage to others.

Focus

There is still another key function you need to perform in rehearsal: *focus.*

Beginning with your entrance for the presentation, it is imperative that every one of your people stay strictly relevant to your message, particularly if the prospect has imposed a time limit.

Those at Leo Burnett Agency diligently apply this discipline because of a costly experience. Some years ago, after considerable pursuit, they succeeded in lining up a presentation with a very desirable advertiser. They were granted 45 minutes. Coincidentally, just prior to this event, Leo Burnett had hired a new senior VP. It seemed like a good idea to bring him along, as it would provide him with an instant agency indoctrination. And he was duly instructed that his purpose in being there was solely to learn—not participate.

One end of the prospect's meeting room was dominated by a massive moose head. As the Burnett team entered the room, despite his vow of silence, the new senior VP blurted out, "Who shot the moose?" The prospect spent the next 45 minutes confessing to the murder. And then informed the agency that their time was up.

Burnett Management doesn't make many mistakes. And never more than once. Thus, they incorporated what they'd learned into their rehearsals. Now, when any presenter strays, one of the others will interrupt with, "Who shot the moose?" This immediately makes the point—without offending any sensitivities.

Duration of Rehearsal

Just short of being confident. You need *some* anxiety, to guard against complacency, and to keep the juices flowing going in. You want to go into the pitch ready to kill, so don't overkill in rehearsal for it.

Finally, remember, whether involving an individual or a team, there are three requisites for a successful presentation. The first is rehearse, the second is rehearse, and the third is rehearse. If you haven't got time for rehearsal, you haven't got time for the presentation.

Selling Team No-shows

When a presentation team is used, provisions need to be made for any no-shows. Failing to anticipate this possibility can be disastrous.

We can learn from what happened to D'arcy Masius Benton & Bowles—and what they now do about it. They have a smoothly-honed opener. Diamond polishers could gain from their performance. The DMB & B list of clients is very impressive. But so is that of their peers. Yet not many have a spellbinder like their CEO, Jack Bowen. Therefore, they lead from strength by using his ingratiating charm to recount their achievements for their blue chip clients.

Although this is basically a new business solicitation tactic, circumstances can require other applications, like this one: One of their largest clients had a total top management change. To DMB & B's credit, they decided to treat this venerable client as a prospect who had to be pitched all over again. They decided they would start with the device which had always proved so effective.

The format consisted of a draped table—underneath which was a representative group of their prestigious clients' products. Upon removing the cloth with a flourish, Jack Bowen would casually reminisce about his agency's remarkable contribution to these clients' success.

Among Jack Bowen's positive attributes are his reliability and punctuality. Yet, on this occasion, for whatever reason, he never even showed up. The agency team did a soft shoe number until they couldn't fake it any longer. With the situation becoming tense, they decided that the management supervisor on the account had better fill the breech and do Jack Bowen's shtick.

Afterwards, he told me, "I heard Jack do this countless times; I was reasonably familiar with the case histories—but I had never done this before. I was uncomfortable, lacked confidence—and stunk."

The experience drove home to DMB & B the necessity of having an understudy for each star in the cast. The assumption that every scheduled participant will always be available is an unaffordable luxury. Therefore, in your preparation for the unexpected, provide for adequate back-up support.

You can also use rehearsal as an opportunity to anticipate any ridiculous situations, such as this scenario: A prospect stupidly slates five presentations in one day. You're third. When you enter the room, they "request" that you cut your presentation in half because they are running far behind schedule. This can be shattering unless you have an alternate plan, whereby you can rebound with a condensed version. So it's in your best interest to expect the worst—beginning with the prospect being totally unreasonable.

At best, a presentation is an anxiety producing experience. Vital to its success is minimizing speaker tension. If you spare them the further worry of having to deliver more than they are prepared for, you will have presenters who can control rather than react to an opportunity.

The Presentation Agenda

There is an opportunity available to you at presentations that is seldom exploited. It is the use of an agenda, which is distributed just prior to the meeting. Admittedly, an agenda is more appropriate for group events. However, there can be instances in a one-on-one situation where this evidence of your organizational ability would be very impressive. And it would certainly distinguish you from your competitors.

Besides its obvious purpose, the agenda must function as an introductory ad for your company and you. You want the agenda to generate interest in your product (service) and presentation. Accordingly, the standard for development is that it be good enough to be published. Here are some suggestions for enhancing your appeal. You can choose those which best fit each situation.

◆ *Create the appearance* that will represent you in the most desirable manner—and provide a visual incentive for the agenda to be read.

◆ Write the *subjects* to be covered in so intriguing a fashion as to put the prospect in an anticipatory frame of mind.

◆ List the names of your *participants*, their functions, and their involvement if you are awarded the account. You could also include a small photo of each so the buyer or committee will know to whom they should direct their questions and comments.

◆ Feature the prospect's *logo* on this sheet. This implies that your presentation was developed especially for them.

◆ Cite the *reason* for your presentation. This should establish in advance why this event will be worthwhile for them.

◆ Include your company's *Unique Selling Proposition*. This keeps before the prospect the reason your product or service can best fulfill their requirements.

◆ Prominently note that you welcome their *participation* throughout the presentation—so you can talk *with* them—rather than at them.

So, while the function of your agenda is to inform, it can also be a worthwhile sales tool. As with every other component of your selling activity, it should be used to compound the potency of your total effort—beyond the basic purpose for which it is intended. Use this prelude to whet the prospect's appetite, build acceptance, encourage involvement, and create preference for your company.

Prospect Objections

Finally, here are four forms of insurance you can take out to overcome prospect objections to your company, product or service, or presentation:

1. Throughout the development of your presentation, continuously apply this acid test: Is this worth a portion of someone's life? Not yours, theirs. In effect, that is what you are asking for. Prospects rate most presentations as "a waste of time." So the first criterion your pitch must satisfy is that it is worth the prospect's while. If so, you are on your way.

2. Don't forget the smarts in basic salesmanship. Specifically, forego any false pride, and anticipate whatever objections might occur. Then prepare your rebuttals—to be held in reserve in the event they're needed. (But don't bring up any unless they do!)

3. The only way you can put on a sales pitch is as a winner. Otherwise, your negative attitude will be reflected in the material developed and

your presentation of it. And the prospect is sufficiently experienced to sense it.

4. Don't ever forget your status in this buyer-seller relationship. Your objective is to convince prospects—not compete with them. So never try to look good by comparison with them. No one-upmanship, no condescension, no putdowns. Even if you should win the battle this way, you certainly won't win the war.

Extent of Preparation

I am often asked, "How far should you go in preparing a presentation?" There is only one answer: whatever it will take to win the account. Remember: a pro seldom putts short of the hole.

In fact, *over-prepare* so you can under-present. If your material is so thorough—and incisively applied—you won't have to include a soft shoe number.

"Any error ... can blow the credibility of your entire presentation."

Capitalize on Selling Circumstances

Perspective ◆ Prospect Ground Rules
Positioning ◆ Duration ◆ Location

Perspective

If there were a single commandment for new business presentations, it would be this: Regardless of how dynamic your concept, THOU SHALT NOT LOCK IN ON A SPECIFIC SWAT TEAM, FORMAT, CONTENT, OR SEQUENCE.

There is a tendency to try to develop a generic winner—and then stick with it. However, what may be impressive to one prospect could antagonize another. So remember, *dynamism exists only if it is pertinent.*

Prospect Ground Rules

To prevent being finished before you get started, you need to comply with the prospect's ground rules. If the prospect stipulates duration, format, content, or sequence of the presentation, don't fight them. They have determined their needs and established a basis for comparison between presenting suppliers. Your cooperation indicates your willingness to work with them.

When ground rules are set, suppliers that don't adhere to them are usually eliminated. Despite a highly appealing presentation, if it can't be held up to their judging criteria and compared to the other presentations, the contrary supplier is usually dropped from consideration.

The direction furnished doesn't need to be restrictive. There can be ample opportunity for innovation within the parameters prescribed. Just remember that at this stage, prospects want evidence of your cooperation—not your independence. So satisfy this need if you want to remain in contention.

Playing the game can pay off. Here is an example that can also be useful for you. Prior to my critiquing an ad agency new business presentation recently, I was shown the sheet of instructions the prospect had given each candidate, which listed the subjects they wanted dealt with—and in what order.

The agency president said to me, "Of course, we'll cover most of these—and work them into our usual format."

I asked, "Why are you fighting them? The prospect specified what they want to hear about—and in what order." And he fired back, "Well, what the hell do you want us to do: blow up this sheet to poster size and prominently display it throughout the presentation?" I said, "Damn right. Then have each presenter check off their topic upon completion with a red magic marker." And as further evidence of their compatibility I proposed they reproduce the instruction sheet, imprint AGENDA on it, and distribute it before the meeting.

The agency apparently figured they might as well cash in on their investment in me, so they applied my recommendation—and landed the account. Granted, this device of itself wasn't responsible for the agency winning. But the new client confided that it was the tie-breaker among rough competition. This strategy graphically demonstrated, more than any claims or promises made, that the agency is client oriented.

But what do you do when a prospect says, "Alright, come on in and we'll just talk. Don't bother preparing anything." (Translation: they don't want to pay for it.) And then some other suppliers comes in with lifelike mock-ups, schematic diagrams, elegant illustrations, etc. and blows you out of the water.

If you want to go beyond the prospect's ground rules, here is your alternative. After having followed their instructions to the letter, acknowledge that you have, and then mention, "There are some further matters worthy of your attention. Shall I cover them?"

Having proved your willingness to cooperate, they will probably acquiesce—if you can be reasonably brief. You can then dip into your case and come up with the plus desired—without having violated the prospect's requirements.

Positioning

Positioning refers to the order of presentation. The prospect views supplier solicitations as a competitive event. Do you? If it is a missionary presentation, the prospect is comparing you with their present supplier. And if they are planning to change, they are thinking in terms of you versus the others.

So in addition to communicating what's in it for the prospect, you must convincingly register why your product or service is preferable to any other. And the way the solicitation game is being played now, your velvet glove better have an

> ## ❝ The way the solicitation game is being played now, your velvet glove better have an iron fist in it. ❞

iron fist in it. Because in this league, the meek shall not inherit the earth—only the dirt.

So, for instance, don't lead from weakness by requesting a specific positioning when a series of presentations are to be made. Some salespersons swear by going first because they coincidentally lucked out in that position once. Others shoot for going last—assuming that this final exposure will increase their memorability. However, there is the risk that after the first couple of pitches the prospect may have already made up their minds—the remaining presentations becoming a mere formality.

Superstition about positioning demeans you—and is interpreted by prospects as a lack of confidence. All that matters is the effectiveness of your presentation—not its sequence vis-a-vis the others.

If the prospect does give you a choice, though, avoid being slated right after lunch. That's too tough an act to follow.

Actually, the best timing for presentation is first thing in the morning—before the prospect has become fatigued, bored, or concerned about other matters.

Duration

When a prospect is receptive to buying, and will interview a quantity of suppliers, in some industries a length of time for presentation is usually specified by the prospect. If a screening procedure is customary, a brief period will be granted.

As a finalist, the amount of time you will be allotted by the prospect is usually whatever amount you need to put on the most appropriate presentation—and do it justice. (Show the prospect the courtesy of informing him of the amount of time you desire—so he can plan accordingly.)

A presentation is hardly ever too long if it is pertinent to the prospect's interests. It only drags if it becomes irrelevant.

Because the agreed-on time limit is usually exceeded, much to the prospect's annoyance, here is an ingratiating device that will increase your memorability—favorably. Open by announcing that your presentation will take a few minutes less than the time specified. This rare cooperation will pull them forward in their chairs. (Of course, this makes adequate rehearsal all the more necessary.)

Because this matter of timing is so important, let's clarify what the prospect means by, for instance, 60 minutes. It is simply that you are not to go beyond 60 minutes; they aren't expecting that your presentation necessarily run up to 60 minutes.

If you determine that for a certain prospect you can be most effective in 35 minutes, do so—and get out. Don't be like the salesman who had everything going for him—except being able to take yes for an answer. In other words, don't sell for so long that you end up buying it back.

Finally, here is the most important reason for complying with timing requirements. Prospects interpret violating this requirement as fighting them—and indicative of the relationship that would exist if such a salesperson were awarded their account. Consequently, ignored timing is sometimes the first, and easiest, means used to eliminate suppliers.

Location

I appreciate that your selling activity occurs most often in the prospect's office. If circumstances ever permit, though, arrange to hold your presentation at your office. This affords you more effective planning, better staging—plus the confidence that comes from familiarity with your own turf. Presenting on your turf will also minimize the risk of Murphy's Law: "Whatever can go wrong, will go wrong." Actually, you're better off applying O'Toole's Law: "Murphy is an optimist."

However, if the prospect requires that the presentation be conducted on their premises, it is essential that you check out the room in advance, because wherever the meeting is held, you—the supplier—is responsible for the logistics. Don't just take a cursory walk-through. Draw a diagram of the room's configuration:

- ◆ Indicate windows and doors, so you can consider their effect on your speakers and materials.

- ◆ Locate electrical outlets and light switches. (Do they have dimmers?)

- ◆ If necessary, decide on positioning of audio-visual equipment.

- ◆ Determine facilities for display (ceilings, walls).

Further, if the prospect stipulates that the presentation be put on at their place, ask if you can hold your rehearsal in their meeting room. This will provide you or your team with the knowledge and confidence of a familiar environment, which is bound to improve performance.

If this request is refused for any reason, you can do what DDB Needham/Chicago does in this situation. They ask if a photographer can come over when the room is available. This request is invariably granted—and he takes 360° shots of the room.

Based on the photos, the agency rearranges its own conference room (adding or removing furniture as appropriate) to simulate the prospect's room. Then after rehearsing under these conditions, when their presentation team arrives at the prospect, they have a feeling of déja vu.

The importance of being adequately familiar with the prospect's meeting room was proved recently in an exceptionally dramatic manner. This experience was played back to me at dinner by Kelly O'Neill who headed up Gardner Agency in St. Louis. Their flagship account was the pet food business of Ralston Purina.

One day, Kelly got a call from his contact at Ralston Purina informing him they had to hold still for a pitch on their dog food portion from another agency that afternoon and he didn't want anyone from Gardner to hear about it on the street. The client went on to stress there was nothing to worry about because this is just a political accommodation—"And we'll get rid of them fast." Further, he promised to phone Kelly the next day to confirm this brush off.

Sure, there is nothing to worry about! Then why the hell is the Ralston Purina client seeing them? Instant panic sets in. Imagination runs amuck—winding up by fearing the worst possible scenario.

To Kelly's amazement—and relief—his client contact phoned that same afternoon to notify him that the soliciting agency had left. Kelly said, "You sure *did* get rid of them fast." And the client replied, "Nope, they got rid of themselves."

He went on to explain that the agency CEO opened the purported extravaganza by exclaiming, "Not only are you going to love the advertising we are proposing, the dogs will love it, too!" At that (as rehearsed in their *own* conference room), one of the agency staffers, dressed in a dog costume, bounded into the room, barking gleefully.

The dog head part of the costume apparently obscured his vision and he slammed into a low glass-top coffee table. His barking quickly changed to howling. Having lacerated his shins, he bled profusely and the prospect had to call the paramedics.

Time elapsed: one minute, 27 seconds. And that was that. Their dog act turned out to be a dog. Adding insult to injury, the agency was out a bundle because nobody presents pencil rough layouts to Ralston Purina.

So be intimately knowledgeable regarding every aspect of the prospect's meeting room. As much as your own. Because the location should work for you—not be a trap.

Beyond this "your-place-or-mine" consideration, prospects are making increasing use of a third location: *a neutral spot*. Usually this is a room at a hotel or club. There are two reasons for choosing a neutral spot:

1. The prospect may have some interest, but doesn't want to risk having their present supplier(s) find out about their infidelity. They would rather not chance being seen at a soliciting supplier's office by a third party who might play it back. Nor do they want the presentation held

on their own premises—and risk being discovered by someone from the incumbent supplier.

2. They have decided to switch suppliers and schedule a series of consecutive presentations. However, they want to get away from their office distractions.

Further, the prospect wants the common denominator of the same environment for all contenders. Instead of being unduly influenced (favorably or otherwise) by each supplier's quarters.

When a neutral spot is used, it can make for a difficult situation. First the prospect may have carelessly slated too many candidates. Then they are harried all day about the time factor. In addition, you are up against their growing fatigue.

Complicating circumstances is the matter of logistics. When a string of suppliers is being run through the grinder, if you are using A-V equipment and displaying material, set-up becomes a serious problem, especially if this needs to be done while the prospect is present. And invariably you are rushed, clumsy—and uptight.

Here is how a Cleveland agency took the lemon of a situation and made lemonade. They rented the room next door to the prospect's hotel room, and arranged it to their advantage in advance. Then they held their rehearsals in it. When their turn came, they invited the prospect to simply step in—with the agency being relaxed and confident.

After having set up the prospect for a score, they applied the coup de grace— to the other agencies. The night before, they had their agency name posted on the hotel directory of events—right under the advertiser's name. The next day, when their competitors arrived and saw this, they assumed there was collusion—and that the listed agency was wired-in. I was told the effect of this device was demoralizing to the other agencies. Of course, the agency having this foresight won.

Of course this strategy, and the conduct of it, was highly risky. However, from the agency's appraisal of the situation, they concluded it would take this kind of boldness to win. Most important, they sensed from their pre-presentation experience that the prospect would react favorably to this aggressiveness. This was based on the gung-ho attitude of the prospect selection team—and the extent to

“ Don't sell for so long that you end up buying it back. ”

which they stressed wanting to be challenged via the agency's initiative and innovation.

Summing up, comply with the prospect's ground rules. But this shouldn't inhibit you from enhancing them—in your favor.

Hopefully, you are now comfortable with what you can expect of the prospect—and what is expected of you. Then you're ready for the selling tactics that should be applied under these circumstances—as detailed in the following chapter.

Selling Tactics That Work

◆ Perspective ◆ Creating Appeal for Yourself
◆ Promotional Activity ◆ Extent of Effort ◆ Honesty ◆ Contact by Prospect
◆ A Prospect Changing Suppliers ◆ A Prospect Using a Consultant
◆ Travel With Prospect ◆ Protection Against Theft ◆ The Prospect Visit
◆ The Antagonistic Prospect ◆ Buyer/Seller Status

Perspective

Here is the most critical matter you need to know regarding the prospect's attitude toward solicitation: Switching suppliers is deadly serious to them.

In effect, you're touting divorce. And regardless of how justified the divorce is, there isn't any room for being flippant. Thus, by whatever means an impression is made—appearance or dress, conduct or language, claims or promises—treat this matter with the same level of seriousness the prospect does.

The depth of the feelings was exemplified by the following experience. An ad director, who was my client, once asked me, "Jack, have you ever spent any time on this side of the desk?" And I told him, "No, my entire tour of duty has been on the other side." So he said, "Then you've never known what is means to lay awake at night, knowing you are forced to fire your agency and trying to figure how to cope with the three personal factors involved. How many jobs will be lost? How many lives will be affected? And finally, how much of a sonofabitch can I be?"

I had always assumed clients had ice water running through their veins.

It nets down to this. When a prospect decides to change suppliers, it is an admission of failure on their part. Either in the selection made or in their inability to work with them. Be aware of this tender nerve. And don't rub it the wrong way.

Creating Appeal for Yourself

The stature of your company and the quality of its product or service is a given. Yet, the prospect must buy *you* before they will buy who or what you represent. To make this first sale, help your contact relate to you. Might the two of you have anything in common? What is there about you that would be of interest to him or her that would be especially admired, or respected? Therefore, be sensitive to any prospect references to sports, armed forces service, hobbies, university, vacation spots, etc. Then, when possible with a minimum of digression from your selling efforts, capitalize on your mutual interest, especially if there is any means by which you can take this beyond conversation (i.e., playing golf or tennis, swapping stamps, attending an appealing event, etc.). By contrast, steer clear of any discussion of politics, religion or sex!

These personal matters, gracefully interjected into conversation to avoid any I-I-I impression, this familiarity, diplomatically applied, will establish the rapport necessary for him or her to be receptive to your claims and promises.

Promotional Activity

Supposedly, promoting your company's product or service is a corporate responsibility. This refers to any impersonal effort to sell through avenues such as advertising, sales promotion, and public relations.

You have more than you can handle pounding the pavement. But the purpose of promotional activity is to create acceptance for and to compound your direct selling activity. Since it affects your results, what are you doing to assure that this promotional activity best serves you? You have two opportunities:

1. It is in your best interest to not only be cognizant of the promotion planned by headquarters, but of what should be expected of it. Then if you have reason to believe this activity isn't being executed most productively, blow the whistle. This nets down to communicating the right message in the most persuasive manner.

    Too often, you are inclined to complain about the caliber of headquarter's support, claiming they don't know the real world. And then you suffer in silence. However, you are just as much at fault if the assumed error of their ways isn't made known to them.

This can be accomplished without jeopardizing your job if it is apparent that your contribution is positive and constructive, and if you recommend ways to strengthen the promotional program.

2. You probably receive some direction regarding how to take advantage of the sales catalysts developed. These could range from ads and commercials to point-of-purchase material and publicity, to buyer inducements. Obviously, the direction furnished to you is generally intended to be applicable to all sales personnel.

Beyond this direction, what action are you taking to adapt corporate strategy to your individual style and selling environment?

Challenge yourself. Can you possibly augment or improve the instructions for follow-through? If you don't try, your efforts will be ordinary and so will your sales. Then the sequel can be written about you: *Death of a Salesman II.*

Here is why your input and initiative are so necessary. Companies tend to equate aggressiveness in selling with *exposure.* I'm frequently asked, "We're active in the following respects. Have we missed any?" And then they cite a list something like this:

◆ Scheduling advertising campaign

◆ Conducting direct mail program

◆ Using "old boy" contacts

◆ Getting the word out to suppliers

◆ Capitalizing on a county club membership

◆ Exploiting civic involvement

◆ Delivering an occasional speech

I'll ask, "Why are you doing all this?" And they will say, "To create awareness."

66 Promotional tools for their own sake are luxuries.

They presume that familiarity with a company's existence, of itself, will generate prospect response. That's like assuming that if you advertise, you can get rid of your sales force. Of course these various promotional devices are of value if there are coinciding plans to exploit them. Develop the reasons for each activity and what you will do to gain from it.

◆ Sure, your company should advertise—but only if they intend to merchandise this activity.

◆ By all means use direct mail in your selling efforts. However, provision need be made to follow through with phone calls seeking an appointment.

◆ Certainly take advantage of contacts with your suppliers, but establish procedures and expectations in advance.

◆ Don't rationalize club dues unless the membership includes an adequate number of prospects and you have a *discrete* angle to solicit them.

◆ Civic involvement as an entree for selling is meaningless except if there is the opportunity to rub shoulders with desirable prospects.

◆ Accepting an invitation to speak is an ego trip unless there is a means to work the audience for your purposes.

In short, creating awareness doesn't produce results, just a warm feeling. It is only valuable when used as a vehicle to eventually stimulate prospect response. Thus, promotional tools for their own sake are luxuries. Rather, they should be planned as the first in a series of events geared to culminate in your closing sales.

Extent of Effort

A new business presentation is the culmination of all the activity it took to get the prospect to this event. However, you won't reach this stage unless each contact along the way is sufficiently intriguing.

Yet, salespeople often don't take a prospect seriously enough until they can taste blood, believing that in the competitive showdown that occurs, the winner is not selected until after the shootout. But this is not necessarily true. During all the preliminary activity (initial contact, pre-presentation meeting, screening pitch, tour of facilities, etc.), the prospect forms impressions of the various suppliers. As a result, when they get to the short list, their preference has already been established.

Therefore, *every* contact with the prospect should be considered a form of presentation. There should be no such thing as *just* a letter or *only* a phone call, because if these inducements aren't appealing enough, there won't be further contact.

So don't hold back until it's too late to win. If a prospect is worth whatever the presentation effort and expense necessary, *all* types of communication to lure them into your tent should be irresistible. *Gear up for all prospect contact as if it were the deciding factor in supplier selection.* Not only will this discipline increase the likelihood of your show going on, but it will prime the audience and make them more receptive to your performance.

Honesty

I would be remiss in not revealing this raw insight regarding prospect reaction to solicitation which answers the question "When is it okay to lie in selling?"

At best, you're suspect. Often, they just don't believe you. It's assumed you will promise them anything to get the business. Therefore, the only answer is *Never!* This advice applies equally to *every* circumstance—ranging from a basic one-on-one situation to a grand scale presentation.

Instead, to receive objective consideration, you must persuasively communicate having a very unusual attribute: *Honesty.* This is the first criterion used for judging salespeople. After you've left, the very first question the prospect asks is "Did you believe her (or him)?" If you are unable to satisfy this initial requirement, the finest performance will be down the drain.

Further, honesty will furnish the discipline to prevent offending the prospect with the tendency to exaggerate, which they have become very adroit at smoking out. Honesty can also provide a competitive edge. In fact, depending on whom you are competing against, it could supply you with an exclusive. In the prospect's vernacular, the first compliment you need to receive after your pitch is "They're straight." If you don't get this compliment, there won't be any others.

All right, how can you convince them that they could even buy a used car from you? By not making any claims about your product or service, or promises regarding your operation, which could be in any way suspect. If there is the remotest doubt that a statement will wash, omit it. Or it can blow the entire pitch.

What is honesty? Just this. Whatever you say should be able to stand up to their checking on it. That's your best test for truthfulness. And the best reason for telling the truth is that you will never have to wonder afterwards what you said.

There is a variety of tactics used by suppliers to convey honesty—with varying degrees of success. For instance, there is the device used by an agency in St. Louis. They make provision for stating in their presentation (just once) "I don't know." It is assumed that this candor will make all else said believable. Another

66 Serve the prospect prior to selection and their choice could be you. 99

agency offers to "make the books on your account available to you." (As a client, they are entitled to this anyway. But verbalizing it can be impressive.)

In the final analysis, for whatever angle you may come up with to communicate honesty, first try it out on the mirror. And then ask yourself, "Would I buy it?"

Contact by Prospect

Ask a prospect what she is looking for in a supplier and she will say "A better product (or service) at a lower price." However, this doesn't occur by spontaneous combustion. Rather, that which is developed and the marketing of it, emanate from *people*.

Since it is people that the prospect is ultimately buying, to whatever extent possible encourage them to contact any of your staff who would be assigned to their account and furnish the list. Invite them to get to know the proposed members of their team, to find out directly why their talents and experience would be of particular benefit.

How many of your competitors are making this offer? It takes courage, and indicates that your people must be especially right for them. This tactic also provides your company with the most valuable form of contact: personal, under relaxed circumstances, and gives the impression that your company is a completely above-board operation.

A Prospect Changing Suppliers

In soliciting a prospect planning to change suppliers, your objective is to convince them why your company is best for them. It might appear as though they could only benefit *after* you have been awarded the account. Yet, whatever you could do for them *before* selection would not only be appreciated, it would provide you with a competitive advantage.

Their immediate concern is the procedure for conducting a supplier search and establishing the criteria for evaluating the contenders. Therefore, in addition to being a great door opener, any insight you can furnish to make the prospect's job easier and faster will be highly valued, and bound to influence them to some extent in your favor.

Your service to them would consist of providing input and direction in the following areas:

◆ Performance and relationship expected of supplier

◆ Supplier search/investigation

◆ Use and content of questionnaire

◆ Analysis of response

◆ Screening suppliers for presentation

◆ Criteria for evaluating presentations

◆ Appraisal of results

◆ Decision-making process

Your amount of effort in providing this information would depend on the size and importance of the account. Thus, the method could range from informal conversation to a written detailed plan.

You say you don't know all that is necessary to perform the above functions? You're more knowledgeable than you think, and in some of the above categories, more knowledgeable than the prospect. Thus, if there are a few gems they are unaware of, or better organization for this program, you have tangibly demonstrated being the kind of person they need.

Needless to say, the insight supplied will be subtly geared to your interest. And why not? This strategy should enable you to at least qualify for the list of candidates and increase the possibility of becoming a finalist. Further, properly parlayed, your contribution will create a special relationship because you have illustrated you can relate to them. So serve the prospect *prior* to selection and their choice could be you.

A Prospect Using a Consultant

This subject may apply to only a few of you, and be experienced infrequently. However, when this situation arises, it always involves a very large prospect. Thus it's worth covering the insight you will need.

Occasionally, a major prospect planning to switch suppliers will retain a consultant to provide direction in conducting the search and selection process. It's often assumed that this introduces a new and complicating element. But it doesn't. Your objective is still to land the account. Not the consultant.

Don't change your strategy from what you originally considered necessary to score. But with this ringer participating, you will have to be prepared for closer-than-usual scrutiny of your appearance and behavior, as well as the claims and promises you make, because they are first looking for a cause to eliminate you.

Actually, it would be well to apply this discipline whether or not a consultant is on board. It will leave less to chance and assure a more professional job.

Travel with Prospect

After a prospect nets down to the finalists, the human equation often becomes the deciding factor in supplier selection. However, if the chemistry is a stand-off, the supplier perceived as having greater knowledge of the prospect and their market will probably win the account.

This is what made the difference in picking the winning agency by a super-market chain recently. Agency "A" went the full route in conducting both quantitative and qualitative research, and gave the impression of being intimately informed regarding this advertiser's operation and market.

But Agency "B" arranged to travel extensively with the chain's store supervisors. This also gave them considerable contact with individual store managers. They kept a diary of this experience, which included conclusions drawn, recommendations made and photos taken. Of course, this hands-on experience was strongly merchandised throughout their presentation and helped them to win the account.

The upshot was that Agency "A" came off as having gone that extra mile. But Agency "B" gave the impression of having walked it in the prospect's shoes. The moral of this story is this: conducting research for the prospect is admirable. Doing so *with* them is likelier to land the account.

Protection against Theft

You have a missionary presentation coming up. (You're not sure whether or not this prospect is even receptive.)

As part of your presentation, you come up with a sexy idea that you are certain the prospect will latch onto. So although unsolicited, you attempt to persuade the prospect with irresistible mock-ups, systems, etc. Whatever it will take to help them understand,—and buy—your idea.

They become excited by your idea, but are not totally convinced you are right for them. They ask if you will leave your proposition and support material for their consideration. Then you become struck with the fear that the prospect may try to steal what you conceived. However, they can't if you require a legitimate adoption procedure.

Here's how to protect your idea. First of all, don't cool off your live one by putting a copyright on any evidence of what you have to offer. They've been around. And know that there is a fair amount of ambiguity in the US copyright laws.

Instead, streetwise suppliers are finding they don't have to surrender their "creative gems." Rather, when the emotions are running high, the salesperson will righteously produce a letter of agreement. That is, a simple sheet setting forth in effect, if you would love to use any of this desirable stuff, it has to be bought from us. Please sign here.

In this way, they can't try it before they buy it.

So go ahead and tease the prospect by hinting just enough to get their commitment. Just so they understand you have a price: *partnership*.

The Prospect Visit

Your head-to-head pitch isn't the prospect's only opportunity to judge your company. In addition, there is the tour of your office or facilities to which they attach considerable importance. The impression made has disproportionate influence in the buying process. For some of you, due to your method of operation, a prospect visit is impractical. But for others, it can be an important part of the selling procedure.

What are they looking for? In regard to your people, the prospect wants to determine whether they are three-dimensional or social security numbers waiting to get the day over with. As to the appearance of your quarters, prospects are strongly opinionated. They are sensitive to a supplier looking too posh because they assume you would play it loose with their money, too. Yet, they are quick to counter that they do not want a supplier that looks ticky-tacky. So I've asked, "Then what are you seeking?" And they will reply, "One that looks successful." Probing further, I'll inquire as to what that means. And finally, the attitude that emerges is, "A place we would be proud to bring someone."

Prospects believe that in the supplier tour they can get a feeling of whether the supplier is extravagant or cheap, friendly or cold, imaginative or dull. Thus, the tour should never be conducted as an impromptu event left to chance. Rather, it ought to be as well conceived and structured as a formal presentation, including what they will be told, what they will be shown and who they will meet. These people need to be briefed on the prospect's needs and interests so they can come across as being particularly perceptive. In other words, don't surprise your production manager with a prospect, and then ask, "Charlie, say something cost-efficient."

Beyond achieving the desired effect on the prospect, a well-planned tour provides an excellent opportunity to further explore what a prospect really wants of a supplier. Assign an individual tour guide to each prospect representative. (If there are more than three of them, set up teams.) Prepare your people to ask them pertinent questions regarding their production or marketing and supplier needs, and their attitude toward these matters.

In this relaxed environment, the prospect is likely to reveal inner feelings which they wouldn't express under more formal conditions. After the prospect group departs, your guides can hold a debriefing session to identify insights they received beyond the prospect's official pronouncements.

By augmenting the prospect's corporate statements with their casual comments, you gain an understanding that allows you to present to them as people rather than functionaries. And with the discreet familiarity that results from a planned tour, they will be able to relate to your operation more than to your competitors'.

Sure, you may not have the authority to schedule and orchestrate a tour. You don't need it. It is only necessary for you to instigate this action.

Don't assume that *anything* which could contribute to your success is beyond you. You can only be faulted for not trying. And if you receive the necessary cooperation from others, and it pays off, you will be credited as the one who made it happen.

The Antagonistic Prospect

Occasionally, you will come across an egocentric prospect who seems to work at being offensive. How much heat should you have to take? That depends on these three factors:

1. The account's appeal: profitability, compatibility, growth, etc. Are they worth you toughing it out?

2. This contact's importance. Is his or her conduct representative? Are there others in your company who would be more appropriate in dealing with this person?

3. Your own sensitivity.

Given the above, can you come into the kitchen?

Rather than hastily taking a "To hell with 'em" attitude, objectively consider these matters. You may conclude that while the prospect is as rough as a cob, the account is so desirable that it would pay to play with pain. Pain is relative, anyway, as the following story shows.

Jack Reynolds and I started out together at Dancer Fitzgerald Sample after WWII. Having been a Navy Beachmaster, he soon concluded that the agency business wasn't rugged enough for him. So he got a job peddling space for *US News & World Report*.

66 Even if a meeting turns out to be a bummer, you can still learn from it. 99

They had Jack doing grunt work in the office until they felt safe letting him out in public. Then for his baptism under fire, the midwest sales manager sent Jack to call on the most miserable sonofabitch he knew. And Jack went to attack this person with the same ferocity he'd used to storm beaches. Little did he know that his boss had set him up to prove it is a jungle out there. And as he expected, he was brutally cut up.

Jack returned, looking as though he had just been hit by a kamikaze. In reporting to his manager, he said, "Y'know, maybe I'm not cut out for this business". And his boss asked, "Did he hit you?" Jack replied, "No, but he really worked me over."

And again his superior asked, "Did he hit you?" Jack repeated, "No, but he was ruthless." So pressing the issue, he was asked, "Yeah, but did he hit you?" Jack finally replied, "No dammit, he didn't *physically* hit me." At that, the midwest sales manager said, "Then what the hell are you complaining about?" As Jack came to think of it, he wasn't bleeding. He wasn't the walking wounded. Therefore, he could try it again without fear of risking permanent injury.

Apparently, Jack learned his lesson well because he eventually replaced his boss in the catbird seat. And his rough indoctrination was literally compensated for. During all those years, he diligently squirreled away *US News* stock. Then, when the magazine was bought by Mortimer Zuckerman, Jack began to live wealthily ever after.

That learned by his experience can also stand you in good stead when it comes to contacting those higher up the ladder. You needn't be squeamish due to their imposing position. Even if a meeting turns out to be a bummer, you can still learn from it. However, you may be pleasantly surprised because this person can afford to be gracious.

Buyer/Seller Status

I began this chapter by dealing with the prospect's attitude toward solicitation. Just as important though is *your* attitude. Sometimes a salesperson starts playing a cold hand, and isn't scoring despite what are believed to be excellent presentations. This often happens after a hot streak when he or she begins to forget who is the buyer and who is the seller.

For instance, there is an agency in Minneapolis that was scoring so well they thought they'd found the new business Holy Grail. They concluded there are two requisites for winning: (1) the presentation must be held at the agency's office, and (2) a minimum of two hours is needed, and they began specifying these requirements to prospects.

Despite the shop's meteoric rise, their growth flattened out just as quickly. Because as important as the environment and duration are to selling, the prospect also needs to be *receptive* to buying your product or service. And since prospects equate seller terms with arrogance, setting ground rules is as far as you'll get.

So tell them *what* to buy—not how.

Section IV

Street Smarts Selling

Most people in sales assume that their sole function is to sell whatever is produced or whatever service is performed by their company. However, that is just for openers.

What the prospect really needs to be sold is the *result* of their purchase. Maybe it's product enhancement or a competitive edge. Possibly a solution or a price break.

Thus, any product or service you're selling is the vehicle for the *benefit* they will receive. This concept was given life by Charles Revson, founder of Revlon, when he said, "In the factory, we make cosmetics. In the store, we sell hope."

So get to the payoff point faster with the advantages the prospect will gain and the opportunities they will realize. Here is the net-net: of itself, your product or service is an expense. What it can do for a buyer makes it an investment.

In conclusion, having simplified your selling operation through this one selling strategy, the ensuing six chapters clue you in on all the factors for implementing it.

14. The Science and Art of Making Claims and Promises

15. The Two Most Sensitive Factors: Price and Payment

16. Reducing the Risk of Mistakes

17. Controlling, Rather Than Reacting to, Competition

❝ Any product or service you're selling is the vehicle for the benefit they will receive. ❞

14

The Science and Art of Making Claims and Promises

◆ Perspective ◆ Promotional Support
◆ Corporate Philosophy ◆ Objection to Size
◆ Combatting Larger Competitors ◆ Supplier Location
◆ Successful Performance ◆ Toughest Lesson

Perspective

There is a tendency to get so involved in the components of your sales plan that you begin to overlook its purpose—to convince prospects of *why your product or service can best fulfill their requirements.* Every aspect of your prospecting, solicitation, and presentation should contribute to proving this claim. That is all the prospect is interested in. Anything else is self-gratifying and distracting.

You may claim to already know this. But according to buyers, sellers do not hone in on what is most pertinent to them—and then stay on target throughout. Thus, to whatever extent you digress from justifying *why your product or service can best fulfill their requirements,* you weaken your impact to the same extent.

137

Promotional Support

Teamwork Sells More

Salespeople are the front-line troops—with personnel at headquarters their be-hind-the-lines support. Although each has her or his own function, no battle has ever been won without a combined thrust.

Those who support your activity with their specialized skills have indirect selling responsibility. Correspondingly, it is conceivable for you to inspire and contribute to their efforts, especially when their selling help is needed or an idea can be offered. Because your results are influenced by the effect of their performance.

Sure, you can't lay claim to being expert in the areas of advertising, promotion, public relations, etc. But neither are those performing this work experienced in confronting prospects. Ultimately, both groups have the same objective: increasing sales, profitably. And the companies that are most successful are those that synergize the abilities of both sources.

To what extent should you initiate suggestions in these sales support areas? Regardless of anyone's qualifications, no one has a monopoly on what will generate sales. And nowhere is it written that this direction can only be a one-way flow from headquarters to you. Teamwork involves more than your implementing the instructions and materials furnished. Rather, it is only as good as the degree to which you *compound* the selling strategy and material developed via your input and application of it.

If you need any further incentive, never forget this. With all due respect to those who indirectly contribute to sales, in the final analysis, it nets down to who physically gets the order. And this is, or isn't you. Therefore, justified or not, eventually you get the credit or blame. From this perspective, then, it is not a matter of *if* you should initiate ideas for increasing sales—only how much you are able to.

Having brought this matter into focus, here is the insight you need regarding direct support activity: promotional mailings.

Strategy

Whether I am at an advertiser or an agency for seminar or consulting purposes, invariably I'm asked for my opinion of their promotional material. They haul out their kid, with buck teeth and pimples, and hope I have the same paternal feeling.

Sure, I can play it safe and answer like the pediatrician, "Now that is a boy!" But there is one pattern that emerges across the board which can't be glossed over. Whatever the mailing piece, by whomever, they all have two faults in common:

1. It is an ego trip on behalf of the company because its content does not pay off for the prospect (i.e., following through with "This is the kind of

> ** The only meaningful claims are those directed to the prospects' interests and needs. **

value or performance you could count on if you order our product or service.")

2. It does not involve the reader—giving them a reason why it would be to their advantage to contact you.

A prospect will not bother to decipher or interpret your message.

These mailers vary from a folksy letter from the company CEO to lavish five-color heavy stock pieces in a variety of sizes and shapes. The appearance is usually attractive. But what happened to the message? It seems written to satisfy and insure approval from the sender's boss, rather than to excite the recipient. But, the only meaningful claims are those directed to the prospects' interests and needs. How well have you explained how the features of your product or service will benefit them?

Themes

Further, the communication, whatever its form, should associate your company with the prospect throughout, frequently referring to "we," and "us," and presenting the relationship as desirable.

The advantages of your product or service are only as impressive as the degree to which the prospect perceives they stand to gain from them. So stop assuming that a photo of your CEO (usually pictured on the phone) accompanied by a gut-wrenching exposition of your company's philosophy is going to enrapture anyone. Instead, target the only matter of interest to a prospect: "What's in it for me?"

Your product or service is the most obvious evidence of what they can expect. And since prospects are authorities in two areas—their business and yours—suppliers will try to represent their value in the most dynamic manner. Unfortunately, some confuse *startle* with *convince* in their promotional material. This occurs when using provocative descriptions of their product or service for their own sake, for example, proudly referring to it as being "too good to be true," or an "unbelievable" price. Too often, these claims are taken literally, resulting in rejection.

Hopefully, you can legitimately instill want by expressing yourself as being innovative—not desperate. To do this, promote in an intriguing—not shocking—manner. Be as imaginative when selling on your behalf as circumstances permit, but not at the expense of your credibility.

Here, too, I'm not moralizing. If the content of a headquarters letter, promotional piece or advertising is at all suspect, you the seller, are indicted with the offender. Therefore, the harm that could occur from this guilt by association provides the best reason for you to be at least a devil's advocate: *to protect yourself.*

Devices

Yet, when your company is developing promotional material, it shouldn't naively assume the prospect will bother to think. They won't. Unless this reality is compensated for, some of your strongest selling appeals will be seriously weakened.

This especially applies to the use of customer testimonial letters and press coverage in your promotional pieces. As proud as you are of this recognition, others aren't salivating to read it. And even if the prospect does, they may be happy for you—but won't make the effort to relate to your accomplishments. Therefore, to lure them into the tent, precede the reproduction of the letter of publicity with an intriguing statement. Then add a brief comment at the end, explaining what this achievement means to them. Otherwise, the recipient will lump these endorsements with all the other puffery received.

There is still another respect in which these promo folders are lacking. In effect, these are a presentation on paper. However, unlike its human counterpart, it fails to ask for the order.

Admittedly, its primary purpose is to generate interest and pave the way for personal contact. Yet, why not use *all* of it to sell for you? This needn't violate any aesthetics. But it can convert this item from a promotional device to a *selling* device.

Finally, in regard to the closer, practically all suppliers use the same wrap-up. Each will conclude with the statement: "Please call John Doe, President, for further information, (987) 654-3210." First, because this is a standard closer, its effect is a wash. Second, why should the prospect do so? Via this request, the supplier seems to forget who's who in this buyer-seller situation.

Instead, break the mold. Dare to be different. Show your respect for the prospect by wrapping up with the opposite tack: "You shouldn't have to call us. We'll phone you." This deference will surely distinguish your mailer from the sameness of the others.

Summing up, the impact of your company's sales support via promotional mailings will be strongly influenced by your involvement. The importance of your merchandising what is developed is a given. Even more valuable, though, could be your hands-on input from the trenches. So don't only finish the job. Get it started right.

Corporate Philosophy

Corporate philosophies are usually interminable, vague, pompous, esoteric and pedantic—seemingly prepared by a Tibetan Monk. And when presented, bore the prospect to death. Instead of wasting time on this ego trip, there are two approaches that can do you proud. Rather than being abstract, both of these offer a promise of concrete benefit—with which a buyer can associate. Significantly, both should be brief.

The first is provocative—and right to the point. State that your company doesn't have a philosophy; rather, you have an individual objective for each customer—to best fulfill their product (service) requirements.

The other option is to set forth specific standards for operation in respect to performance and relationship. For the impression desired, credibility is essential. Whatever proposals and claims are made must be believable and realistic, the criterion being, if called upon to prove that stated, you can deliver. And then, to enhance acceptance it should be written in plain language: "people talk."

In both instances, the appeal is based on what's in it for the prospect—as opposed to what you want to boast about. So, if your company feels compelled to have a philosophy, its intent should be to impress the prospect—not itself.

In presentation, don't belabor your philosophy, or prospects will suspect you lack ideas. For it to come alive and be meaningful to the prospect, translate how you will use your philosophy in your relationship with them, and how they will specifically benefit from your conduct. This is what it finally takes for your philosophy to have the impact you want.

Objection to Size

Unless you are with an international mega-conglomerate, there may be concern about selling against larger competitors. Salespersons assume that being with a company that is smaller implies being less desirable in respect to personnel, product, services, or facilities. By contrast, sometimes a prospect is reluctant to consider your company because it is *too big*. They fear they might get buried and receive short shrift.

The best way to defuse prospect objections to size is to constructively refute them *before* they occur. Go beyond the usual impersonal claim of being able to fulfill all their needs. Provide the prospect with a list of the specific people—by name and function—who will be assigned to their account, and cite the back-up personnel ready to serve them. (Unless touting bodies for the sake of numbers, no competitor can offer more than this primary and back-up team.)

This commitment, in writing, can dissipate the prospect's reservations about your size, by providing proof that there is already a designated team on line that would be held accountable for performance.

❝ To the prospect, you are what makes it happen.❞

Combatting Larger Competitors

Yet, with few exceptions, there will always be particular concern regarding the difficulty of pitching against larger competitors for new business. Admittedly, you're not going to make it with transparent claims such as, "What we lack in numbers, we make up for in ideas," or, "Just think, you'd be getting our first team." The prospect has already yawned through these and a variety of other attempts by suppliers to compensate for being smaller than their competitors.

Instead, you can overcome the misconception that a larger supplier must be preferable in the most logical manner: by citing the economics of any business. Namely, a supplier can only allocate employee time to a customer based on the income received from them. And this cold fact applies to any supplier—regardless of size. Sure, some suppliers will over promise. But eventually they will be confronted with the moment of truth: the balance sheet. Then the supplier will discover it trapped itself and has to start cutting back on time—particularly from among the heavyweights they've promised. Now it is only a matter of time until this wheeler-dealer supplier receives a "Dear John" letter. Because customers take a jaundiced view of being deceived in presentation.

Therefore, if it becomes necessary, explain that supplier size cannot be equated with the amount of attention they will receive. Anyway, that's not the criterion for determining preference. Rather, the difference lies in the *quality* of personnel assigned. So you needn't be beaten in the numbers game. You can win by convincing the prospect that your people are better. After all, they wouldn't hire Goliath if they knew David was looking for a job.

Supplier Location

The factor of supplier location is a two-edge sword. Local or otherwise, it can be used to your advantage—or might need to be compensated for. Although supplier selection should be based essentially on price/value relationship and compatibility, sometimes proximity is a consideration. Since your location could work for or against you, here are your recourses:

◆ If in your favor, cite your distance from the prospect in minutes and miles. (You needn't mention the substantial difference in distance that applies to any of your competitors. The comparison by inference is strong enough.)

◆ If location can be to your detriment, note that their objective should be to have the supplier of greatest value to them—irrespective of distance. Anyway, the substantial progress made in telecommunications significantly minimizes the importance of location.

Successful Performance

Every noteworthy achievement should be viewed in terms of how it can serve as an inducement to attract more business. Suppliers spend a lot of time trying to dream up clever selling devices—that usually just tout themselves. But what could be more impressive than your *actual* accomplishments—and what they could do for the prospect? And this should include not only that achieved corporately, but also what you personally contributed. Because to the prospect, you are what makes it happen. Whatever you achieve for your current customers can also be used to your advantage with prospects.

This approach is success oriented, which is what prospects want. How well are you merchandising your ability to deliver? It should be S.O.P. to parlay customer success into your success.

Toughest Lesson

You felt really good about that presentation. And you should. Everything was right on the money. Requiring a team effort, it consisted of those likeliest to appeal to and impress the prospect. The pitch was relevant to their interests and needs. And the results promised were believable, and better than they are presently getting. So when a buyer asks the standard question, "What's new?" you sure have an answer.

You were on a roll in both concept and execution because you flushed out the necessary information in your pre-presentation meeting with them. And your team came across as pros because of the discipline and confidence gained in rehearsal. In fact, you felt euphoric about that presentation—since this kind of preparation and conduct is what resulted in your winning the last three times.

Then came the cold grey light of dawn. Another supplier was selected. What particularly hurt is that they aren't as experienced in the prospect's field—and don't have your depth and caliber of personnel. Where did you go wrong? You didn't. Apparently the chemistry wasn't right. And you can't do anything about the human equation. Difficult as it might be to accept, as maybe Confucius said, "Everybody ain't gonna love you, baby."

It's important that you don't panic into changing a strategy that has proved itself successful. You can't become emotionally unglued because you're not always irresistible. Recognize that even with everything going for you in presentation, your charm isn't going to work all the time. Just hang in there—and don't let a letdown that doesn't make any sense throw you off stride. Have the faith to stick with the necessary basics, and you will get more than your share of additional business.

The Two Most Sensitive Factors: Price and Payment

◆ Perspective ◆ Prospect Attitude◆ ◆ Method of Payment
◆ The Unsophisticated Prospect ◆ Desirable But Unaffordable
◆ Appealing But Risky

Perspective

In simpler times, the method of compensation wasn't as much of a factor in supplier selection as it is today. Everyone played by essentially the same rules: whatever was standard practice for the industry involved. But at some point, tradition gave way to negotiation. Buyers now expect the same cost efficiency from suppliers as is required of them.

As a result of the demise of the status quo, price has become a key criterion in supplier selection. And since it enters into many areas of solicitation activity, price is dealt with in many areas of this book. There are certain matters, however, that warrant being singled out for special attention.

Prospect Attitude

As is being made amply evident, prospects aren't holding still anymore for the historic system of payment just because it is tradition. Few are willing or can afford to make this concession to sentiment. They no longer feel bound by past industry practices for charging and billing which were appropriate back then—but not necessarily now. They are taking this stand because the increasing market pressure to operate more economically in all areas has resulted in their becoming more knowledgeable regarding supplier finances. Many now have a fair idea of how much (or little) their suppliers need to charge for their product or service.

Many prospects realize there are circumstances in which a supplier couldn't break even in fulfilling their needs. They also recognize that in other situations routine pricing for nominal requirements could be a license to steal. In either case, adjustments need to be made. Contrary to the assumption by cynics that prospects and customers are out to gouge your margins, actually most of them want you to make a satisfactory profit for a basic reason: they want to be associated with a winner. In essence, the prospect wants a supplier they can respect—not one that can be had.

However, they are concerned about, and intend to protect themselves against, your making an unjustifiable profit. That's why, for instance, there is growing objection to being charged according to a standard formula (fixed mark-up, inflated margin, cost plus, etc.). They would now much rather pay on the basis of work performed. The crux of the matter is that as customers, they want payment to be equitable: commensurate with output.

Thus, whatever the mechanics by which you charge, it must satisfy the first two most basic necessities for consummating any sale:

◆ The supplier must receive a realistic profit

◆ The customer should be able to pay according to what they get—instead of gambling on some generic system, pawned off on everyone.

The bad news is that you won't get fat on this type of arrangement. But the good news is that your company will be assured of an acceptable profit. Most important, selling a method of payment geared to productivity rather than chance offers customer satisfaction in the most meaningful manner: value received.

Method of Payment

There is an important development taking place in compensation strategy, a smart move, long overdue. Because suppliers can no longer afford to get hung up on intermediate words like *commission* or *fee*—having been deceived (and burned) by these front-end terms—they have come to realize that the only word that matters is *profit*.

As a result, these converts are evaluating prospects more realistically, according to projected workload and estimated income. Then the amount of dollar profit deserved is established—not some cockamamie formula, but the exact number of dollars to which the supplier is entitled.

This net-oriented approach prevents being dazzled by an account's assumed size or appeal. Either they are affordable based on your financial requirements, or they aren't. If this concept seems too cut-and-dried, you need bring into focus the purpose of your company: a profitable enterprise or a charitable institution. The application of this discipline is contained in the following case history.

One of the most wonderful prospect inquiries you can receive after a presentation is, "In our particular case, what would be the most appropriate form of compensation?" Here is how Bill Biggs, major domo of Biggs/Gilmore in Kalamazoo, Michigan handles it. Being exceptionally charming, he disarmingly replies, "Whatever will make you happy."

Bill isn't giving anything away. He couldn't care less what the prospect calls the method of compensation. His only concern is that the account returns the predetermined amount of profit. I've heard his own people ask, "But Bill, what if some other agency undercuts us?" His Socratic reply was, "We'll wish them the best of luck. We have a responsibility to serve our agency as well as our clients."

In the final analysis, charity begins at home. So develop a two-way street mentality regarding compensation. Because you can only take care of a customer if your company is adequately cared for.

The Unsophisticated Prospect

There are all kinds of ways to make—or lose—money in your business. The obvious factor is payment for product sold or services rendered. However, your profit is directly affected by the amount of selling time needed to justify what's been developed.

If a customer has a working knowledge of supplier operation and work performed, you can concentrate on the presentation—needing only a minimum of time for indoctrination. But if they are lacking this knowledge, the period spent educating them in addition to your presentation can become unaffordable. Therefore, a key consideration in determining a prospect's profitability is their sophistication in dealing with suppliers. So to whatever extent applicable, take this matter into consideration when negotiating compensation.

Desirable but Unaffordable

Don't arbitrarily turn away a prospect of acceptable size by assuming they couldn't be sufficiently profitable. Granted, based on estimated income and projected workload, they may seem unaffordable. Rather than writing them off, though, present the amount of *supplementary* income necessary for you to realize a legitimate profit. (Sure you can be had. At your price.)

If they accept, great. This prospect has just graduated from appalling to appealing. However, if they refuse, they will still respect your acumen. And you didn't offend by rejecting what might be a worthwhile prospect down the road. So don't eliminate; negotiate. Sound out the prospect. Your value to them may be such that they would be willing to work out a financial arrangement that would accommodate you.

Appealing but Risky

In any industry, there are certain accounts whose substantial size make them especially attractive. But getting them to pay their bills is something else. Granted, this business is very tempting. Thus, there is the tendency to salivate when thinking of the killing that could be made. Even when aware of the considerable financial risk in having this type of customer, on occasion suppliers are compromised by ambition or greed.

Although other suppliers have been stiffed, you believe you could succeed where they have failed because of *personally* staying on top of their payment schedule.

That's idealistic. Ad agencies learned this the hard way in handling political candidates. For instance, an agency head in Atlanta was approached by a state senator to handle his re-election campaign. Although the agency has a policy against accepting *any* political advertising, this candidate happened to be a close personal friend. The CEO knew that his buddy was in such good financial shape that he felt it wasn't even necessary to stipulate the standard prepayment of charges for this type of advertising.

This naivete ignored the nature of the political beast—and the ground rules for the game. As a result, six months afterwards, the CEO was still trying to collect the $24,000 still owed to the agency. At this stage, he desperately stated to the deadbeat, "I never dreamed you would try to stiff me!" The state senator vehemently denied this accusation and countered with, "I'd rather owe you this money for the rest of my life than renege on my word to pay you!" This sadder but wiser agency learned from this bitter experience the first law of compensation when dealing with such volatile accounts: C.O.D.

In the case of a prospect who is historically "poor-pay," negotiate getting all or enough of your money up front. Would this be impolitic? What have you got to lose? They are unaffordable otherwise. However, if your proposal is appealing (and aware of their own reputation), they may acquiesce to this arrangement. And then you can have it both ways: making the sale and getting paid for it.

In conclusion, price must be more than a cold number by virtue of the value of the product or service you sold the customer. It should stand for their purchase being worth more than that paid. And you should periodically remind them of the soundness of their buying decision as an incentive for them to pay promptly.

Reducing the Risk of Mistakes

◆ Perspective ◆ The Two Major Causes for Coming in Second
◆ Describing Your Company ◆ Evaluating Prospect Performance
◆ Materials vs. Presenters ◆ Gimmicks ◆ No Written Commitment

Perspective

Usually the successful salesperson is the one who made the fewest mistakes. The major reasons for failure are

◆ Inadequate pre-presentation input

◆ Insufficient rehearsal

◆ Poor chemistry

◆ Irrelevant presentation

◆ Offensive conduct

◆ Unsatisfactory handling of prospect zingers

◆ Poor chemistry

Beyond these obvious traps, there is a variety of other pitfalls that could scuttle your success. We had better examine the more dangerous ones because any of these could do you in. However, since criticism carries with it the responsibility to contribute, I've also furnished the alchemy to make a silk purse out of a sow's ear.

The Two Major Causes for Coming in Second

Before we go any further, let's establish top-of-mind awareness of the two major causes for a salesperson coming in second—and what it takes to win.

1. First, there is the belief that no one would know better than you how to develop a presentation. After all, you're the one who is beating doors down and getting roughed up. So no ivory tower theories, just what works on the street. The strategy is based on the assumption that the prospect is holding still because they want to get to know you. Sure they do—but only after you've explained what is in it for them.

So you sell hard rather than smart, concentrating on promoting your product or service—and dealing with the prospect's perceived needs only as an afterthought. As a result, the pitch becomes an ego trip—based on past performance and professed successes. This nostalgia turns the prospect off because they can't relate to it.

Instead, open with what your research has taught you they want to hear about. Then devote the rest of the time to proving why your product or service can best fulfill their requirements. This involves targeting as quickly as possible what they consider their most important needs—and why your company can best fulfil those needs. This is the best strategy for satisfying their expectations—and distinguishing your presentation from routine ones.

Again, remember, the prospect is holding still to first find out what's in it for them. And to then find out why your company can best provide it. Keep bearing in mind they are sold by the benefits—not the availability—of your services.

2. Second, upon developing a dynamic presentation, you assume it is so compelling that the prospect can't help but infer why your product or service is preferable to any other.

But the prospect becomes numb very easily. (How often have you seen that glazed look?) Further, they will not make the effort to think. As far as they are concerned, a presentation is a buyer-seller situation, in which it is your responsibility to attract and hold their attention. Consequently, only that presented which

❝ Forego the hackneyed sales ploy of claiming your company is different. ❞

is readily apparent—and so intriguing—will penetrate the prospect's psyche and be absorbed.

How can you achieve all this? First, *critically appraise* whether your presentation was developed to appeal to and satisfy the prospect—or those to whom you report. (Too often, the latter is the case.) Then *test* your sales approach and delivery on a devil's advocate, someone not encumbered by pride of authorship, and who has the clout to be objective. It would be especially desirable if this person also has *in-depth industry experience* and knowledge of supplier presentations. Having these three qualifications, he or she becomes the most valuable person in your rehearsal.

Where can you find such a person? He or she is a customer, who by virtue of past or present involvement, is an authority on your prospect's industry and/or market and, of course, has a track record in choosing suppliers.

This action was taken by a Minneapolis agency. They have a major bank client for whom marketable results have been produced. Thus, they decided to expand their horizons and parlay this success among other nonconflicting banks. Having a good relationship with the client's ad VP, the agency invited him to cut them up at their rehearsal. Result: the agency credits the hands-on insight and objectivity of this ad VP with providing the clincher for winning.

Thus, when appropriate, capitalize on this secret weapon—prior to going into combat. If your presentation can withstand the disciplines of a critical appraisal and devil's advocate, then you know that at least you are on the right track.

Describing Your Company

Forego the hackneyed sales ploy of claiming your company is *different*. Regardless of philosophy, size, or specialty of location, a supplier is a supplier, is a supplier—with essentially the same problems and opportunities. Your potential for distinction lies in being *better*—not different.

Is this just a matter of semantics? No. "Different" could be construed as being "odd." However, there is no doubt that "better" conveys "superiority." Of course, this differentiation applies to your product or service, too.

Evaluating Prospect Performance

Sometimes an evaluation of prospect performance is initiated by the supplier for use as a selling device. On occasion, a prospect will request this service. The former tactic warrants little attention because you probably already know it is suicidal. Regardless of how well your criticism is cloaked in the guise of a constructive contribution, the impression you convey is that they fouled up in having approved this inferior work. Their ineptness revealed, their jobs may now be threatened. How anxious will this prospect be to get involved with you and risk being finished off?

So no matter how lousy their operation, there can *never* be any justification for trashing it. In this way, you allow the prospect to buy you from a position of strength.

The reverse situation is more complicated. When a prospect asks a supplier to evaluate any aspect of its operation, they may be being sincere or setting a trap. But either way, it can be a heads-you-lose, tails-you-lose situation. Don't get sucked into this supposed opportunity without having options. This is a gamble that serves the prospect's interests—however, it is usually stacked against you.

There are four reasons why you can get hurt—terminally:

1. You can't possibly be familiar enough with the prospect's strategy and objectives. Not being qualified to pass judgment, you are bound to make an inadvertent blunder.

2. It is inconceivable that there wouldn't be anything critical in your analysis. Accordingly, those responsible for approving what you're criticizing become instant enemies.

3. There is the risk of your judgment being used to resolve internal political differences. Then you are remembered as the hatchet-man—and have outlived your usefulness.

4. Your conclusions are bound to be suspect because your self-interest is involved.

Yet, you don't want to flatly refuse their request. Whether it is on the level or you're being conned, here is how to salvage the situation. But first, let's set the stage for the solution with this nightmare.

An agency president in Toronto recently told me about a prospect enticing him into a very tacky position. This involvement cost him much time and effort—and the respect of his peers at two prominent agencies. I'll protect this agency president by referring to him by only his first name: Bob. Bob had been romancing the senior VP of marketing of a major package goods company—any portion of whose account would be highly desirable. It had been determined that this contact had the clout to hire or fire agencies. The opportunity to ingratiate himself with the prospect arose—but in a dangerous way.

The senior VP offered Bob tapes of TV commercials just produced by the two incumbent agencies—and asked that these be critiqued. Supposedly this cooperation would provide the incentive for Bob's shop to be given active consideration. Despite this devious tactic, Bob salivated—rationalizing that the potential was just too great to resist. Bob not only assigned his creative staff to analyze these commercials from a concept and production standpoint, but also involved his marketing people to identify objectives and determine the appropriateness of the approach taken. Then, for further impact, Bob called upon the resources of his agency's other offices for their input. Obviously, the combined time and cost was brutal. Needless to say, the report was impressive, so much so that the senior VP sent copies of it to the presidents of his two agencies.

They were appalled at this client subterfuge—and their competitor's acquiescence. But who were they going to get mad at? Certainly not their valued client. Instead, Bob became the villain. And whereas there had previously been a good fraternal relationship, the other two now froze him out. To compound the injury, this favor didn't pry loose any of the prospect's business.

Sure Bob was used—but there was no need for him to be had. He could have gained stature—and profit—by proposing to undertake the project on a fee basis. Instead of giving the store away, Bob should have submitted a recommendation detailing the following:

◆ The professional, objective approach to be taken

◆ The service to be provided

◆ The results that could be expected

◆ The direction for applying the findings

◆ A justification for the charge

This approach makes the assignment a legitimate business deal—serving both interests. The supplier doesn't come off desperate. And if nothing occurs afterwards, at least they are compensated for an above-board job. On the prospect's behalf, this arrangement is clean—and they are not beholden. As a result, the prestige of each remains intact. And the supplier can continue to ethically solicit the account without any loss of face—or financially shafting itself.

The moral of this case history is best expressed by the credo of Harvard Business School: "If you can't sell it, sit on it; but don't give it away."

Materials vs. Presenters

There are probably as many ways for blowing a sale as there are salespeople. One of the more common causes is the attempt to impress the prospect up front with a portfolio of material. The portfolio usually contains a variety of information about your company, its product or service, and achievements, and is given to them at the beginning of the presentation. It is assumed that this tactic will favorably precondition them.

But you are really only fighting yourself. The portfolio is a distracting device that competes with what you will be saying and showing. Even reference to its content is difficult and confusing because people read at different rates. Finally, most damaging, it sacrifices eyeball contact.

Instead, you retain control by *presenting* what you want shown—in the sequence you've deemed effective. Rather than distributing an ego trip in a packet, simply hand out a one-page agenda—whose brevity and clarity will not interfere with your selling effort.

Gimmicks

The prerequisite for scoring is the relevance of your pitch—in an environment conducive to the prospect's receptivity. Yet even the most sophisticated of salespeople keep looking for a by-the-numbers formula for winning. For example, here are a couple of "hooks" used by some heavy hitter agencies in New York. Unfortunately, each approach has recently worked—once. As a result, both agencies assume they have found the New Business Holy Grail, and are diverting their efforts from proven successful strategy to these cockamamie devices.

The Hokey Approach

This approach consists of showing the prospect samples of exciting creative work—and then informing them they can't have it because you don't know the prospect's business. That's being a lousy host. You invited the prospect over for cocktails—and then didn't serve any, since you don't know what they drink. This supposedly realistic angle is a letdown—and negative. A prospect wants to know what's in it for her—not what she can't have.

Actually, you *can* present viable proposals based only on input provided by the prospect. Then there isn't any concession of ignorance on your part—and you have registered your capacity to satisfy their needs according to the direction furnished.

The moral of this story is to give the prospect what they expect: the reason to buy.

The Cutesy Approach

The agency responsible for this case history concentrates its activity on those accounts wanted—as opposed to those who happen to be available (the rifle shot method discussed in Chapter 4). Fine so far. Then, for this missionary purpose, a woman with a British accent and a sexy voice phones the targeted contact *every day*—until this person agrees to come over to the agency for a get-acquainted luncheon meeting with its top management. Ostensibly, this persistence will wear down the prospect's reluctance. And the curiosity of meeting the body that goes with this intriguing voice will be irresistible.

Granted, this woman is well-trained in telemarketing. But the concept is offensive. Although it may appeal to the voyeur type, it will antagonize most others. Further, this conduct will ruin a supplier's chances with the prospect for as long as that contact is there.

> **❝ There are probably as many ways for blowing a sale as there are salespeople. ❞**

Instead, a person making contact should be able to represent himself or herself as having a very responsible position. And use a legitimate door opener rather than come across as a shill.

This time, the moral is that there isn't any single miracle, regardless of how unusual, that will provide a quick-fix for landing new accounts. There is only the sum of all the necessary sound activity it takes to win. You have a much greater opportunity for winning using a strategy based on synergy rather than relying on a single tactic.

Anyway, even the cleverest device of itself will not make the sale. There are too many factors that must be considered. Further, the purchase usually needs to be justified. And no one is going to attribute their decision to a one-shot gimmick.

No Written Commitment

Some suppliers pride themselves on their handshake arrangement with customers. It is assumed this lack of formal commitment is indicative of respect for their excellent relationship. But all this casual arrangement means to the customer is that they are less obligated. A written agreement provides you with two vital opportunities:

1. *Protection*: The agreement details how your company operates—and the method of compensation. Then if any doubts arise regarding your relations, you have tangible evidence that you kept your word.

2. *Promotion*: The agreement states the variety of products, or services and functions your company can provide, and explains why it would be to their advantage to make maximum use of them.

An acknowledgement of purchase, or an operating agreement could range in format from a personal letter, to a purchase order, to a contract. Granted, to some prospects, a contract is an anathema.

But if you call it a letter of agreement, it often becomes acceptable. As to appearance, how you read this new customer will determine whether the document should be in a printed or typed form. The printed version implies this letter of agreement is the standard industry form, one for which there is overall acceptance—with obviously nothing between the lines. By contrast, the typed version is less awesome—and indicative of the personal nature of your relationship.

This confirmation of claims and promises made should preclude any misunderstandings or unwelcome surprises. Further, it is evidence of your operating on a professional rather than casual basis. This distinction has become increasingly important to customers. So after you ask for the order, give them a receipt—for their signature.

The matter of blunders is so critical it warrants being given this chapter of its own. For this reason, in this fiercely competitive climate, the time-tested adage is truer than ever! "Often, the winning salesperson is the one who made the fewest mistakes."

Controlling, Rather Than Reacting To, Competition

◆ Perspective ◆ Developments ◆ Size ◆ Prestige
◆ Advantage ◆ Treatment of Opponents
◆ Attitude ◆ Cost of Presentation

Perspective

The subject in selling is the prospect—not the other suppliers—and why your company is best for them—not why the others aren't. So don't distract the prospect. Your purpose is to create a winner—not a loser. Let the others defeat themselves.

Of course, you need to be aware of competitive activity. But don't waste time *worrying*. It's counter-productive and blows the situation out of proportion. Instead, devote all your energies to proving that your product or service is the most desirable—and the other candidates will end up eating your dust.

Developments

Currently, there is more intensive solicitation activity than ever before. Significantly, the game has changed in the respect that suppliers are no longer limiting themselves to soliciting only the accounts of their peers. Nor are they restricting themselves to pitching accounts of prescribed size. Therefore, it has become open

> ## ❝ There is no such thing as a 'small' supplier, only suppliers with people who think small. ❞

season on *all* your accounts. This sheer weight of effort is making your customers more vulnerable than ever. Further, with traditional payment systems becoming an anachronism, suppliers are now wheeling and dealing like never before. And not only under the table; whenever possible they are throwing *in* the table! So, you had better do unto others—before they do unto you. How? By having one goal; to outsell them all.

Size

To begin with, let's dispel a misconception. Unless a supplier is mammoth, there is a tendency to be defensive about its size. This self-deprecating attitude is defeatist, minimizes prospect impact, and infects your entire operation. There is no such thing as a "small" supplier, only suppliers with people who think small. If, however, your company has fewer employees than a competitor, and the matter of size comes up, you are never smaller—you operate *leaner*.

Granted, you may not be as big as some of your competitors from the standpoint of sales. But you intend to grow to their size. For that matter, your product or service is already better than theirs, isn't it? Better believe it—or there is no reason for anyone to become a customer of yours.

Get rid of any paranoia regarding larger suppliers—and the assumption that you are stymied because you can't fight fire with fire. You don't have to. Usually water will suffice. This is because all suppliers have the same common denominator: people. And even though a competitor may have more, they don't put on their pants both legs at a time. Actually, you're all starting out even, with the same thing going for you: opportunity. And the sale is made by the one who makes the most of it. Besides, the prospect may not be looking for an elephant. They may want a tiger.

Prestige

While we're at it, let's tackle any defeatism that exists regarding the prospect's supposed desire for the prestige of using a big-name supplier. Suppliers that assume this are conceding accounts. The megasuppliers don't have a sure-win advantage. Nor are they necessarily invincible.

The most meaningful proof of this is the success enjoyed by suppliers who are relatively new kids on the block. You've come up against these hot operations. But how did they pull it off? They didn't buy the negativism that it couldn't be done. Instead, they set about to convince the prospects that they have better people, with better ideas, who can execute them better. Functioning from this base has also resulted in a better product or service. By concentrating on what a prospect must first buy—*people*—these suppliers succeeded in competing against the establishment. And you can, too.

So instead of falling into the cynical trap of assuming that presentations have been rigged in favor of old-line suppliers, critically appraise yours to determine how it can be made more appealing. Because if a supplier can do so well from ground zero, you—with momentum going for you—surely ought to make out. Bring the importance of size into perspective. Remember, bigger isn't necessarily better. Only better is better.

Advantage

Salespeople get so wrapped up in their product or service they tend to overlook its origin—the persons who conceived and produced it. And since what you are selling can't be any better than the people behind it, you will want to stress why your people are preferable to any elsewhere, particularly since your competitors are usually derelict in promoting the caliber of their personnel.

Treatment of Opponents

Suppliers get very concerned about who their competitors are when pitching an account that is planning to switch. Unfortunately, sometimes they use information about the competition in a negative way—to make the case for their own operation being preferable to the others being considered.

However, the extent to which you devote your presentation to combating the competition is the amount of time you sacrifice for convincing the prospect your product or service can best fulfill their requirements. And hardly any salesperson can afford to concede this advantage to the competition. So sell *for* your operation rather than *against* the others. That is, concentrate on what it will take for you to win—instead of how you can cause them to lose.

Admittedly though, sometimes it can be to your advantage to know who your competitors are. This will enable you to capitalize on your strengths and compensate for weaknesses—of course, always positively and constructively. I'm not moralizing, because if any attempt is made to instill doubt regarding your competitors, the environment created could boomerang to include your company.

Then, in presentation, you can get as competitive as circumstances permit—as long as you *never mention another supplier by name*. After all, this romance is between you and the prospect. Why acknowledge anyone else? You only afford them further recognition—while forfeiting your own objectivity.

In some cases the prospect may press you to discuss the competition. But don't dilute your effect by falling prey to this tempting but shabby tactic of sniping at competitors. You might wind up with the prospect's gratitude—but not the account. You can righteously state, "We're here to present our strengths—not their weaknesses. Our approach is strictly positive, entirely prospect-oriented."

Remember, the question is why your product or service should be selected—not why the others' shouldn't.

Attitude

Here is another selling situation that may at first seem remote. Nevertheless, the strategy revealed can be of direct value to you.

A frustrating question was popped at me in a recent ad agency network meeting. "In a competitive presentation, if you know that another agency has better TV commercials than yours, what should you do?" I replied, "Don't."

The inquiring president snapped back with, "What the hell kind of answer is that?" This desired reaction enabled me to explain: "Their commercials won't beat you. Your defeatist attitude will." Although a little heavy, the end justified the means. Because as I have previously stressed, the only way you can go into a new business presentation is as a winner.

After this explanation, he simmered down and asked, "Okay, since we are up against Coke commercials, how do we combat their advantage?" Now that he was receptive to positive action, success was possible. Here's the solution I gave him. "You can overcome their seeming superiority in appearance of material by the conduct of your presentation. Your competitor may assume that their more expensive commercials will speak for themselves—and rely on them to do so. By contrast, you finish the job by selling how the strategy of your commercials can fulfill this prospect's needs. Namely, giving them tangible reasons why to buy rather than coasting on pizzazz. Because the prospect won't bother to associate the other agency's efforts with their requirements.

Thus, in your case as well as theirs, relate your product or service to the prospect's operation—and how they will gain from it. Because your vaunted competitor may be indulging themselves in the ego-feeding luxury of merely taking credit for material produced.

Then, upon comparison, your product (service) will come off as being preferable. So despite what may seem like insurmountable odds, stop whining and start winning.

Cost of Presentation

Some smaller suppliers forego soliciting larger accounts, assuming they can't afford to spend as much as bigger suppliers can for major presentations. This misconception is caused by rumors of the astronomical amounts spent on these presentations. As a result, many suppliers have seriously limited their potential.

Apparently, it is necessary to identify what all this money is spent on. It is not on the physical requirements for the presentation. How many slide or film projectors or VCRs can you rent? And the price for processing slides, tape, or film is approximately the same for any company. What runs up the cost is the content. And if you feel that the audio-visual component of your presentation needs to look like a soft drink commercial, you'll pay accordingly.

Beyond this, the heavy part of the expense you hear about is accounted for by spec material: expensively constructed mockups, time-intensive schematics, costly research, etc. By contrast, the investment in the vehicle for presentation, the medium used, is just about a standoff.

Therefore, unless the production of your AV message must be especially elaborate, or you are required to submit replicas of that proposed, it *is* possible to compete against bigger suppliers.

So don't restrict your opportunity for significant growth by figuring you're at a disadvantage in this respect, particularly if you have the confidence you should have in your ability to persuade via the supporting materials you've developed.

❝ ... the prospect may not be looking for an elephant. He may want a tiger.❞

Selecting the Most Appealing Presentation Team

◆ Perspective ◆ Strategy ◆ Size and Participation ◆ Composition
◆ Qualifications ◆ Star Presenter ◆ Anyone Objectionable?

Perspective

Most often, the selling encounter is one-on-one—between you and your contact at the prospect. But there are circumstances in which it is to your advantage to bring along others from your operation to enhance your efforts. And there are organizations that sell primarily on a team basis. Even if you can't conceive of being involved in a multi-person selling scenario, the only constant is change, and either at your current employer, or elsewhere, this type of soliciting may be your eventual approach. When pitching as a group, the tested direction furnished in this chapter can compound your impact.

Strategy

There has always been a dichotomy of opinion regarding the composition of the selling team. Some suppliers maintain that the team should be composed of only those to whom the customer would have access once the sale is made. By contrast, others hold that since the objective is to land the account, the participants should be those who can sell best. The tie breaker is a simple one: the prospect's attitude. As far as they are concerned, anyone present from the supplier will be involved on their account. Otherwise, why are they there? The prospect isn't shopping for a corporate logo, but for the specific people who will deliver the actual talent and experience promised.

Granted, sometimes the "swat team" concept can increase your rate of success. However, it can also result in a higher incidence of account losses. If ever a customer discovers that one of the presenters by whom they were smitten isn't available, they believe they were deceived in the pitch. And after that, the supplier is on borrowed time.

Size and Participation

The chemistry factor requires that the size and composition of your team be based on that of the prospect team. Obviously, you don't want to outnumber them because, psychologically, they would feel placed at a disadvantage (or as a prospect might express it, "ganged up on").

Further, every member of your team must have an active role in the presentation. You can't afford any observers. Otherwise, the prospect could suspect that you brought along empty suits to compensate for something lacking in your message. I'm asked, "But how else will a young salesperson learn?" Easy. By attending your rehearsals. Trying to train them while you're in combat is just too risky.

Composition

Create a presentation team as you would a product or service: for its appeal to its market. To begin with, seek personality balance. Besides the dynamo, the team should also include your solid citizen (the one who wears white socks to the office). This person is likely to receive greater overall acceptance.

Some suppliers mistakenly believe that each member of their team must be cast from the same sensational mold. But the prospect selection team isn't composed in this way. Without sacrificing your ability to put your best foot forward, include the variety of characters the prospect can best associate themselves with. This would be based on how you read them in the pre-presentation meeting. All else notwithstanding, there must first be rapport between the presentation and selection teams before there will be acceptance of the supplier. If you were to have 20 presentations coming up, hypothetically they could require 20 different combinations of your people.

I am aware that it is unlikely that you, individually, are calling the shots on the composition of your presentation team. But this is *your* potential customer. And the responsibility for making the sale is laid at your doorstep. Therefore, it is worth the effort to attempt to influence the selection of those who can best contribute to selling this prospect.

❝ There is no such thing as a man for all seasons. It takes a person for each.❞

Qualifications

The most important criterion for selecting your presenters is their ability to communicate and their likeliness to appeal and impress the prospect. Regardless of how well qualified they are in their function, an inability to register this clearly and persuasively will seriously weaken your effect.

Star Presenter

There is probably only a nominal number of you with organizations who sell primarily on a team basis. However, for the sake of those who do, here is a crucial caveat requiring your attention.

Despite suppliers having learned the preceding truisms early—regarding strategy, size/participation, composition, and qualifications—most have forgotten them long ago. This is evidenced by suppliers continuing to feature their same star presenter wherever possible for whomever the prospect. This is the person who has earned the reputation of being dynamic on his or her feet.

But hold it. Maybe you discovered in the pre-presentation meeting with the prospect that they are the laid back type. Your dynamo could overwhelm, and possibly offend, them. Your star can't be a designated hitter for use in all situations. Instead, your best presenter is the one most appropriate for the prospect. He or she may not be as articulate or charming—but more important, this person is the prospect's kind of people.

Anyone Objectionable?

Since sellers need to cover themselves for any eventuality, even concerns such as this one surface: "Is there any type of person who might be unacceptable to the prospect as a member of our presentation team?" No. None. Whomever your members, there is built-in acceptance because the prospect assumes the team consists of those who can best represent your company. However, they are accepted for admission only. Your objective—approval—still has to be earned. And this is achieved by evidence of professionalism and vitality—at which no one excels or is lacking because of race, religion, nationality, or sex.

Consider this: Psychologists claim that any individual appeals to only 25 percent of the others. The feelings of the other 75 percent range from apathy to hostility. Therefore, when soliciting new business, there is no such thing as a man for all seasons. It takes a person for each.

Conduct Likeliest to Impress

Perspective ◆ Appropriate Dress
Necessary Behavior ◆ Evidence of Teamwork
Use of Humor ◆ Effect of Taste
Profanity ◆ Personal Stature
Prospect Questions ◆ Unexpected Interruptions

Perspective

In the ideal selling situation you would only have to concern yourself with the value of your product or service. Then you could be as misanthropic as the selling functions can cause a person to be. However, while a prospect realizes they need to buy the product or service that will best fulfill their requirements, they also want the very best *relationship* they can get. A prospect must first buy *you* before they will buy your product or service. Only after you have convinced them of your compatibility can they be impressed by what you are selling.

You have to take into account the chemistry factor, (you vis-à-vis them), from that learned in your pre-presentation probing. And you have to apply this consideration in the selection of your presenters. This insight and action will now allow your company to position itself as the prospect's kind of people.

Appropriate Dress

Let's start with the first basis by which a prospect forms a judgment of you: your appearance. What's right? You can best decide that by honestly answering for any presentation, "Do I look like a winner?" That's your objective, isn't it? Then *dress* like a winner! And that means dressing in a manner that shows your respect for the prospect. This is not only desirable. It is essential. Emery Lewis felt compelled to punctuate this point during my seminar at his McCann Erickson office in Louisville.

He said, "Let me tell you about the time we came in fifth out of four agencies." At that time, they were doing collateral work for Kentucky Fried Chicken. On one occasion, Emery's client contact mentioned, "I meant to tell you that our co-op account for West Virginia is open. Although we're down to three finalists, I can still get you in. It bills about $1,000,000. Want a crack at it?"

When Emery acknowledged they would be delighted, the KFC contact cautioned, "But remember: We're dealing with good old boys. So don't make your grand entrance in your usual swallow-tail coat, ascot, and spats." Emery agreed and thanked him for this perceptive advice. I was then told, "So the five of us went there dressed in nice plaid sports jackets and clean golf slacks—mirroring the prospect's supposed informality.

You can see what's coming. The other three agency teams all showed up in three-piece, blue, pin-stripe suits. As Emery put it, "We looked so different, we were eliminated off the top. We couldn't have *given* the agency away." This experience proves the importance of evidence of your respect for the prospect. Without it, there can't be a relationship—or a sale made.

Necessary Behavior

Your behavior during presentation has a much greater influence than you may realize. All your professional qualifications notwithstanding, sometimes the final criterion for supplier selection can be as arbitrary as, "Would I want to have this person to my home for dinner?" So mind your manners. The best strategy is to conduct yourself throughout as if you were applying for a job. In this context, here are two tips for making a better impression.

The first is based on a question that was frequently asked of Vince Lombardi: "How come your teams are always so great?" And he would reply, "Because the players have such respect for each other." Well, when pitching on a team basis, the quality of your relationship is every bit as important, and should be demonstrated by your interaction at the presentation. Further, beyond the claims and promises made, you're scrutinized for vitality, attitude and professionalism. How? Consider this. Only 20 percent of communication is by words. The balance is accounted for by body language. So, in addition to your sales pitch, the prospect is directly affected by the other 80 percent of your communication. While

66 A prospect is more impressed by deed than word. 99

body language plays a key role *throughout* the presentation, the time when you, as a presenter, may forget its importance is after your portion. Remember, you're still communicating when you've finished speaking.

I can appreciate there is an emotional letdown when you finish your pitch. (Further, in a group effort, the letdown is compounded by the fact that you've heard your next speaker 39 times before—and not only know his part word for word, but could probably deliver it better.)

Your alertness is vital, though, since it sets the pace for the prospect. Throughout the total meeting, you need to give the impression of momentarily expecting The Second Coming. Remember, even when your contact is speaking, you are on just as much as this person is. (For instance, always try to lean forward. This body language conveys that you consider what he or she is saying to be important.)

As proof of this, think back to a team sell. You couldn't help but notice how the members of the prospect team surreptitiously eyeballed each of you during your presentation, and then their level of attention was no higher than that of your least-interested team member.

How can you exhibit the necessary absorption? Here is a tactic for giving the impression of being totally enraptured by your own speaker or theirs. Listen for the first word used beginning with the letter "A." When this occurs, move on to one starting with "B," then "C," and so forth. For each of the speakers, see how far you can get through the alphabet. This game will not only serve the purpose of conveying a high intensity of interest—but will help keep you awake. (This device, of course, could also cover for you in rambling customer meetings.)

Evidence of Teamwork

A prospect is more impressed by deed than word. Verbalizing that your product or service will fulfill their expectations is worthwhile. But it won't convince until it's been demonstrated in the presentation. This concept was proved in a novel manner recently. I was working with an advertiser who decided to switch agencies. They went through the cattle call/questionnaire/screening presentations process.

Upon selecting the finalists, this advertiser stressed to both that they would be strongly influenced by the capacity for agency teamwork. (The apparent dissension at their previous agency had caused loss of client confidence in their performance.) Both finalists took this direction literally. Agency "A" voiced their dedication to teamwork throughout their pitch. Agency "B" didn't make any mention of it. However, they *demonstrated* their belief in the importance of teamwork via the planned interaction of their presenters.

Thus, Agency "A" came across as offering contrived lip service, while Agency "B" was convincing as a result of their conduct. And the latter was clearly the winner. So remember, what you *do* in presentation speaks louder than what you say.

And, even if a prospect doesn't specify their desire for teamwork, your evidence of it will still be impressive. Because a customer assumes that if you can get along with each other, there is a much better chance of your getting along with them.

Use of Humor

The first impression of you that the prospect wants is one of buttoned down professionalism. The initial meeting is your first chance—make sure it isn't your last. They want to experience a sense of confidence and trust in you; they're not there to be entertained. I've been told by prospects, "There have been presentations that we've heartily enjoyed. But that's not how we select a supplier." So be careful that the last laugh isn't on you.

This is not meant to imply that the use of humor is forbidden—only jokes told for their own sake. When it is relevant, humor can make your point in a more appealing, memorable manner. Further, the use of humor can create a relaxed environment—one in which the prospect will be more receptive.

For instance, Rumrill Hoyt in New York uses a delightful icebreaker for this purpose. They open their presentation by saying, "Before we tell you anything about ourselves, let's first check whether you can pass our fitness test for clients, whether you can qualify for our shop." Then they quickly add, "Actually, no advertiser has ever flunked this test." This is because the "test" turns out to be the agency's qualifications as they would benefit this prospect. So of course, they always pass. This has proved to be a great warmer-upper—getting everyone off to a friendlier start.

But again, humor is to your advantage only if it is appropriate to the prospect's interests, and only if you have a knack for delivering it. Everyone can learn from the title of the longest running show on Bourbon Street: "Nobody Likes a Smart-Alec."

Effect of Taste

If you satisfy the human equation, then the impression you make is based on two factors: professional qualifications and presentation skills. Beyond this, though, there is an intangible that, of itself, can wipe out your credentials. It is the matter of taste. Playing it safe to avoid offending doesn't require being rigidly programmed, or self-righteous. Rather, it amounts to not taking anything for granted. This includes anticipating the unexpected. Otherwise, even a rigged opportunity can be ruined.

Here is a case in point. An agency was contacted by a substantial advertiser via an intermediary. This prospect's president was smitten by one of the agency's campaigns and wanted to set up a one-to-one meeting with their CEO. The intermediary confided that if the chemistry was right, the agency would be home safe with an upper seven-figure account. The agency CEO came in well-prepared, was totally relevant, highly persuasive—and couldn't give it away. Afterwards, he reported to the intermediary that he was baffled by the president's fickle about-face.

The third party said, "You're not very observant." He went on to explain, "His office is liberally decorated with crucifixes and religious artwork. Nevertheless, you repeatedly sprinkled your pitch with 'Jeez' or 'Kee-rist' or a combination of both." The advertiser's president was obviously a Christian gentleman. He was properly, deeply offended by these irreverent references. End of prospect.

So be loose, confident—but never so relaxed that you overlook the fact that this is a buyer-seller relationship.

Profanity

Even if your prospect contacts punctuate their sentences with profanity, this does not give you the license to use such language. Initially, they consider themselves to be a private club—and resent such familiarity on your part. So for openers, play it safe. Express yourself as if you were talking to your mother.

Recently there were three finalists for a very desirable account, one of whom had been given an indication of having the inside track. After the final presentations were made, I ran into one of the participants from the agency. I asked how it went and he said, "If we don't score on this one, we never will. We really related to them."

But when it came down to the bottom line, a different agency was selected. By now I was quite curious regarding this turn of events. Knowing the advertiser involved, I phoned to ask about their choice. My contact said, "On the surface the preferred agency was certainly more appealing. But, in the final analysis, we

" Come in with your best shot, what you can be proudest of: your own self."

concluded we just couldn't risk having our company represented by such foul-mouthed people."

Never blow a fine opportunity by conducting yourself as if you're already one of them. You're not. And won't be if you act as though you are.

Personal Stature

For all of the reasons you should know only too well, you can be very proud of your occupation. Yet many salespeople are defensive about what they suspect is a negative image of their function. They fear they are categorized with used car dealers who sell "cream puffs" which were only used by a suicide club. And with real estate agents peddling ocean front property in Kansas. So they attempt to compensate when selling by bending over too far backwards to establish an "aw shucks" image. Usually at the expense of their self respect.

This was proved again at an agency presentation I was critiquing recently. After an excellent demonstration of their advantages, they platformed their heavy hitter for the closer. His credentials were remarkable—and he was very charismatic. Apparently he had everything going for him. Nevertheless, this person sent in for the kill felt the need to develop acceptance via a "Mr. Humble" approach. He opened by announcing, "I'm not going to be modest." And then attempted to establish credibility by quoting Golda Meir: "Don't be modest. You don't have that much to be modest about."

This angle brought a few chuckles. Mostly at him, not with him. Then, to try to ingratiate himself, he conceded some apprehension by quoting Winston Churchill who said, "Never speak to an audience that knows more than you do."

After he put himself down a second time, it was obvious he'd lost the selection team. Because if a representative of an agency was honestly that self-deprecating, the agency was not for them. Further, this false humility was transparent. It ranked with statements like "It's in the mail." So come in with your best shot, what you can be proudest of: your own self.

You didn't get where you are by being a wimp. Rather, your position is the result of ability and dynamism. So don't ever sacrifice that which is responsible for your success by minimizing its value. You've proved what works. Encore!

Prospect Questions

You're on a roll in the presentation. You have that undefinable rhythm that inspires confidence. Then the prospect hits you with a question requiring some thought. It could probably be answered—if you just had a few moments to think without dead air time. But they seem to be expecting a solid reply—now.

Don't panic. Instead of blurting out an answer, ask them a question about their question—or for some elaboration on it. This will buy you time to formulate a knowledgeable answer. However, if your response requires investigation, don't risk an off-the-cuff remark (for instance, if it involves a technical matter that has to be explored). Explain that this inquiry requires preparation. Then, inform them of how soon you will return with the information they've requested.

Yet, how about when the prospect confronts you with, "How much do you recommend we buy?" Expecting you to pull a figure out of left field is loading the request. You've been placed in a no-win situation. Because regardless of how sound your estimate, it is based only on assumption and desire. Yet, in your eagerness to score, you scramble to come up with a figure that is bound to be vulnerable. Obviously, you can't recommend without any input.

You've been baited. And seemingly stymied. Since there is no way in which you can conjure a defensible amount.

But you don't want to concede being unable to meet their challenge. So go on record regarding your ability and willingness to deliver—if you are provided with the basis for specifying the quantity, specifically, their marketing circumstances and objectives.

It is improbable they will release this proprietary information. But you will have called their hand. If they are on the level, this "how much" zinger will not be used as a factor in considering your product or service. Otherwise, you'll know they are just jerking you around.

Do these tactics sound like gamesmanship? They're not. Rather, they embody the pragmatism necessary to win it all. And that is the only way to compete. Because in the selling Olympics, there is no such thing as a silver medal.

The gold is won by those who proact. Going with the flow is no longer enough. Now it takes anticipating whatever surprises—and preparing accordingly for them. This will reduce the possibility of your being thrown off stride—and any "Oh no!" reminiscences.

Unexpected Interruptions

Even with these protective measures, though, there can be an unexpected interruption. And it will produce the amount of cold sweat that deodorants aren't made to overcome. The slide tray is dropped. Or the prospect's decision-maker is called out—and asks that you wait until she returns. In both instances, you are confronted with a maddening void. The way you handle these calamities will indicate your resourcefulness—or lack thereof.

Therefore, prepare a transitional filler for use in the event that such a situation occurs. Where do you get this material? You will discover in rehearsal that your presentation well exceeds the amount of time allotted. The portions that need to be cut can become your filler in case of an emergency. Then, whatever is said is relevant—and you don't have to come up with an impromptu soft shoe number. In the event the opposite happens, and their decision-maker says, "Keep going," that's okay too—unless you're the only one remaining in the room.

Section V

Go for the Jugular: The Presentation

Yᵒᵘ have now arrived at the moment of truth—the payoff for all your efforts and expense: the presentation.

However, so much solicitation activity consists of the salesperson telling the prospect how great they are going to be, and in his or her eagerness, the seller fails to notice that the prospect has either fallen asleep or gotten up and gone home.

There isn't any secret for getting and holding their attention. All it takes is getting back to the basics. It is simply a matter of answering up front *the first and most important thing a prospect wants to know: "What's in it for me?"—both personally and corporately.*

Having established that your pitch is based on their wants, not yours, you have accomplished the first half of your goal: an alert audience. Now you can become passionate about what you are selling.

The series of four chapters in this section deal with the other half of your goal: converting the prospect into a buyer. To receive the commitment desired, detailed are the ideas, conduct, and tactics that work (or don't). All learned the hard way.

❝ In his or her eagerness, the seller fails to notice that the prospect has either fallen asleep or gotten up and gone home.❞

Presentation Skills Honed on the Street

◆ Perspective ◆ Fear ◆ Nervousness ◆ Assumption of Inadequacy
◆ Control ◆ Comfort ◆ Preparation ◆ Audio-Visual Devices as Clinchers
◆ Use of Sales Aids ◆ Content vs. Conduct ◆ Performance
◆ Technique ◆ Level of Communications ◆ Idiosyncrasies
◆ Qualifying Phrases ◆ Offensive Characteristics
◆ Knowledge of the Prospect

Perspective

I t is worth the risk of offending you by bringing up something as elementary as your vocal delivery in presentation. This is what determines your power to persuade. As proof of the importance of this attribute, Motorola conducted an in-depth study of the effect of their sales training programs. They learned that of all the factors involved (i.e., location, content, format, timing, etc.), the one with the greatest influence is the speaker. The study showed that the impression the speaker made was the deciding factor in subject appeal and retention. Significantly, the ability to speak well also fulfills the prospect's personal objective of buying from someone with the charisma that will make them look good.

177

Fear

You are usually comfortable with the value of the *content* of your sales message, but invariably have misgivings about its delivery. The feelings experienced by most of those in sales could provide a field day for psychotherapists. They range from inferiority to paranoia—capped off by fright. In addition, you can be physically hampered by a dry mouth/cold sweat reaction. I didn't realize how universal this hang-up is—or how intense—until I came across a startling study on this subject. The findings, which reveal the solution to the speaking problem, can immediately improve your performance.

This survey was conducted among top management of the Fortune 500 companies. The sum of their response was that second only to death was their fear of having to address a group. The survey further revealed that the cause of this fear is *inadequate preparation*. Therefore, plan and rehearse enough so your energy can be devoted to your sales pitch rather than to fighting stress. When you have control over your material, you can come across as able to fulfill the prospect's needs.

Thus, you *can* do something about this mental block. And all it takes is preparing to the extent necessary to do yourself the justice deserved. This breeds confidence, which in turn provides empathy—resulting in acceptance of you and your product or service.

Nervousness

The most charismatic speaker I've ever heard was Bo Kreer. As to who ranks second, no one even comes close. He honed his skills when serving time at such institutions as J. Walter Thompson, Campbell-Mithun, Clinton E. Frank, and Young & Rubicam. And he became so good on his feet that people were either totally captivated by him—or they resented his exceptional ability.

For a while, I fell into the latter category—because too often, I had to follow him in new business presentations and client sales meetings, something I undertook with a deep feeling of inadequacy. After one of these humbling experiences,

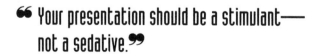

66 Your presentation should be a stimulant—not a sedative.99

(and a few Beefeaters with him at dinner), I said, "Bo, it would be awfully easy to hate you." This confession was startling—and not conducive to job security—since he was my management supervisor when I was an account supervisor.

So I went on to explain, "Presenting comes so goddam easy for you. You're always so cool up front." His response: "You're not very observant." Then he went on to explain, "Regardless of how hot a summer day, if I have a talk to give, I always wear a winter suit. Otherwise, in a summer suit, it would be apparent to the audience that I perspire right through it."

But he wasn't complaining. He felt this nervousness was one of the greatest things he had going for him. It got the juices flowing—and reduced the possibility of a mental lapse. And he *used* it to get up for the event and to stay at the necessary level of intensity. He summed up by saying, "If ever I get to the point when I can address a group in a summer suit, I'm in trouble."

However, Bo realized that the charge generated can become self-defeating if it's not harnessed. He found this can be achieved by way of the control provided by confidence. That's great, but what is the formula for creating confidence? Bo believed the clue lies in your knowledge of the subject. If you're familiar enough with it, you can handle whatever the situation. Of course familiarity doesn't absolve you from needing to prepare your material; you still need to develop your presentation. Attempting to wing it can give the impression that you take the prospect for granted—and then you will have plenty of reason to be nervous.

Assumption of Inadequacy

In weak moments, top management of some suppliers will describe their performance at presentations in terms ranging from, "We're nice mice" to "We're so boring!" And they are somewhat resigned to these afflictions because "That's just the kind of people we are." They aren't alone. Most people deprecate themselves as speakers—minimizing their ability and appeal. Their assumption that they lack the innate magnetism required borders on masochism. ("I'm just not the flamboyant type.")

But lack of magnetism isn't the problem. Most often, a presentation is dull because it is irrelevant—and/or delivered in an unenthusiastic manner. Both of these causes of boredom can be overcome if you are willing to apply the discipline necessary to land accounts.

Specifically, your presentation should be a stimulant—not a sedative. Regardless of how fabulous your materials and ideas may be, if they're not communicated in a fired-up, inspiring way, you aren't going to create the *want* for your product or service.

The only way to do this is to come across as really believing in what you say—and being truly excited about serving this prospect. Conveying this impression won't be difficult for you. Because emotions don't have to be memorized.

Control

Your big picture in presentation is only as good as its strokes: all the components culminating in this effort, ranging from research to preparation to rehearsal.

In solicitation activity there is no room whatsoever for assumption regarding the prospect's company, industry, and market, especially, who and what is likeliest to appeal to and impress them. Thus, whatever is said or shown must be beyond reproach. Because the winning supplier can be the one who made the fewest errors. Therefore, being on a sales force is like working on a bomb squad: you don't get more than one mistake per prospect, since it will be your last one.

Sounds too cynical? Not really. It takes an attitude of expecting the worst to protect against fouling up.

Due to the precarious nature of presentations, suppliers are coming to realize that they must prepare themselves in every respect. The goal is to exercise optimum control—thereby leaving little to chance. Usually, this is based on lessons learned the hard way. Here are some that won't happen again—and how they were corrected.

◆ *Having personnel from the prospect located in various parts of the room.* This makes it difficult to present to them as an entity—and complicates visibility if audio-visual equipment is used. For a more effective environment in which to operate, permission was obtained to rearrange their furniture as necessary—and tent cards with names were placed where it was desired that each person be seated.

◆ *Violating prospect's comfort level.* If your presentation will exceed one hour, it's difficult to hold their attention if their teeth are clenched and legs are tightly crossed. Thus, provide a break for a pit stop. Your thoughtfulness will be much appreciated.

◆ *Calling prospect person by the wrong name.* To preclude this unforgivable blunder, provide name tags for prospect personnel—and yourselves so they can direct their questions and comments to the appropriate individuals.

◆ *Loss of presentation material.* It's very difficult to come up to bat without a bat. Thus, prepare *two* sets—each to be brought to the presentation by different individuals, traveling separately. I know, you already have more than enough to carry. And you were hired to be a seller not a schlepper. But if you don't accept taking this precaution as something that comes with the territory, you could wind up *without* any territory.

◆ *Unpleasant climate.* The prospect will be less receptive if the meeting room is too warm or too cold. If the event is scheduled at your place, you should be able to make provisions to control the temperature. If it will be held at the prospects' company, inquire as to whether arrangements can be made for a comfortable temperature. (If anything, err on the side of being cool. They will stay awake longer).

◆ *Prospect becoming fidgety due to thirst.* Some may be coffee, tea or soft drink addicts. If the presentation is held at your place, provide refreshments. It it's at their office, bring it with. They will never forget you.

Protection then, begins with the basics. Having been through them many times before, you are inclined to take them for granted—and become careless. However, since prospects eliminate rather than select suppliers, no detail is too small—or can be second guessed. That's why when I conduct seminars and consult for agencies, they are now grilling me on the nitty-gritty. They don't want conjecture. They want to know what works and what doesn't.

For example, here is a matter that seems so elementary that the question belies its importance. "Is it best to deliver from a standing or seated position?" Don't brush off this factor as being inconsequential. Unless there are so few people involved, or if the room layout or furniture arrangement would make it awkward, *the presentation should always be delivered from a standing position.* By creating a focal point, you provide a visual reason for the prospect to pay attention to you. And, as significant, this format establishes authority.

Admittedly, to some people, being this prominent seems more difficult. There are suppliers who will rationalize their decision to give their presentation seated around the conference room table, talking informally, by claiming "We're more of the laid-back type." Although they may feel more comfortable, sitting forfeits discipline. When you are at the prospect's physical level, you don't seem any more important than they are. This makes it more difficult to attract and maintain interest—and to deter them from rudely talking among themselves during your pitch.

So take command by at least *appearing* to be in charge. While the prospect may set ground rules, they expect you to take over from there. And they will place much emphasis on how well the ground rules are implemented. Consequently, the method by which you *conduct* your presentation will have a strong influence on its outcome.

But what if you have a person, vital to your presentation—who can't get up in front of a group? It's probable that this key individual can communicate well—but only on his or her terms.

I was called in by an agency to critique a presentation they'd lost—and to smoke out why. We decided they would go through the entire pitch exactly as they had performed it for the prospect. However, in the interest of determining what it would take to win the next time, anyone could interrupt with questions and suggestions. As it happened, I sat next to their creative director. I was immediately struck by how valuable and interesting his comments were, and in particular, by how well they were articulated.

When it came time for his turn at the podium, the president proudly platformed him. The creative director leaned back and said, "We all know what I did. Let's move on to the next presenter." The president objected with, "Now look, we agreed to reconstruct this for Jack. Let's do it right."

The creative director snapped through gritted teeth, "Awright, damn it. But you know what happens when I stand up to present: I freeze!" At that he stomped up to the podium—and froze. His white knuckles clenched the podium; he became livid—and speechless.

Obviously, the presentation of the creative aspect is critical. And this creative director had everything going for him—except his mental block on speaking from a standing position. The solution was to let him deliver while seated—representing this as a change of pace. This alternative provided the creative director with the necessary comfort and confidence—and enabled him to unleash his extensive abilities. Result: he blossomed into a dynamic presenter. And the agency's rate of scoring increased substantially.

Summing up, plans for every sales pitch, regardless of size, should be totally buttoned up—with all fail-safe precautions applied. And then each opportunity should be orchestrated for maximum impact.

Comfort

Suppliers are becoming more sophisticated in the preparation of their new business presentations: more research, more ambitious presentation materials, and substantially more time and money spent on their development. This greater thoroughness is intended to provide for every conceivable factor—all except the most critical: *the presenters.*

Can you relate to the concept? Are you confident with the visuals? A presentation is not only show; it is also tell. And if you are ill at ease with either, in any respect, the most well conceived presentation will be like the dodo, a wonderful bird—that couldn't fly.

This isn't an academic assumption. It was inspired by an agency that recently had this experience. The president told me that the creative staff had come up with a delightful (not cutesy) cartoon approach—to be delivered in a whimsical manner. Management loved this fun tactic for dealing with otherwise heavy matter. It communicated why their agency was preferable to any other in an especially clever, distinctive style.

Then came the moment of truth: performance. In rehearsal, his people discovered that the presentation wasn't *them.* It was great in theory, but not implementable by these presenters. Nobody had caught it because the presentation wasn't wrong. It just wasn't right for this agency. He concluded, "The materials cost a bloody fortune. But my people just weren't *comfortable* with it. And there is no sense in trying to convert them into something they are not. So we're biting the bullet and going back to square one." Sadder but wiser.

There is a valuable lesson to be learned. Whatever the presentation created, it is meant to be delivered. While it is in the conceptual stage, apply this acid test: is

" If you're not selling, you're being sold."

it appropriate to *our* presenters? Remember that your objective is to achieve the most effective blend of message and speakers.

You're bound to agree with this premise, but may assume the matter is out of your hands. In your capacity, you don't develop selling strategy. But you are held responsible for its application. So if you strongly doubt that a selling approach can be executed, make your misgivings known to the appropriate authority. You may be concerned that this initiative could jeopardize your status. Well, you surely will be in trouble if you agree to the approach but don't succeed with it. Then it won't be the author who has failed, but you. So go on record before you can be blamed for disappointing results.

Preparation

A presentation can be only as good as the thoroughness with which it is planned. Any portion relegated to "winging it" becomes a crapshoot. Acknowledging the necessity of preparation, on occasion salespeople will write out their pitch. Fine. This discipline gives the matter the thought it deserves. As a result, you will appear well organized and authoritative on the subject. And if there are other participants, this control precludes any repetition among speakers.

But there is one caveat. People don't talk the way they write. And if you deliver from a written script, you will seem stilted, and the presentation will sound canned. So that you speak *to* them rather than at them, translate your formal message into "people talk." By speaking their language, you are more understandable—and you become more acceptable.

Further, you need to make the effort to make your presentation as *effortless* as possible for the prospect. (The prospect expects *you* to work, not themselves.) Avoid any lengthy dissertations on slide or poster board. No Lord's Prayer on the head of a pin.

Suppliers attach a spiritual quality to their corporate philosophy. However, in whatever the medium used, they complicate their presentation by filling it from top to bottom, side to side, with this deathless message.

Then what do you do? Insult them by reading it word for word? Or shift around during this dead air time hoping they will read it. Instead, use a few buzz words and/or illustrations to intrigue them—while you just tell them about it. Because the most impressive presentation is one that is conversational. Yet, throughout this casual scenario, remember, if you're not selling, you're being sold.

Using Audio-Visual Devices as Clinchers

Again, I realize that for most of you, selling is an individual, head-to-head situation. No extravaganzas. Just your capacity to make a believer out of the prospect.

But how about the day when you get a shot at a humongous account? The use of audio-visual support could be the clincher. So it is worth your having this insight now, rather than scrambling when this opportunity arises.

Here is why these smarts are so necessary. As appealing as you and your material may be, when appropriate, intriguing use should be made of audio-visual techniques to attract and hold attention.

However, remember, if the prospect is willing to hold still, they want to get to know you. Thus, *the degree of use of AV equipment depends on the extent to which it is worth sacrificing eyeball contact.*

While this medium can substantially improve the impression made, there are some situations that can cause you more harm than good. You may be familiar with these—but let's flush them out anyway. Because if overlooked, the damage can be irreparable.

Function

Many suppliers go into a presentation with everything selling for them—except their visual aids. However, your presentation is only as good as its weakest link. There are two tactics that lessen your impact:

◆ Visual aids are annoying and distracting if used as a substitute for your notes. This code is only meaningful to you—and a diversion to the prospect. Therefore, these aids should be prospect- rather than presenter-oriented.

◆ These visuals also fail to pay off if used just to identify the subjects. Actually, their function should be to persuade on behalf of whatever is being covered. In particular, include action words (i.e., probe, prepare, recommend, evaluate, etc.), rather than passive ones that just identify the subject.

So put whatever visuals you plan to use to this test: Are they working as hard as you are to land the account?

Production

Production techniques. Your use of AV technique should not be so fascinating as to be more memorable than the message. Rather, it should support and enhance your presentation.

I've been told by prospects of instances in which they were so mesmerized by production techniques, they couldn't recall anything that was said. So in regard to the relationship of technique to message, usually less is more.

Multi-media

Some salespeople assume that presentation impact depends on the quantity of slide and film projectors and VCRs used. Undoubtedly, this can have a very desirable effect. However, in developing a multi-media program, apply this three-word criterion: "Will it travel?"

If not, you're severely limiting its potential. Because too often, the prospect will require that the presentation be held at their office. Thus, whatever your presentation, it should have the versatility for optimum effect—wherever it is used.

The Narrator

If a prospect is so important as to warrant developing a slide, videotape, or film presentation, it's axiomatic that it should represent your company in the most impressive manner. Its production should be indicative of your dedication to quality and customer service, and should register the vitality of your people assigned to their account. Beyond all else, its ultimate objective is to convince a prospect that your product or service is best for them.

As a final touch, a professional announcer is sometimes hired to provide polish. But this surrogate presenter isn't one of you. This is a paid stranger making claims and promises—causing your message to lose some credibility. Replace this formal narrator with one of your own who will talk *to* the prospect instead of *at* them. He or she may not be as much of a smooth talker—but will be more believable because of the authority with which this person can speak.

Remember, one of the most severe indictments a prospect can make of a pitch is that it is "canned." Selling on your own behalf removes this stigma from a produced presentation—and enables better transition to the "live" portion. (Who is your Lee Iacocca?)

Equipment

Don't leave anything to chance in regard to equipment. The best conceived program can go down the drain if a mechanical problem occurs. Further, regardless of circumstances, any foul-up is considered your fault. Therefore, *bring your own*

66 Acceptance begins with the prospect's vibes: their gut-feel for the type of person you are. 99

(and if appropriate, your own person to operate it). You're more familiar with this equipment—and will have checked it out in advance to assure that it is operating properly.

Then don't relent, and get trapped by good intentions. This happened when an ad manager told a soliciting agency that they would provide the AV equipment. The agency demurred, explaining they would prefer to bring their own. The ad manager, to assure them that this arrangement would be risk-free, said, "Not to worry. We'll even furnish an experienced technician to operate it." The arrangement seemed safe enough, and simplified matters, so the agency acquiesced.

The agency was then notified of the ground rules. They were to supply their slides, films, and tapes prior to the meeting. The prospect's operator would have everything set up and ready to go at the designated time. Then the prospect's president would be informed that the group was assembled and ready for his grand entrance.

Upon entering, his majesty signaled the operator to begin. But nothing happened. And despite the operator's desperate fumbling with the switches and dials, still nothing. After a few minutes of this frustration, the president turned to the agency team and said, "If you people can't even handle a presentation, you can't handle our advertising."

Most prospects aren't as pompous as that. Even so, it is generally felt that putting on the presentation is your show. And accordingly, you are liable for its success or failure. So play it safe, safer, safest. Despite all the precautions taken, there is always the risk and fear of something going wrong. Therefore, prepare an emergency kit containing all possible life-saving items.

To begin with, provide for any contingency by bringing along spare parts, bulbs, reels, the all-important extension cord, and of course, a three-way plug and an adapter plug. (In addition, this kit could also include valium, a screwdriver, tape, vodka, etc. For that matter, a person at the agency handling the N.R.A. account suggested a gun.)

It hurts enough losing to a competitor. But being beaten by AV equipment makes the pain almost unbearable. I know of some agencies that would no more leave for a presentation without this tool box than they would take off without their creative material.

However, don't use any equipment that could be counterproductive. Obviously, circumstances determine the type and amount of equipment to be used (i.e., presentation strategy, size and configuration of the room, number of attendees, etc.). Yet, except for unusually extenuating circumstances, *don't include an overhead projector*. Because invariably this type of equipment is misused.

The speaker begins by placing the materials to be projected on crooked—and spending the rest of the presentation trying to straighten them. Then, instead of using some form of notes, the visuals serve this purpose—and the obvious is drolly read to the audience verbatim. Finally, this deadly performance is compounded by its being delivered with the speaker's back to the audience. And to all: good night.

Lighting

Understandably, you want to screen your films, tapes, and slides in the most impressive manner possible. This can best be achieved by killing the lights. But that's also a sedative. Further, the prospect may want to make notes about your company, product, or service—hopefully favorable. Don't deny them—and yourself—this opportunity.

Thus, compromise on the showmanship somewhat by just dimming the lights. This will enable them to do the necessary writing, won't totally sacrifice eyeball contact—and will reduce the risk of their minds going out with the lights.

Use of Sales Aids

There is a relationship between a salesperson and the support material she or he uses. These visuals are only as good as your skill in employing them. Further, regardless of how appealing they are, they can't compensate for a dull speaker.

So don't ever count on audio-visual materials carrying you. The effect of your message begins with your delivery. It depends on your enthusiasm, the relevance of your message—and its value. So be constantly aware of your respective roles. It is your responsibility to sell—the sales aids are there to assist you by enhancing the impression you make.

Content vs. Conduct

When I first started critiquing new business presentations for agencies, I assumed my concern would be essentially for content. I used the following criteria:

◆   Is the message and communication of it relevant?

◆   Does it register what's in it for the prospect?

◆ Is your product or service represented in so appealing a manner as to persuade the prospect to buy?

Beyond this, I figured that unless the agency's conduct was offensive, the importance of behavior was incidental.

Then came the greening of Jack Matthews. Working on the other side of the street with advertisers on agency selection, I found they have a different set of priorities. It all stems from the fact that this is a people business—and that is what the advertiser is buying. To what extent is the human equation a factor in your relationship with customers? Personal chemistry is only a matter of intensity.

So take a page from what agencies learn the hard way every day. If the prospect is willing to hold still, they want to get to know you. They wonder, "Are you our kind of people?" "Could I live with you?" "Would you be good for me?"

Becoming privy to these criteria, I began evaluating pitches from a different, more realistic perspective. Obviously, it would behoove you to also role-play the prospect's mind-set—and do whatever necessary to satisfy it.

Therefore, with all due respect to the significance of the content of your presentation, acceptance begins with the prospect's vibes: their gut-feel for the type of person you are. Only after you have established a rapport they would be comfortable with can they be impressed by your company, product, or service.

Performance

Now that you're psyched to do yourself proud, we can deal with performance. There are various strands in the tightrope you walk during a pitch. Specific provision is made for demonstrating the quality of your operation and the relationship the prospect could expect. But the prospect is also scrutinizing you closely for *attitude*. They are trying to determine in advance how you would be to live with.

It is crucial to convey your respect for the prospect in the conduct of your presentation. (So don't lounge in your chair—or blow smoke at them.) Of course, you want to come across as being confident. And you want to register your dedication to challenge them, namely, the initiative and innovation you will bring to this relationship. However, there is a fine line between this conduct and arrogance.

Convey conviction, and you're respected. It is evidence of your commitment to selling—which the prospect feels so strongly about. If, in the heat of presentation, though, you become too overbearing, you seem domineering. And no prospect wants that. So be sensitive to not getting carried away.

To further prevent any misconception of arrogance, guard against these two common pitfalls:

◆ Acting too familiar

◆   Being adamantly right—all the time

Although the perils of both are well known, salespeople will inadvertently drift into this behavior. Unequivocally, any such lapse offends—and is a handicap you can't afford.

By contrast, here is how you can especially ingratiate yourself. Maybe because it's so basic, this strategy is usually neglected: provide evidence of *your willingness to listen*. The prospect's opinions should be sought—and your interest in them made apparent. Too basic to bother with? I know of a high-scoring agency that attributes much of their success to positioning themselves as seeking prospect input—and then hearing the prospect out. Try it. This gives the impression that you really care—and intend to take whatever action is required to satisfy their needs.

Technique

Don't resort to any of these crutches which seriously lessen your ability to convince prospects:

1. Don't *read* to them. This approach forfeits eyeball contact—and implies that you are not adequately prepared.

2. Don't *act* out your sales message, namely, delivering in a manner assumed to be expected of a presenter. This role-playing sacrifices sincerity.

Even though this admonition is self-evident, it warrants elaboration. After I finished critiquing an agency presentation in rehearsal, the agency CEO wrapped it up by observing, "We're probably as ready as we will ever be. Yet I have a gnawing apprehension." He went on to explain that this was by far the biggest account they had ever gone after, and that they were spending substantially more money on the pitch than they ever had before.

Then what had been welling inside him erupted. He fired off, "Look Jack, we didn't bring you in to win a popularity contest. If you have any reservation whatsoever about anything we've said or done, for God's sake do me a favor and level with us."

Apparently this challenge triggered a concern I was harboring for some time. Being given this license was the incentive I needed. I let loose with, "Okay, I had breakfast and lunch with you people. You are delightful, impressive, and stimulating. Tell me, what happened to you on your way to the podium? You had a complete personality change. You were robot-like, mechanical, certainly not yourselves. But that's who the prospect wants to meet."

I wound up by offering a two-word recommendation: *Don't change*," and followed it up with the following direction: "Let the prospect get to know you for who you are. Don't make them interpret what exists behind the facade of a programmed reciter."

To improve your odds, sell according to the best of *your* ability—not that of a stereotype.

3.   Finally, don't deliver from a *memorized* script. It will sounded canned—and if someone interrupts, you're wiped out.

Instead, if appropriate, and you're comfortable with it, work from a series of buzz words that will trigger the components of your talk. This will allow you to talk for understanding instead of effect. Further, it will keep you on target, prevent rambling—and require you to think. This organized spontaneity will enable you to come across in the most believable, authoritative manner.

Level of Communications

A common concern when selling is the risk of offending the prospect by talking *down* to them. But a putdown occurs only if you speak in a patronizing manner.

By contrast, you will suffer much more if you speak *over* anyone's head. If there is a single word used that any individual can't comprehend, they will tune you out thereafter. And you can scratch one buyer for your product or service. It's not that you will purposely try to impress by playing mind games: by using "in" expressions or references to situations they are unlikely to be familiar with. But you can be derelict by assuming that everything you say is intelligible to everyone.

Here is what can happen. I was critiquing a run-through for one of the top agencies in Canada. These heavyweights did a great job, particularly the person proposed as account supervisor if they were awarded the business. He covered the agency's marketing capacity in a remarkably knowledgeable manner. And without a single note. His only prop was one poster board containing nine numbers—which he eloquently brought to life.

As this spellbinder was wrapping up, he felt compelled to justify these figures. So for credibility he announced, ". . . and these mnemonics were extrapolated from empirical sources." That set my head to shaking—sideways. He stopped

---

❝ You can only persuade if you are both understandable and sensible.❞

and asked, "What's the matter?" So I told him, "I don't know what the hell you're talking about."

He was amazed. This erudite language wasn't an affectation. Rather, I found he is just that articulate, and was expressing himself in what was for him a normal manner.

If this hadn't been caught in rehearsal, and he had rattled off this series of mind-boggling words in presentation, the selection team would probably have gone blank. And an agency is never chosen in a vacuum. So beware of committing this presenter's inadvertent error. Rather, be sensitive to your objective: speak for understanding, not effect. Your purpose is to convince, not dazzle. Otherwise, your product or service may be an easy sell—but a tough buy.

Idiosyncrasies

Apropos of being understandable, it is incongruous to ask, "Are you understandable?" Supposedly, clarity is a prime requisite for a person in sales. But there is a fair amount of comment by prospects to this effect: "We don't know what the hell they are talking about."

You're not dazzling a buyer by bringing up *the advisability of fractionating their demographic quintile.* Instead, it's a putdown. And no on will be receptive to buying your product or service after having experienced that. So to prevent shooting yourself in the foot, it is imperative that you speak at a comfortable level of understanding. Use "people talk." This means expressing yourself in a manner they can readily relate to. It is the first step towards their becoming amenable to your proposal.

But don't loosen up to the extent that you put the foot you saved in your mouth. For instance, in high ticket industries, by describing the amount of their expenditure as "200 thou" or "two mill." As far as the prospect is concerned, there is never anything frivolous about their money. You can only persuade them if you are both understandable and sensible.

Since this matter is so basic, it's often taken for granted. As an example, at a recent agency seminar, the president punctuated this point by stating, "Y'know, Jack's right. We use too much obfuscating patois."

Consciously or otherwise, salespeople pepper their pitches with trite phrases. These are used in an attempt to convey humility and honesty, and to thereby gain acceptance for the claims they're making. These phrases include senseless prefaces like the following:

◆ "Frankly, to tell you the honest truth . . ."

◆ "Trust me."

◆ "Please bear with me on this one."

◆ "This can't be proved, but . . ."

◆ "Would I lie to you?"

◆ "You can check anyone on this."

◆ "I'm not sure of this, however ..."

◆ "Don't take my word for it, but ..."

◆ "As everyone knows ..."

◆ "May God strike me dead if ..."

Prospects find these ploys, at best, annoying. And they make everything else said suspect. So in preparation for your meeting, make a point of stripping these hedging remarks from your style of speaking.

Qualifying Phrases

Here is another common weakness in expression that I find across the board. In delivery, people in sales seem compelled to qualify their claims by prefacing statements with the phrase, "We think ..." Or justifying a recommendation by preceding it with, "We believe ..." And to indicate sincerity by starting the conclusion with, "We hope ..."

Actually, the prospect prefers that your justifications be based on a broader, more authoritative source, not just your humble assumption. These qualifying phrases instill doubt because they imply a lack of certainty on your part.

To convince prospects, sell without these restrictions. It is not that you "believe" your product or service is the best for them. You *know* it is the best for them. And it is not only that you "think" it is best, it *is best*. So don't lessen your power to persuade by backing into your claims and recommendations. Sell with conviction—without reservation. Your proposal deserves it. The prospect expects it.

Offensive Characteristics

Regardless of how dynamic a salesperson may be, no one can impress a prospect if they make blunders in conduct. These could range from coming across as arrogant or patronizing, to using distracting mannerisms, for instance, tapping your pen on their desk or jingling coins in your pocket.

Particularly annoying to the prospect is sloppy delivery. This is evidenced by speaking too softly, mumbling, or letting your voice trail off. They will assume you don't think they are worth the effort to communicate understandably. Offensive attitude or mannerisms can wipe out what would otherwise be an acceptable, convincing presentation. So don't turn off a prospect before you can turn them on.

(Incidentally, I'm often asked if it looks all right to talk with your hands in your pockets. It's okay—if you don't move them around.)

Knowledge of the Prospect

With all due respect to delivery though, heed these pearls of wisdom from some-one in the best position to know. I had lunch recently with Brian Palmer, Director of the National Speakers Bureau. He said, "The importance of presentation skills is a given. But first, *you'd better know what you're talking about.*"

This point was never made better than when Bob Noble of Springfield, Mis-souri asked to be included in the agency search by Tyson Chicken some years ago. This request seemed incongruous because Noble's total billing at the time was $2,500,000—and this advertiser's media budget was $6,000,000. Nevertheless, Noble persevered because they were already doing the collateral work for Tyson. And their rationale was "What agency could know more about your operation that we do?"

Even though selecting Noble seemed improbable, Tyson acquiesced to consid-er them. They probably assumed they could afford this gracious gesture because Noble would be eliminated in the screening presentations anyway, since based on the caliber of the competing agencies, they were way out of their league.

But not only did Noble make the cut, even more amazingly, they would up as one of the two finalists. This time though, the odds against them were insur-mountable because their adversary was one of the top ten agencies in the United States. Yet, Noble concluded that they had already invested so much time and money, they might as well see it through—in the event a miracle might occur. It did.

Inasmuch as Noble would be an afterthought, the big-name agency was sched-uled to go first. And of no surprise, the amount they spent on their presentation was comparatively overwhelming. Like the difference between lunch in New York City and Springfield, Missouri.

Unbelievably, in order to customize the presentation, the heavy-hitter agency kept referring to Tyson *turkeys.* Tyson didn't have a single turkey! Only chickens. I don't mean to take anything away from Noble's efforts, but after this fiasco, all they had to do was show up. They were awarded the account.

Of itself, this object lesson should be enough. However, there is more to be learned from this experience. Because of its financial impact on the agency (staff-ing up, adding space, etc.), Bob Noble phoned Harry Paster of the American Association of Advertising Agencies to find out the first thing he needed to do now that he had quadrupled the size of his agency.

Speaking to the money maven of the agency business, he expected financial direction. Instead of "debits-credits" counsel, though, Harry came back with some of the most valuable advice that can be given in any business. He wisely said, "You'd better get more aggressive than ever in soliciting new business to compensate for when this dominant account leaves you." This warning was in no way due to a lack of confidence in Noble's operation. Rather, it just acknowledged a cold fact of business life. Namely, you begin to lose an account the day you get it.

Regardless of how articulate and charming you may be, if anything you say is suspect, you won't be able to give your product or service away. Thus, when developing your presentation, it's essential that you include in your acid test: "you'd better know what you're talking about."

66 You begin to lose an account the day you get it. 99

Organizing a Persuasive Presentation

◆ Perspective ◆ Entrance ◆ Introduction: Your Team
◆ Introduction: Presentation ◆ Opening ◆ Show-and-Tell
◆ Closer ◆ Exit ◆ "Leaver"

Perspective

You are now at the moment of truth. The payoff for all your efforts and expense: the presentation. Because it is intended to create the most favorable impression of your company, the appeal of your product or service, and your capacity to serve them, prospects assume your presentation represents the best they can expect from you.

The prospect assumes this represents your best shot. It evidently must be the most conclusive proof of why they should buy from you.

The prospect is further sensitive to how well your presentation is organized—the logic of its sequence, how well it builds, convinces, and pays off. Here, too, this communicates the caliber of operation you represent.

Since the new business presentation is the most stressful activity in any company, directions follow on how to prepare and sell in a calmer, more confident manner.

Entrance

The most uncomfortable time begins with your entrance—and lasts until the opening of your presentation. What can be done to reduce the awkward factor? Can this period be choreographed?

The extent to which this phase can be controlled depends upon your knowledge of the following circumstances. Granted, for most situations, this lists more than you need to know. But when any of these conditions come into play, you will want to be aware of their effect:

◆ Location: your place or theirs—or a neutral spot

◆ Environment: size and layout of room

◆ Facilities: conference table, theater style, or informal seating

◆ Time: beginning, middle, or end of day

◆ Sequence: first to present—or following other suppliers

◆ Arrangements: able to set up beforehand or have to do so while they are present

◆ Familiarity: degree to which members of prospect group in attendance are known to you

Having this information enables you to plan how to conduct yourself under these conditions. And plan you must. Because it will distinguish your operation from the fumbling uncertainty exhibited by your competitors. By contrast, you can come across as being more confident, organized, and professional.

For instance, being aware of the circumstances under which you have to operate, you can orchestrate the transition from entrance to presentation. This would include the following:

◆ Handling introductions (if you are accompanied by others)

◆ Creating acceptance for your people

◆ Generating interest in your presentation

◆ Arranging the location of presentation and selection teams

◆ Establishing the procedure for getting underway

With this programming, you can control rather than react to the situation. Therefore, what had been a sticky phase, can actually pave the way and enhance your presentation. Further, with this awkward phase planned for, you can open from strength—able to concentrate on convincing the prospect of why your product or service can best fulfill their requirements.

66 A problem defined is a problem half solved. 99

Introduction: Your Team

In the case of a team effort, your people enter the meeting room as strangers to the prospect group. The more quickly this status can be changed, the sooner the necessary rapport can be developed. So instead of the usual practice of withholding the identity of each member until their turn on the program, introduce all of them at the outset. This should include their present function—and their proposed involvement if you are awarded the account. This way, the prospect group can immediately begin to relate to them.

The importance of this tactic is due to the fact that prospects frequently play a silly game when your people come in: trying to guess what each does at your company. The longer you delay in furnishing this information, the longer a distracting element is present—which detracts from your presentation.

Yet, upon arrival, the situation usually consists of a fast round of sweaty handshakes—with both parties anxious to get this amenity over with. Thus, due to this environment, the supplier formally introduces their people—but seldom platforms them. This procedure only identifies your team. To their disadvantage, it does not create the authority and acceptance for prospect receptivity.

The next acknowledgement of each of your members occurs when it is their turn on the program. And then they are thrown to the wolves with not much more than: "Now to tell you about product characteristics, here's Charlie." Then poor Charlie begins that long trek to the podium—during which time the silence is deafening. Next, he has to begin building stature and credibility for himself—which is tough for an individual to do on their own behalf. And valuable selling time is lost while he attempts to ingratiate himself. Obviously, this could be accomplished much more effectively by someone else.

Instead, precondition the prospect to each of your presenters. This will eliminate the dead air interval—and enable each member of your team to hit the deck running by devoting their entire time to selling. Present them intriguingly to generate interest. Introduce your presenters by parenthetically confiding his or her exceptional professional qualifications, and the esteem in which they are held by their peers in your industry. Then cap it off with an anecdote proving why they have earned such respect.

Remember, the prospect will be strongly influenced by the caliber of the people who will be responsible for producing the most desirable product or developing the most valuable service. Therefore, to whatever extent you represent your people as being preferable to those of any other supplier, you will gain a potent competitive edge. This people-oriented tactic will also distinguish your operation from the impersonal impression made by your competitors.

To sum up, most suppliers fail to make the most effective use of participants in their presentation strategy. Specifically, being sensitive enough to their presenters being the medium for the message. In this situation, Marshall MacLuhan was right when he said, "The medium is the message."

Introduction: Presentation

Upon establishing acceptance for your participants, the next objective is creating interest and understanding for your presentation. To begin with, distribute an agenda—the appearance and content of which will represent your operation in the most appealing manner (see Chapter 11).

Then, preface your presentation with the announcement that it is based on information the prospect has provided. This protects you in the event of having received any inaccurate or misleading input. (If so, your misguided approach still provides evidence of your ability and willingness to follow direction.) Further, this tactic establishes the presentation's relevance and identifies where you're coming from. And it precludes the prospect wondering "How the hell did you ever come up with that?"

Finally, pave the way for your opening by intriguing them with a brief highlight of each feature to be covered. This will put them in an anticipatory frame of mind.

Opening

The opening of your sales presentation will establish the amount of prospect interest and receptivity thereafter. Here is a four-step sequence that will immediately attract and hold their attention:

1. First, in your pre-presentation efforts, you flushed out what they need from a product or service—and the reasons why. This insight forms the basis for your most logical and effective introductory statement, one that identifies and brings into focus the purpose of this meeting. Namely, their product or service needs—and why your company can best fulfill them.

    Therefore, your most compelling opener is "As you have informed us, what you need is _____, because (the reasons), and I'm (we're) going to prove why our company can best satisfy your needs.

2. From there, you get into describing your company. (Of course, only as it relates to this prospect).

This should take only as much time as necessary to establish the authority and qualifications for the claims and promises to be made. If you belabor the description, you come across as I-I-I, me-me-me—which doesn't include them. Thus, the prospect becomes impatient—and distracted—because you've strayed too far from the target: them. Thus, the opportunity for developing receptivity wanes.

3. Now proceed with creating the desired prospect frame of mind, one that will immediately start tracking with you. This prelude should also jolt them out of their lethargy.

Set the tone by announcing, "We will start by dealing with your specific product or service needs—followed by how our company would function to best serve them." This will promptly establish an environment pertinent to their interests—one in which they will be more receptive to your presentation.

4. Then you better get right to the point with the answer to the prospect's ultimate question. "Why should we buy your product (service)?" Any approach short of supplying specific, relevant reasons will make your effort a long run for a short slide.

They shouldn't have to discover or assume why your product or service is preferable to any other. It's your responsibility to tell them. So sell early by spelling out up front the six reasons (or five or seven) why your company's product or service can best fulfill their requirements. Your claims should not be just general puffery, but should directly identify with their needs.

To sum up, start winning with your opener—and clinch it with the rest of your presentation.

Show-and-Tell

Now let's get into the "Show-and-Tell" phase of your presentation.

The *promise* in your solicitation activity has gotten you this far. Now you have to convince the prospect of your ability to *deliver*. To do this, provide an insight to their company, industry, or market hitherto unknown—and what to do about it. Much of what you need know regarding their problems and opportunities can be flushed out at your pre-presentation meeting. Since a problem defined is a problem half-solved, you're on your way to coming up with the ideas and solutions that will make doing business with you preferable. Needless to say, your product or service is essential to these proposals.

Then substantiate your proposal with successful, pertinent case histories. In doing so, though, go that crucial step further and explain why the strategy of these achievements is relevant and important to the prospect—and how it can fulfill their needs.

Otherwise, whatever you present or exhibit will be just decorations. The prospect will not make the effort to relate it to themselves, and the desired effect will be wasted. So your criterion for deciding what to show is whether it will be actively used to convince the prospect of why they need your product or service.

But remember, your track record is an opener—not a closer. Beyond all else, they still need to be given a compelling reason why to buy. What is this reason? Any of the various factors that contribute to the appeal of your product or service, (quality, uniqueness, price, availability, etc.)? Not quite. These are the means—not the end. What the prospect will actually buy is the *benefit* received if purchased. Therefore, lead from strength by featuring these attributes—and then finish off with how their business will gain from it.

For instance, you give much emphasis to your product's or service's advantages in presentation. You're proud of these achievements, and justifiably so. But this pride is only self-serving unless you explain what it can do for them. So sell on the basis of the desirable results they will realize, rather than stopping short at boasting. Finish the job. To whatever extent you can convey a mutuality of interest, you will improve the climate for their receptivity.

Closer

It's amazing how a salesperson will go the full route in the development and execution of a splendid presentation—then quit with victory in sight. Namely, upon completion, some are reluctant to ask for the order. That's like spiking the football on the five-yard line!

There are those who feel it is in poor taste or beneath them to ask. As a result, their bells and whistles climax will consist of a grabber like "Well, there it is. . . ." Or "The gang at the home office is really excited about this." That isn't a finale; it's a fizzle.

And then the salesperson wonders why his or her nights and weekends of work on this pitch didn't pay off. Everything was right: specifications, price, delivery. . . But no cigar.

Other people in sales are aware of the need for some sort of "closer"—but are uncomfortable with it. So they will apologetically state: "I guess at this point I'm

❝ What the prospect will actually buy is the benefit received if purchased.❞

supposed to ask for the order. Well, I'm doing that." (This is followed by an insincere chuckle.) This matter-of-fact, lighthearted approach is intended to remove any appearance of crassness.

This thinking is 180 degrees off target. Because a prospect highly respects a salesperson who will forthrightly sell, the way they do. They feel if you don't sell boldly and imaginatively on behalf of your own product or service, what can they expect?

And watch out for the following characteristic. The prospect is nearly as turned off by commonly used, trite expressions like "We're ready to go to work for you right now!" Or "We're really anxious to become members of your team!" The prospect figures you surely ought to be able to come up with something more intriguing than that.

The matter is this basic: the reason the prospect is in business is to sell their product or service profitably. Thus, they are most impressed by the salesperson who is demonstrably selling-oriented. Such being the case, base asking for the order on the ultimate reason for buying: "Did I convince you that my product (service) can best fulfill your requirements?" This registers your sensitivity to their needs, your desire to serve—and your ability to get to the heart of the matter. How much more could the prospect want? If this doesn't get a rise out of them, you can say, "Obviously, you have to ask for the order in your business. We do too. What do we have to do to become your supplier?"

If and when you sell on a team basis, and are not comfortable with either of these, there's another alternative. If you're able to carry it off, admit that "After we leave here, the first thing we do is ask each other: 'Well, how did we do?' Whatever our assumption though, it's worthless. Because the only opinion that counts is *yours*. So instead of our performing this exercise in futility, would you please tell us how we did?"

Finally, All of your activity up until now has been geared to reaching this high. Don't blow it because of an awkward exit. A planned "closer" will prevent this from happening—and your being left in limbo.

Exit

You won't have to wonder about the prospect's reaction to your presentation if they hint, or worse, inform you, that it's time to leave. Because if they say goodbye first, it's your last goodbye. To prevent overstaying your welcome, *you* need to take the initiative. This provides advance evidence of your respect for their time—and indicates that as a customer they would not be taken for granted.

Prior to the farewell lull, acknowledge that they have a tremendous responsibility: selecting the product or service that can best fulfill their requirements. Then you can say, "And since dedication to fulfilling customer needs is the basis of our operation, we'll get back to ours now. But we'll keep the champagne cold in the event we're awarded your account."

Of course, you want to leave gracefully, but your dynamic presentation will be followed by the mundane activity of packing your materials and possibly equipment. It is sort of embarrassing coming down to this menial task after having operated in the lofty areas of how you would solve their production or marketing problems.

The prospect isn't anywhere near as sensitive to this situation as you are. It is an expected procedure, part of the package. But it is still desirable to minimize this wrap-up—and conduct it as efficiently as possible. To do so professionally, include planning for the departure in your rehearsal. Most presenters gather their sales support material in an obviously disorganized manner. But by orchestrating this procedure, with responsibilities assigned, you can prevent coming off as the Three Stooges. Rather, you will give the impression of being the follow-through supplier that knows what it is doing—all the way.

The "Leaver"

Finally, there is a pre- and post-factor that will make or break the impression you make. The first has already been covered: your rehearsal. The latter refers to the "leaver" furnished the prospect after the presentation. Also referred to as a "leave-behind," this is a typed version of the essence of your presentation.

As with the rehearsal, the "leaver" should be accorded as much importance as any other component of the presentation. No pitch, of itself, is so fantastic as to suffice. After a series of presentations, the prospect's impressions of the various products or services proposed begin to blur. Further, this summary is essential because it is used for reference, review, and comparison.

Therefore, the criterion for developing the "leaver" should be how well it can represent what you are selling in your absence. This applies to the vitality of its content and the appeal of its appearance. In essence, whatever you leave should be so compelling as to tip the scale in your favor.

Here's why it deserves your best shot. When a buying committee meeting is held after all presentations have been made, the "leaver" in effect *becomes* the supplier. A member will hold up a copy and ask, "What do you think of this one?" Another will toss a copy across the conference table and say, "How about that one?" These are the *suppliers* they are throwing back and forth. And as such, when the prospect is attempting to arrive at a decision, the "leaver" provides the final impression. Therefore, while your objective is to develop a winning presentation, you still need the clincher: a winning "leaver." For yours to make the difference, here is what you need know regarding its content and appearance.

Content

This is what's necessary for your product or service to come across as being more desirable than others. To begin with though: here's what *not* to do. Because of the amount of work and pride involved, suppliers will often reproduce the entire presentation—assuming they will impress the prospect by the pound. However, because of the need to arrive at a decision, the buyer has neither the time nor inclination to sweat out what looks like a Master's thesis.

Instead, your "leaver" should contain only what is critical to remember. This does not mean that you are restricted to a limited number of pages, only to the discipline of preventing its content from looking overwhelming. If, however, the situation requires a thickness which could be intimidating, preface it with an "Executive Summary."

In particular, the "leaver" should recap the following:

◆ Why your company's functions and qualifications are best for fulfilling their requirements

◆ The pertinence and value of the talent/experience of your team to be assigned to their account

◆ The claims and promises made

◆ How the ideas and solutions offered will serve this prospect's specific needs

◆ How you would operate together

◆ The method of compensation

◆ A checklist/timetable of action to be taken upon being awarded the account ("The first 100 days")

In addition, the "leaver" should do the following:

◆ Ask for the order

◆ If appropriate, include a Letter of Agreement

If having fewer employees than your competitor may place you at a disadvantage, you will want to give the impression of nevertheless having sufficient depth.

Here is how to combat their numerical difference. To a prospect, it shouldn't be a matter of how many are employed by a supplier. But rather, *who* will service their business. Therefore, include a list specifying your employees who will become "their" people. And detail their work experience (ie., where, in what capacity, and for how long).

It will be amazing how impressive this list will be, and how well it can compensate for any quantitative shortcoming. Actually, even if size isn't a concern, this tactic is worth considering.

Appearance

The "leaver" is considered a valuable insight to your vitality. Therefore

◆   The cover should be intriguing enough to encourage its being opened. It should convey your class, your imagination—and that you are the kind of people they would want to know.

◆   Each page should be treated as an ad for your company—laid out attractively, easy to read, providing the incentive to read further. (Note: This does not take some God-given artistic flair. Just common sense.)

Above all, your "leaver" must give the impression of having been developed especially for this individual prospect. The prospect's corporate name and logo should appear on the cover—plus the person's name for whom it is intended. Beyond this, their corporate name should be sprinkled throughout the subject matter. This device will preclude any suspicion of your "leaver" being a stock item.

As to *when* it should be furnished, first, here are two caveats:

1.   Never, I repeat never, distribute the "leaver" *before* or *during* the presentation. It is often assumed these are opportune times because they involve the prospect. However, you actually lose them because people read at different rates. And you sacrifice eyeball contact, and, in effect, wind up competing with it.

2.   Distibute the "leaver" immediately after the presentation. Some suppliers surmise it is a better maneuver to mail the "leaver" the next day. Supposedly the cumulative effect provided by this additional shot at the prospect will compound the appeal of your product or service.

But this strategy also reduces the amount of time the prospect can spend with it. Even worse, you may be slated on the last day of presentations—and they might hold their selection meeting right afterwards or the next day. This lack of presence could cause your elimination. So don't gamble on the benefit of another exposure. Because it might occur after the decision is made. The only right time for supplying the "leaver" is immediately after the presentation.

To sum up, the "leaver" can be accorded much more importance among the mix of factors for choosing a product or service than is often realized. It is your ultimate "closer." Therefore, it should be so convincing that—of itself—it will register the preferability of dealing with you.

Performing for Greatest Impact

◆ Perspective ◆ Objective ◆ Angle or Hook
◆ Capabilities/Credentials Presentation ◆ Emotional Appeal
◆ Style vs. Substance ◆ Move Prospects to Presenter's Office
◆ Ask for the Order—Throughout
◆ When to Promote Your Product or Service Features ◆ Team Proposed ◆
Prospect Involvement
◆ Seek Prospect Reaction ◆ Duration ◆ Gimmicks

Perspective

The previous chapter set forth the step-by-step procedure for conducting your presentation: what to include—and how to achieve the desired reaction. In this chapter, we'll discuss the smarts to be applied—techniques that will improve the potency of your efforts.

They are based on a crucial development: the combination of prospect attitude and economic circumstances is causing a much more critical evaluation of supplier presentation. Thus, you can't count on last year's strategy anymore.

Instead, it needs to be now-oriented in terms of both appearance and content. Namely, it must be visually fresh, must relate to the prospect's current and projected needs, and must explain what's new that is vital to them, and why.

Being fresh and relevant could make your presentation unique by comparison—thereby distinguishing it from the stereotyped ones of your competitors.

Objective

Based on my cross-pollinating among agencies and advertisers each week, I sense a growing need to bring back into focus the function of a presentation. Possibly due to taking the path of least resistance, some suppliers are lapsing into presentation strategy short of what their objective should be. For instance, there are some salespeople putting on full-scale presentations to create familiarity—or in order to cultivate prospects. That's ridiculous!

There is only one reason for a pitch: *to land the account*. Therefore, only apply this time, effort, and expense when going for the jugular. With a supplier's margin of profit, anything less than the intent to score is unaffordable.

Further, when salespeople haven't done their homework, they will make abstract promises that are just fluff, rather than addressing head-on the prospect's ultimate want. All else notwithstanding, what you offer should enhance the appeal and value of their product or service—thereby increasing the likelihood of making the sale. That is the kind of bottom line contribution your prospects want to hear about.

Angle or Hook

People in sales are constantly seeking an angle or hook for their presentation; an approach that will fascinate the prospect. But the angle or hook is so obvious, few notice it. The angle or hook *is the prospect.*

As far as the prospect is concerned, he or she is the most fascinating subject—corporately and personally. Therefore, the only strategy that will work in promoting your product, service, or dedication is one that is communicated within the framework of the prospect's concerns. An approach that does anything less than totally relate to their interests is an approach that was developed to satisfy the supplier—not the prospect.

❝ As far as the prospect is concerned, he or she is the most fascinating subject.❞

Capabilities/Credentials Presentation

It has become trendy for prospects to ask for a "capabilities presentation" or a "credentials presentation." Don't get thrown off stride by this misleading request. What they actually want is a capabilities or credentials presentation that *relates to them*.

Therefore, the generic presentation on behalf of your product or service as such doesn't work anymore. The prospect must now be given specific reasons why to buy from you—that have been developed and customized for them.

At a recent seminar, someone said to me, "Oh hell, Jack, we just produced an expensive slide presentation on behalf of the agency. Does this mean it can't be used?"

I asked him, "Can you afford one more slide?" He replied, "Of course." So I said, "Fine. Then put the prospect's name on it and drop it in the first slot in the tray. And if you're flush, make up a couple of dupes—and put one in the middle and the other at the end. This shows your respect for the prospect—and the importance attached to the presentation." In particular, this proves they are receiving a personal, not an all-purpose pitch.

Here is another effective yet economical means for giving the prospect the impression that the presentation was created especially for them. For whatever the medium used (slide, poster boards, folder/notebook, spec sheets, etc.) subtly place the prospect's logo in the lower right hand corner. If the prospect isn't worth this basic effort, you're just spinning your wheels. Instead, concentrate your activity on those sufficiently desirable—with whom you want to get traction and get going.

Emotional Appeal

Essentially your selling approach is factual and tangible—directed to the prospect's intellect. But logic will get you only halfway there. You also need to provide an organic appeal—to their heart and gut. In a competitive situation, if all other matters seem equal, the prospect's emotional reaction can be the tie-breaker. In fact, if the *impression* made is powerful enough, it could induce the prospect to dump the formal criteria for selecting a product or service and defer to their own good judgment—and select yours.

This impact can be achieved by establishing the following goal for your presentation: its effect should make the prospect wish they had been getting your caliber of product or service and people all along. How? Come up with ideas the prospect would wish they had thought of. Instilling this envy and regret can transcend all other considerations—and competitors. So compound their need with want, since the latter is the deciding factor.

Style vs. Substance

As important as it is to be personally appealing to prospects, demonstrating how your product or service would best fulfill their requirements is just as vital. Your own attraction must be matched by proof of how they will benefit from this purchase. Your compatibility is meaningful only if what you are selling produces the results desired by prospects. And they want to be convinced of *both*.

So don't get carried away with style at the expense of substance. For instance, I know of an ad agency specializing in high-tech accounts that got the jump on competition when they learned of a German company intending to open the US market in a big way. To indicate how well the agency could relate, they delivered the entire presentation in *German*. And they lost, right then.

If language was much of a consideration, the advertiser could have settled for an agency in Germany. Rather, they were seeking an American agency because they wanted one that is US oriented in its approach to the market. Instead of ingratiating themselves, this shop served as a reminder to the prospect of what they don't want in an agency.

So sure, speak their language—but not literally. Instead figuratively put out the sign: SALES SPOKEN HERE—YOURS. So while style provides you with a vehicle, you still need the horsepower to get you there: the substance. Namely, *What's in it for them.*

Move Prospects to Presenter's Office

There are three negative factors you are confronted with in any presentation:

◆ The prospect is not accustomed to holding still.

◆ They have a short attention span.

◆ There is tedium inherent in any pitch.

Why hope that your devastating charm, of itself, will overcome these obstacles? Rather, here is a tested idea to combat these forces fighting you. This applies if the event is held at your place—and if the facilities are conducive.

Instead of the usual practice of bringing all your presenters to the conference room, take the prospect to the presenters' offices (i.e., open in the conference room, next present production matters at their location, and then move on to your service department.) This will provide a refreshing change of pace for the prospect—and break the mold of the stereotyped presentation. This tactic will also contribute to a more relaxed environment—and a more alert audience. (Not incidental, your participants will be more confident and effective performing in their own surroundings.)

❝ Don't hold your trump card until the game is over.❞

But remember, the logistics make adequate rehearsal even more essential. Individually, you may not have the authority to engineer this event. But as far as your management is concerned, what a great idea you came up with!

Ask for the Order—Throughout

Asking for the order is often thought to be a function performed at the end of the presentation. Thus, your attempt to inspire a favorable decision is postponed until you risk its looking like an afterthought. But you're soliciting their business beginning with your opening statement. So why not start landing the account at inception?

Your closer should be the most compelling reason for buying your product or service—now. Sure, it's the climax of your pitch. But its potency shouldn't be sublimated to sequence. So don't hold your trump card until the game is over.

Instead, develop variations of this payoff appeal and sprinkle them throughout. In effect, use the *entire* presentation to convince the prospect to act on their behalf—and thereby yours. This strategy will assure a *total* selling effort—which is what it takes to score.

The best evidence of the effectiveness of this strategy is its application in the biggest "business" of them all: Religion. Whether it's high mass or a snake-swinging revival meeting, the matter of belief begins when the bells chime and is featured all through the service. In fact, by the time the benediction is delivered, it's anti-climatic. So benefit by repetition of message as they do. God knows it works.

When to Promote Your Product or Service Features

One school of thought staunchly maintains it is best to open with your advantages—to get off to a roaring start. Others prefer to close with these features—guessing that a bells-and-whistles climax would be more impressive. They are both wrong! The only right opener is what the prospect told you they want to hear about.

If they indicated in pre-presentation contact that their major concern is with features, then that is what you start with. If they expressed greater concern regarding some other factor (i.e., price, availability, etc.), then features should be slotted after—and complementing—the matter of primary prospect concern.

The prospect is holding still to find out how their needs can be best fulfilled. To whatever extent you delay in answering this question is the extent to which you lose them. If your presentation is anything less than totally prospect-oriented, it becomes supplier-oriented. And you can't award yourself the account.

Team Proposed

When a salesperson pledges his or her good faith to a prospect, the size and caliber of the back-up team promised is limited only by their imagination. And in retrospect, the claims made by various suppliers are often so extravagant that they cancel each other out. Even worse, if not just suspect, they can be unbelievable. And though *your* intended commitment of personnel is legitimate, you can suffer guilt by association. Under these circumstances, how can you make your offer credible? Obviously, you can't bring along all of your staff who would be involved.

Instead, there is the device used by J. Walter Thompson/Atlanta. At the end of the presentation, with flourish, they present each member of the selection team with a handsomely wrapped, jewelry-sized gift box. Obviously, this pulls the prospects forward in their chairs—and causes suspicion of impropriety. Having captured their attention, J.W.T invites the prospect to open "the best gift our agency can give you."

When they do so, they discover that each box contains a stack of business cards representing all the agency people who would be assigned to their account. This imaginative approach has proved to be very impressive. It is accepted as physical evidence of a bona fide commitment. (Note: If your company isn't too big on the use of business cards throughout its operation, offer an album consisting of snapshots of these back-up people.)

There is a worthwhile conclusion that can be drawn from this tactic. Whatever the promise made, if at all possible, deliver it in an idea-oriented vehicle. It's

❝ Whatever the promise made, deliver it in an idea-oriented vehicle.❞

more intriguing, memorable—and indicates that your company can produce beyond what they expected.

Prospect Involvement

Having your game plan in place, it is unlikely you will be too easily startled. For instance, it is not unusual for a prospect's participation in the presentation to consist of opening with the statement: "Go ahead." And then not saying another word until concluding with: "Next." In between, you conduct a monologue—gambling that of itself this will be sufficiently compelling to get their business. However, no agreement is ever reached without communication between the parties involved.

Instead, structure your presentation to be a dialogue, so you can speak with the prospect—rather than at them. This can be achieved by building some questions into the presentation. Preferably those with which they would agree—thereby developing the desired rapport.

Importantly, if there is more than one person present, these questions should be directed to specific individuals—*by name*. Then, to further impress them, casually intersperse one fact you obtained about each of them. Make a key point by stating, "Janet, with your MBA from Harvard, you certainly know that . . . " and, "Phil, you knew back when you were a division manager in Cleveland that . . . "

This tactic confirms that your presentation was developed especially for them; it is flattering—and commands attention. While you're at it, make the members of the buying committee look good. Compliment them on the astuteness of their questions and comments. The interaction generated will enable them to better relate to you—and to favorably remember you.

This involvement should consist of no more than asking them to confirm simple truisms with "Isn't that right, Phil?" This way, you won't put anyone on the spot. But you will serve notice that they will be involved in your presentation. Anyway, all you want is their agreement—not a speech.

Then, since involvement begets interest, invite them to interrupt with questions at any time. This indicates that apparently you must know what you are talking about—and proves that yours isn't a canned pitch. As further evidence of its not being canned, also bounce some questions off your own people to corroborate the claims being made. The spontaneity this injects will, of course, be well planned in your rehearsal. (Don't surprise any of your people with a question and expect a profound reply.)

Seek Prospect Reaction

You led the prospect to water. Now get them to drink. The purpose of your presentation is to obtain a favorable decision in the shortest period of time. To

❝ To whatever extent you digress is the extent of advantage given to your competitors. ❞

succeed requires seeking a commitment—rather than the usual practice of submitting your proposal for the prospect's eventual consideration.

Therefore, how about having the courage to occasionally inquire during presentation about their reaction to it. For instance, "Are these the kinds of product advantages you're looking for?" and "Is this the type of dedicated service that you expect?" This is a catalyst to their thinking immediately—and is conducive to a spontaneous expression of judgement. It saves you from wasting time speculating on their reaction, while they vacillate.

Some people object to this tactic, citing that according to the book you should always conclude with a positive statement—not a question. But your goal is getting a commitment—not observing a formality. So give a little on the textbook to get what you need. Or you may be reluctant to go this route for fear the prospect may say "No." But even that is good. Because you just got them to open the channel of communications. And when this happens, you can ask, "Why?" Then, whatever answer you get will be in your best interest. You see, there can be two kinds of "No." One could be "No"—irrevocably. That in itself serves a purpose because it precludes beating a dead horse. And your margin of profit makes this unaffordable.

The other possibility is "No, but . . . " which can clue you in on what revisions are necessary to make the sale. So this negative can be of value—positively.

Duration

Some prospects, due to policy or circumstances, limit the amount of your meeting time. For whatever the duration—for instance, 30 minutes—if needed, make it a full 30 minutes of selling time. To whatever extent you digress is the extent of advantage given to your competitors. So skip the extraneous warm-up patter — and be strictly pertinent throughout.

Because the period stipulated is usually exceeded—much to the prospect's annoyance—here is an ingratiating device. This will also increase your memorability—favorably. Open by announcing that your presentation will not take any longer than 27 minutes. This rare cooperation will pull the buyer forward in his or her chair. (Of course, this also makes adequate rehearsal all the more necessary.)

Since this matter of timing is so important, let's clarify what the prospect means when they specify 30 minutes. It is simply that you are not to go beyond 30 minutes. By contrast, it is not expected that your presentation go up to 30 minutes.

Thus, if it's determined that for a certain prospect you can be most effective in 20 minutes, do so and get out. Don't be like the salesman who had everything going for him — except he couldn't take yes for an answer. In particular, don't sell for so long that you end up buying it back.

Finally, here is the best reason for complying with timing set forth. Prospects interpret violating this requirement as fighting them — and is indicative of the type relationship that would exist if you were awarded their account. Thus, ignored timing is one of the first and easiest means used to eliminate suppliers.

Gimmicks

Nowhere is it inscribed in stone that you must spring some oh-so-clever device in presentation. Actually, if the substance of your program is impressive enough, there is no need for any sort of gimmick. Here is cold hard proof.

Dennie Davidoff invited me back to her agency in Fairfield. I was looking forward to congratulating her because it is not often that a $9,000,000 agency lands a $5,000,000 account. The new client was the regional co-op portion of Domino's Pizza. After I had offered my felicitations, she humbly countered with, "Thanks, but we just got lucky." I wasn't buying it. Nobody falls into that kind of achievement. However, Dennie insisted they'd lucked out. Since I still objected, she revealed what had happened.

Whatever her agency had done right to become a finalist seemed like it would no longer sustain them because the other shop was five times bigger and had everything going for them to justify being selected. Plus, as feared, they put on a smashing show. But Dennie's contender wouldn't let it go at that. They had to get creative. At the end of what had been a winning presentation, they had a huge cake wheeled in, smothered in frosting. And covering the top was a Domino's Pizza!

The selection team found this to be the most nauseating sight they had ever seen. At that, they called in Dennie's team with the instructions, "Do your thing, and if you don't screw up, you've got the account."

The moral here is *don't force a gimmick*. Certainly not one playing games with the prospect's product. Instead, make the message and the communication of it so good that you're not tempted to hokey it up with something too clever.

This advice especially applies to the wrap-up of your presentation. It's at this point that the temptation is greatest to come up with some jolting attention-getting device. Sure, you want to wind up your presentation in a blaze of glory. But don't ruin a fine performance with a contrived finish. This happened to an agency that was actually wired in—yet couldn't resist the temptation of an off-the-wall clincher. In critiquing their pitch recently, I was tremendously impressed with what they said—and how they said it. It looked like they had confirmed the prospect's preference for them.

However, as it drew to the conclusion, I was told, "Now Jack, get a load of this wrap-up. It will blo-o-ow your mind!" The concept was based on the fact that an annual fee of $100,000 had been negotiated. As evidence of the agency's integrity, they planned on having a Brinks' guard enter at this time carrying a canvas sack. And he would dump its contents on a table in front of the presenter: $100,000 in cash. Then the presenter would announce, "In the event we fall short of fulfilling the advertising objectives established, we will rebate a pro-rata share of the money to you." This statement was accompanied by grandiose gestures depicting the money being returned. Afterwards, the agency president bubbled, "Dynamite, huh Jack?"

I winced, hard. And with whatever calmness I could muster, explained, "You've shot yourself in the foot not only once—but three times."

◆ First, this device is negative—implying you probably won't fulfill this responsibility.

◆ Second, there is nothing more appalling to a client than the specter of their agency playing with its money.

◆ And finally, you've demonstrated that your only concern is money.

I hope the agency didn't use this gimmick. If so, *they* will end up holding the bag. Empty.

Learning from this mistake, when you get to the end of your presentation, use *this* gamesmanship as further proof of why your company is best for them: casually mention having complied with their ground rules for presentation. Because in all likelihood, to some degree, your competitors will have disregarded the prospect's wishes. This reminder will confirm your compatibility—and subtly imply that the others are lacking by comparison.

Overcoming Buyer Objections— Plus "Grabbers" to Make It Happen

◆ Perspective ◆ Four Excuses for Not Changing Suppliers
◆ Prospect Desirability ◆ Customer Endorsement
◆ Support Staff ◆ Compensation

Perspective

There are four basic excuses used by prospects for not buying from you. Here is what you are confronted with—and subsequently, how to overcome them.

1. No reason to change

2. The momentum factor

3. Functional familiarity

4. Emotional overlay

Beyond this, there are the following four factors by which a prospect is most influenced:

1. Your desire for their business

2. Impressive customer testimonials

3. Caliber of support staff offered

4. Appealing compensation system

Their favorable reaction to any one of these could persuade them to come around.

Four Excuses for Not Changing Suppliers

1. No Reason to Change

How many times have you put on a fine presentation, by which the prospect was apparently very impressed, only to be informed that "Actually we have no cause to drop our present supplier."

Obviously, this type needs to be given a *reason* to change. This can be accomplished with some finesse by furnishing them with a list of expectations for product benefits—and ways in which a supplier should serve them.

If for no other reason than curiosity, they will probably evaluate their present source. Such action is bound to reveal some inadequacies—and even problems. By contrast, your having supplied this service implies that these desirable standards represent *your* method of operation.

Euphemistically, this tactic could be described as "creating constructive dissatisfaction." If you have any concern as to the advisability of this approach, Leo Durocher was right when he said, "Nice guys finish last."

2. The Momentum Factor

Prospects fear that change would be disruptive, complicating their operation, and causing downtime that would have to be compensated for.

To minimize this apprehension, register how your support activity will provide a smooth transition. And stress how the advantages of your product or service will considerably offset the modest inconvenience that may occur.

3. Functional Familiarity

Another reason for hesitating is the matter of familiarity. Prospects worry about how long it will take a new supplier to become sufficiently knowledgeable regarding their business.

Put their mind at ease by assuring them that you could be on stream from the moment you are awarded the account. As evidence, provide a timetable, detailing the specific dates by which you will contribute to their operation. This would include what they will receive—and how they would benefit from it.

I've seen a few instances in which agencies wrap up their presentations by revealing a big bar chart. And then they announce, "If we are awarded your account by March 15, you will receive copy and layout by April 1, first proofs by April 15," etc. To the prospect, this graphic visually confirms that these people are set to go.

66 There is much to be said for being wanted. 99

In fact, that is how Ketchum in Pittsburgh got Westinghouse. After explaining this bar chart, they were interrupted and asked to leave the room and wait outside. The agency's reaction was, "How the hell did we screw up?" However, after a brief period, Westinghouse called them back in and inquired, "Can you spend the rest of the day here?" Ketchum, puzzled, replied, "Sure, but why?" And Westinghouse said, "Well, apparently you're ready to go to work right now. So you've got our business."

4. Emotional Overlay

Finally, a prospect will stall because of the discomfort caused by the emotionalism experienced. The prospect wants empathy, understanding—and assurance that they would be doing the right thing by switching suppliers.

Thus, when a prospect seems inclined to change, but you can't quite get them to the alter, help justify why this action should be taken (both corporately and personally). But remember, even if you convince them of the need for a different supplier, you still have to create the desire for *your* company.

By contrast, what if the prospect digs in his heels and snaps, "We'll switch suppliers when there is an earthquake here." Okay, take out earthquake insurance on them—with your company as beneficiary—and send them the policy. The agency that did this didn't score right then. But one year later, when the account was ready to move, this agency was the first one contacted.

Prospect Desirability

The variety of inducements offered prospects by suppliers is probably infinite—all striving to be so unique and appealing as to be irresistible.

However, any inducement other than telling them what they want to know most just clouds the issue. Instead, as I've recommended, spell out up front in your presentation: "Here are the six reasons (or five or seven) why my product (service) can best fulfill your requirements."

Then build to a climax in the wrap-up with: "Here are the six reasons, (or five or seven), why we want your business." Because a prospect doesn't care how much you know until they know how much you care. They view this explanation as indicative of the desired attitude and effort they could expect if you were awarded their account.

Besides whatever reasons you may want to cite, your list should include these two basics:

◆ Make a point of the prospect being especially *desirable* to you. There is much to be said for being wanted. ("Your account would be an exciting one to work on!")

◆ Stress their *importance* to you—with specific reasons why, for credibility. Importance stresses the measurable. ("Your account would be our second largest one!")

Emphasizing these two matters can be very impressive because a key cause for customer dissatisfaction is their assumption that they are taken for granted.

Rather than the usual selling practice of concentrating on why they should want you, this flip-side approach reveals your incentives for being valuable to them. And this desire provides another justification for buying your product or service.

Customer Endorsement

The most impressive tactic in selling is proof of customer satisfaction. Regardless of how great a job you've done for a customer, a prospect considers it only as good as the customer's reaction to it.

Customer endorsement can be communicated in a variety of ways. These range from basic approaches that can be easily used to more ambitious or imaginative ones. The circumstances will determine which of the following options would be most appropriate.

1. *Testimonial letters:* This is the usual evidence. The prospect assumes you must have garnered some of these by now. Thus, this standard, impersonal approach is the least influential.

2. *The slide-audiotape technique:* Projecting the customer's photo on a screen, accompanied by a voice-over pitch extolling your virtues, is a good makeshift means for conveying authenticity.

3. *Videotape:* Today, this has proved to be the most impressive approach. Depicting the customer actually expressing his or her pleasure with your operation is much more effective—and believable.

4. *Participation:* Customer's direct participation in the presentation on your behalf can have considerable impact if staged properly. (But remember, the prospect's main concern is with who will be working on their account.)

The state of the art in the use of clients is applied by a Los Angeles agency. The highlight of their pitch is called "Meet the Client." This consists of installing a closed circuit TV hook-up at the offices of three key clients. At a predetermined time in the presentation, the prospect is invited to ask any of the clients why they selected and continue to retain this agency. (The clients will presumably follow the script provided.)

5. Finally, here is how you can best capitalize on a customer's respect for your company:

The usual practice is to offer the prospect a list of impressive (safe) customers and say, "Call any of them; they all love us." But why should the prospect call? The burden of proof is your responsibility.

Here is an intriguing alternative. Ask the prospect if you can have three of your customers phone *them*. Sure it's rigged, but no more than any other customer testimonial.

This strategy registers that you have customers who think so highly of your operation and product or service that they are actually willing to promote it to other companies. What greater evidence is there of their satisfaction with you?

One important warning, though. If you are going to use a customer personality to tout your company, be sure this person isn't controversial or someone who might antagonize the prospect. I ran into this just recently. The customer endorser was outstanding. But unbeknownst to the soliciting supplier, the prospect hated him. And the advantage backfired. Admittedly, you can never be really certain of one person's appeal to another. However, if there is the remotest doubt regarding compatibility, scrub your first choice in favor of a less risky one.

In the final analysis, to what extent can you exploit customer influence? Obviously that depends on the status of your relationship with them. And on your using the option most appropriate to the circumstances—in the most logical, least contrived manner.

Support Staff

Regardless of how personable you may be, a customer will not accept being totally dependent on any single individual. They expect that there will also be an across-the-board support staff to deal with all of their needs. Thus, a highly appealing inducement to prospects is offering to assemble the best team for their purposes—consisting of their kind of people. Your promise to take such action not only fulfills the requirement of proficiency—but also satisfies their desire for the right chemistry.

This has been proved time and again when I'm consulting to advertisers on ad agency selection. Understandably, the one chosen will have a considerable effect

66 What you are ultimately selling is the people responsible for your product or service. 99

on sales. Therefore, advertiser attitude toward which agency they will hire is also pertinent to you. After these meetings, I always ask the reason for the choice they've made. At first I'm told, "They seemed right." Or, "They felt good." The advertiser has answered but hasn't really said anything until explaining, "I think I can live with them." This is usually followed with the final justification: "I believe they'll be good for me."

It boils down to this. Unless your company has totally converted to robotics, what you are ultimately selling is the people responsible for your product or service. And it is their performance that the prospect is buying.

Now for the application of this concept—and why. A prospect being pitched may be vulnerable, or planning to change because of dissatisfaction with the type and amount of support they have received. Granted, a customer will usually assume that they are not getting enough attention. However, they may also have misgivings about the caliber of supplier personnel assigned, and their turnover. Or worse, they may suspect that their account is being used as a training ground for your new or junior employees.

The customer has invested in their supplier team becoming functionally familiar with the account. When this has been achieved, and the customer is satisfied with the relationship and performance, they now want *stability*. In essence, they are buying a total supplier, and feel entitled to whatever personnel, functions, and facilities they need.

The prospect's first concern is with which individuals will be assigned to them, who—specifically—will be responsible for each function on their account. So, in presentation, assure the prospect that those present from your company will be *their own team*—not a swat team sent to the presentation for the kill, that they will never see or have access to again.

This matter may seem minor to you, but it isn't to the prospect. So make this commitment up front—if you want them to do likewise.

Compensation

Suppliers will use a variety of financial inducements in attempting to close a sale. This could be for any of the following reasons:

♦ Needing cash flow when first starting out

♦ Wanting to break into an industry with which they haven't been previously involved

♦ Being anxious for an account that would enhance their reputation

♦ Competing under such rugged conditions

Suppliers may assume the most appealing incentive is money. But it is also the most dangerous. Specifically, sometimes I am asked, "Should we offer the inducement of working on a break-even basis for the first year? This recognizes that a supplier has to go to school on them for that period."

Never! As I stated before, this concession has a negative connotation. Further, it is an admission of inadequacy. And finally, by this act, you're demonstrating that your only interest is in money. A year later, it would be tough to hit them for enough of a price increase for you to achieve a satisfactory profit because you have already demonstrated your willingness to sacrifice profit. Now it is just a matter of the customer determining the extent to which you'll shaft yourself again.

The ultimate variation on this theme was tried recently by an agency in the southwest. The bait used in promotion was: "We will prove our worth by performing any project that costs up to $2,750—free!"

What happened? The agency reported that it generated "considerable awareness." How about additional business? None. Because the agency didn't specify to prospects what they could do for them. And worse, it established a value for their work: zilch.

Whatever the income-cutting device, it characterizes the seller as being, to some degree, desperate. Prospects think of them as one that can be had. However, as a customer they want to be associated with a winner. So while you may land a few small fish, you won't get the catch desired! Because the overall impression made is that of a supplier whose work isn't good enough to be priced accordingly.

Remember, there is only one financial incentive for a prospect: the *price/value ratio* of your product or service—not your willingness to give it away. Therefore, the inducement of your investment spending should be in the people you provide and in the improvements you make to your product or service—not in cutting legitimate charges.

I didn't venture into the subjects of price and value without realizing that these are determined by management policy—which is probably out of your realm. Nevertheless, they are counting on you to execute their game plan. Being in the trenches, you may conclude that what is played in the office won't score in the field. If you adopt an "ours is not to reason why" attitude, management will assume you concur with whatever pricing strategy is developed. Then, if it's been

66 Whatever the income-cutting device, it characterizes the seller as being desperate. 99

miscalculated, any failure won't be attributed to the headquarters' plan. Instead, since there wasn't any objection or criticism, it evidently must be your fault.

So if you have any reservations, speak up from where the sales are made—not planned. Even if your hands-on experience isn't accepted, it is less likely you will be blamed if you are on record. What about risk? If pricing strategy that is off target will cost you sales, the hand plays itself. Anyway, your input for preventing a blunder or correcting the course can make you a hero in the most important area: *money*—some of which could be used to reward you.

Finally, for whatever the financial incentive considered, it is essential that you have a sense of the person to whom it would be offered. What is likely to impress or offend that individual?

Here is why you need know in advance how he or she would react to your bait. It is based on the overture by the head of a New York city agency to a wavering prospect. His shop was one of the two finalists. Having exhausted all rationales to break the stalemate, the agency president decided to appeal to his contact's professional pride. The dialogue went like this:

Agency: "If you select us, how would you like to write your ads on the account?

Prospect: "I don't know how to write ads."

Agency: "You know how to write an invoice, don't you?"

Prospect: "If that's the case, why don't you just pay me in cash?"

Agency: "What the hell do you take me for?"

The offer left little doubt. Yet, the agency president vehemently defended his pristine integrity right through Chapter 11 as to how he was perceived.

So be scrupulously careful about the kinds of financial inducements you offer—and to whom. For whatever angle occurs, play Devil's Advocate. Otherwise, in this crapshoot, you'll lose more than the dice.

You've planned for everything that can be expected in your solicitation activity. Everything except the unexpected. However, if you're caught flat-footed by a prospect's misgivings, it can cost you the sale. To prevent a sale from slipping from your grasp, anticipate, play devil's advocate, apply Murphy's Law—whatever it will take for you to counter any reservations. In effect, prepare for surprises—so you can actually use them to your advantage.

Section VI

The Extra Mile

The activity you undertake between presentation and the prospect's decision can probably make the difference between winning and coming in second.

The initiative necessary won't be exhibited by the order-taker. This is the one who makes their product or service available. By contrast, the person who is sales driven scores—because he or she creates *want* for their product or service.

This gung ho attitude especially applies during this white-knuckle period. It begins with your realizing that this isn't waiting time. Instead, it is your opportunity to become preferable to your competitors. Thus, when the others slack off, take a final shot at making yourself more memorable—favorably so.

But how are you going to come up with the fabulous idea necessary to clinch the sale? Recognize that you're not a one-man band—nor are you expected to be. There is an entire marketing machine backing you up. They are depending on you to bring in the business to keep them employed. So you can bet the ranch that they will be more than willing to assist you in this respect. So think of generating ideas as a networking procedure instead of a lonely, heavy-duty chore.

In addition, your initiative and follow-through, of itself, is very impressive to prospects because these are two key attributes sought by them.

To enable you to lead from strength during this final stage, these four chapters divulge what succeeds or fails:

24

The Follow-Up That Pays Off

◆ Perspective ◆ The Discussion Following Presentation
◆ Critique ◆ Misgivings/Regrets ◆ Pre-Finals Activities
◆ Pre-Finals Inducement ◆ Post-Finals Activities
◆ Post-Performance Gimmicks ◆ Post-Winning Devices

Perspective

One matter has become increasingly evident regarding how prospects select suppliers. There are certain aspects of solicitation activity to which they attach more importance than you might expect (i.e., presentation materials, "leavers"). Of themselves, these may not seem crucial. But if a tie-breaker is needed, the prospect's impression of any of these factors could tip the scale either way.

One aspect that is particularly important is the discussion that takes place after the presentation. Prospects are strongly influenced by the way you handle yourself. They believe that the spontaneity of this phase strips away the veneer—revealing your actual personality and method of operation. To prepare you for this phase, this chapter will deal with the three matters of greatest consequence—from which most conversation will emanate.

Prospects are also very sensitive to your activity between presentation and purchase. Your conduct during this delicate period can either improve your chances—or blow them.

66 As to identifying your company's worst fault, don't be a masochist. 99

The Discussion Following Presentation

Grilling

It is axiomatic that your objective is to sell—and that of the prospect is to buy. They realize that their responsibility goes beyond merely relying on your sales pitch. Thus, they will probe—and even bait—to help themselves make a decision.

Your best strategy is to expect a trapping effort—and to be prepared for it. Because this book can't be endless, I can't give you an extensive list of zingers to watch out for. But some examples are when they zap you with "What do you consider to be your company's worst fault?" Or "Explain a recent failure of yours." Or "Other than yourselves, if you were us, which one of the following products/services would you select?" These are cheap shots. And despite the temptation to counterpunch, keep cool. Give them a straightforward answer and you'll be home safe.

As to identifying your company's worst fault, don't be a masochist. Don't assume that conceding some shortcoming will make all else said more believable. Dead wrong! Don't ever bare your soul by admitting to anything that could cause the prospect to doubt the value of your company.

In regard to confessing to a failure, you have a legitimate response in, "If this occurred, it would involve confidential customer information which we could not reveal. This is the same protection we would afford you as a customer." If this answer isn't acceptable, neither are they. Because there isn't a court in the country that would require you to testify against yourself.

As to which product or service *you* would select, you can logically state: "Much of the judgment needs to be based on their presentations. Not having seen any of them, all I can offer is a subjective opinion. And you need one better informed than that."

Your greatest incentive for these honest answers is that if a single reply smacks of double talk, your best effort will have been just that. For that matter, if you even hesitate, you will be more than proverbially lost. That is what happened to the agency that was informed of being the front runner for the Cadillac Dealers Association account in a major market.

Seeking final evidence of the agency's good faith, the association chairman asked the agency the toughest question you might be confronted with. He began by acknowledging, "We realize our account is desirable from a prestige standpoint. But we are also aware that the Chevy, Ford, Toyota, and Honda Dealer Associations spend a helluva lot more money that we do." Then he turned the screw with, "If as a result of the fine job you do for us, the opportunity arises for you to get one of them, would you drop us?" The agency president snapped right back with: "Well, we-uh-er-we . . ." and the chairman said, "Don't call us . . ." You know the rest.

Obviously, the only answer to that is an honest one. Namely, "As long as our relationship continues to be satisfactorily profitable and desirable, we would have no interest in a competitive account."

Don't shrug off this case history because you're not restricted to non-competitive accounts. The point is still well made: you need to be prepared for even the farthest out question. To the prospect, your response to this question may be the deciding factor. Significantly, in addition to *what* is said in your response, the prospect is also affected by *how* you answer their questions. This indicates to them whether they would be getting a cohesive team—and how well organized it would be.

So prepare for this "informal" phase as diligently as you do for the structured presentation. Specifically, in the case of a team effort, all prospect inquiries should be accepted by the same person (usually your top executive present) who would hand them off to the member best qualified to reply. This procedure precludes any unauthoritative answers being blurted out, and it prevents contradictions—both of which make your team seem like it doesn't know what it is doing.

So don't win the game at bat and lose it in the field. Practice. There is much to be said for defense, too.

Supplier Involvement

Much is made by the prospect of wanting more supplier involvement. And in your eagerness to get the business, you heartily concur—and say something profound like, "Oh yeah!"

Okay, you registered your good intentions. Now better find out precisely what is meant by this vague phrase. It could range from being available when phoned to coming to their office on an instant's notice.

Based on estimated income, projected workload, and the dollar profit goal you have established, determine the extent to which you can *afford* to become involved. Further, decide on whether any additional involvement would generate enough extra income to be worthwhile. This information will also enable you to convey more believably how much you *can* do for them (i.e., in respect to preferential treatment, price concessions, inventory warehousing, etc.).

Compensation

The tenderest matter that will come up in post-presentation discussion is that of payment for your product or service. Recognize that the prospect has become more knowledgeable regarding supplier finances. They are fairly well acquainted with the current price/product or service ratio.

So when negotiating compensation, while being aware of their growing insight, constantly bear in mind that your objective is to produce profitable income as skillfully as you produce your product or service.

It's recognized that payment practices vary widely among industries. Thus, whether its based on straight commission, fee, cost-plus or any combination thereof—there is only one kind of good marriage for you. And this doesn't mean just marrying for money. It means marrying for *enough* money.

Critique

Agencies estimate that they should close on approximately one out of nine solicitations. After receiving the input provided in this book though, I have been told the hit ratio can be tripled to one in three.

A very important practice for contributing to at least this projected record is conducting a thick-skinned critique after every presentation. This should be scheduled soon enough that all matters are still fresh in everyone's mind. Imperative to the critique's value is the realization that this is not a witch hunt. Rather, it is a means for objectively determining how your future presentations can be improved. What you are looking for is twofold:

◆   Better reaction to subjects and materials

◆   More effective use of team members

If, for the most part, you sell solo, don't rule out this assessment. You can still be introspective, and probably more effective because you can come down on yourself as hard as necessary without any fear of embarrassment.

These sessions usually consist of the participants congratulating each other on their outstanding performance. This ritual is conducted for job security. Keep it short—and get on with evaluating the presentation experience. Then, since this is not intended to be merely a bull session, provide for the application of what you have learned by assigning responsibility for follow-through.

The findings of this post-mortem, implemented as necessary, can significantly increase the potency of subsequent solicitations. This discipline will also preclude becoming complacent or stale, either individually or as a group.

This procedure is the second half of the one-two assessment of your presentation. In the first phase, *rehearsal*, it was critically evaluated prior to actual performance. And improvements were made beforehand—while they could still benefit

66 Don't win the game at bat and lose it in the field. 99

you. The payoff punch, *post-mortem*, will reveal what needs to be done to strengthen the impression made hereafter. How important is this? Since you're selling for a living, you'd better believe in the hereafter.

So pre-test and post-test your sales pitch. After all, its for your most important customer: your company.

Misgivings/Regrets

In the post-presentation critique, the warts and wrinkles show up. Invariably, it is discovered there were some sins of omission and commission that lessened your effectiveness. This involves matters such as

◆ Your people who should or should not have participated in the presentation

◆ Too much or too little attention paid to the various members of the buying committee

◆ Changes in sequences and emphasis on subject

◆ Need for more and better visuals and props to explain and enhance your message

◆ Greater amount and intensity of rehearsal.

Then regret sets in. And a lot of sentences begin with "If only. . ." The next reaction consists of wondering whether to write a letter to the prospect to compensate for these shortcomings, or to request another shot at it—for whatever contrived reason.

Never. Both tactics are negative. The letter calls attention to something being wrong—which the prospect may not have perceived as such. And as to a repeat performance, it is suspect. Your follow-through activity should not cast any doubt whatsoever on the worth of your pitch, or product or service.

If however, your misgivings are that strong, any subsequent effort should be strictly positive and constructive. Further, whatever your communication, it must be of value to the prospect. Otherwise, it is considered a self-serving gimmick—

resulting in a loss of respect for you. Thus, any supplementary activity should come across as leading from strength—not compensating for weakness. As to specific action, these are detailed under "Post-Finals Activity."

Pre-Finals Activities

There are many instances in which a prospect will consider a broad spectrum of suppliers. From these they will narrow down the list to the finalists from which selection will be made.

Congratulations: you just made the short list. Your product or service is still in contention. Is there anything you can do between now and the final pitches to improve your position? There sure is. But first, let's consider the circumstances at this time. Upon selecting the finalists, the prospect may speculate (with some justification) that little difference could be expected in product or service quality and support activity.

Now the chemistry factor comes into play. Which supplier would wear well? Who would make them look good? At this stage, the matter of relationship becomes increasingly important. Therefore, at this point, greater emphasis should be placed on the team to be assigned to the account, in particular, their appropriateness to the prospect and their compatibility.

Of course, your people will be platformed in the presentation in the most appealing manner. Further, they should be highlighted in your "leaver"—in a warm, pertinent way, featured as persons rather than functionaries. Beyond this, develop means for creating preference for your people during this sensitive period. For instance, here is an idea that will particularly impress the prospect. Try to engineer this. It beats chopped liver.

Provide the prospect with a videotape, (approximately ten minutes), to be delivered several days prior to the final presentation. (Loan them a VCR if necessary.) This would feature your forthcoming participants, each of whom would speak on the theme: "I asked to work on your account. Here's why." The desire expressed to achieve on their behalf will create not only familiarity, but also acceptance for your presenters in advance. Since the prospect's attitude toward

❝ For any promotional device, the more imaginative it is, the greater the risk of it backfiring. ❞

the finalists is skewed more toward the human equation, satisfying this concern is bound to influence them in your favor.

Having softened the prospect with this warmer-upper, you will want to take whatever other action you can to enhance your appeal as a finalist. Circumstances may trigger an idea that is a blast—and begging to be used. However, for any promotional device, the more imaginative it is, the greater the risk of it backfiring. Thus, for a favorable reaction, it is essential that you know the character of the prospect representatives for whom it is intended.

There is no better evidence of the validity of this advice than the experience of the Della-Femina-Travisano agency when pitching Kohler Company. Upon being selected as one of the three finalists for the $5,000,000 account, the agency came up with a hilarious thought. What materialized was an ad in the *Sheboygan Press* (Kohler's headquarters city). It contained a photo of the agency's president, Jerry Della Femina, in a bathtub (assumedly a Kohler product). The headline featured this prospect's theme: "The bold look of Kohler." And was followed by, "The bald look of Della Femina. They belong together."

Anyone with the remotest sense of humor would have to love it. But Kohler is very straight. Straight-straight. So before the ink was dry on the ad, Kohler notified this agency not to return for the final presentation.

The lesson here is, for whatever the device, be sure you're on the same wavelength as the prospect—or both of you will be turned off.

Pre-Finals Inducement

You have just survived the baptism of fire in the screening of all suppliers. Now comes the shootout: the finals. You've made the cut; now make the difference. Wouldn't it be great if you could skip OK Corral and just put another notch on your gun?

You can—by tantalizing the prospect with your development of a marketing idea so dynamic that it shouldn't be held until the scheduled series of final pitches. In fact, waiting until the formality of the other suppliers' presentations would result in sacrificing substantial potential sales. Inquire as to how soon you can present this irresistible opportunity. (Of course, your idea had better be plenty damn good.)

Here is one that met this standard—and aced out their competitors. The co-op account for a national fast-food chain in a major market opened up. After the make-work procedure of a cattle call, they netted down to four finalists. Since the account was worth several million in billings (which could pay for a lot of hamburgers) it was worth going the extra mile. But how, without violating the traditional ground rules?

It so happened that the prospect's major push—a breakfast promotion—wasn't getting off the ground. Coincidentally, one of the remaining candidates had the morning newspaper as a client. What could be more of a natural than a free copy

❝ Play the game. But control it by supplying the bat and ball.❞

with breakfast at any of these outlets? The newspaper was delighted to participate because of the heavy advertising exposure and trial this tie-in would provide. And the fast food co-op flipped—so much so that they awarded their account to the agency that had taken this initiative. The others were still preparing for the finals—which never occurred.

Granted, it is unlikely you're in a position to arrange such a complex maneuver. However, the *concept* is right—and possible. Surely you can come up with some means to compound the situation. Going the distance is expected. It's whomever goes the extra mile that gets the sale. So, *think like a winner*: boldly, imaginatively—and clincher-oriented.

So sure, play the game. But control it by supplying the bat and ball.

Post-Finals Activities

The time between final presentation and selection is the most delicate period in the solicitation process. To the prospect, your activity during this phase can be the final influence as to whether you rate thumbs up or down. From your standpoint, you want to do something so impressive that it will clinch your being chosen. However, because there was a fine reaction to your presentation, you don't want to risk an impetuous device that might queer it. Since your pitch isn't over until the fat prospect sings, here is what your reprise shouldn't and should do.

Employing a do-nothing strategy to be discreet will accomplish just that—nothing. Yet, a prospect doesn't like to be hustled. (This is because he or she doesn't want to appear to associates as being on the take.) Thus, while more than silent prayer is necessary, don't resort to any subterfuge in using their people—or any transparently clever devices. Instead, here are two safe, yet effective, tactics that you can apply that will distinguish you from competitors—and enhance the favorable effect of your presentation.

The first tactic consists of assuming that all presentations wound up in a tie. Now, what kind of tie-breaker can you come up with that will make you preferable to the others? Nothing cutesy—or that might be demeaning. Rather, when critiquing your presentation, determine what the prospect's hot button was. What tender nerve did they reveal? Then take whatever ethical action to register final proof of your sensitivity to their needs—and why your company can best satisfy them.

Second, during this critique session, also objectively identify what aspects of your presentation received a favorable reaction. Then follow through by capitalizing on these strengths in a letter to the prospect: briefly, imaginatively, and in a businesslike manner. The payoff is that you are confirming the soundness of their judgement.

Of course, personal contact with the prospect can be especially valuable. However, during this decision-making period, the prospect's relationship with the potential suppliers must be very circumspect. They need to come across as being totally objective—unable to be had. Therefore, your follow-through must never give the impression of being romance designed to influence them beyond legitimate considerations. Rather, whatever contact suggested should be vital to their business needs.

Post-Performance Gimmicks

Usually, gimmicks should be forbidden. However, there are exceptions. They can be justified when they are able to make your point in an especially appealing manner—as interpreted by the prospect. The concept needs to be relevant, and in good taste—a sense of humor also helps.

One example involves a major loose account which was coveted by an agency too small for consideration. This "David" agency felt that while they did not have the size, they had the firepower. Therefore, the "Goliath" account was worth their best shot. Afterwards, although the prospect was very impressed—and liked them—there was no way of rationalizing awarding so large an account to an agency of such modest size.

Yet, even though they'd been rejected, the reception was so good, the agency couldn't accept defeat. Anyway, they reasoned that landing even a portion of this account would be great for them. So, after all the presentations had been made, and the advertiser was getting the selection process underway, the agency sent them a freshly baked pie with the enclosed note: "Save us a piece."

No mistaking the message. Nothing suspect about it. And it was both figuratively and literally in good taste. There was a happy ending: The agency got a "piece" commensurate with their size—and are living with this client happily ever after.

This experience certainly proves that a promotional effort needn't be extravagant or a hoopla event to succeed. And significantly, it is something that you too can dream up and implement. Because sometimes the simplest novel communication of your message can be the most potent.

Post-Winning Devices

Granted, you begin to lose an account the day you win it. But this shouldn't actually happen the *first* day. Yet, there isn't any grace period during which you are safe. You're on probation from the outset. So don't mistake a new customer's surface cordiality for acceptance.

Since your conduct and back-up support determine the duration of the honeymoon, think twice about using any device to launch your relationship, such as a contrived final shot to confirm the soundness of their judgement in having selected your product or service.

This was learned the hard way by an upstate New York agency. They were jubilant in landing a major baking account, because it became by far their biggest client. The victory wasn't enough for them, though. They felt compelled to further prove their desirability.

Thus, upon receiving the good news, the agency decided to immediately deliver tangible evidence of their devotion. And to no less than the new client's CEO. Unfortunately, they got "creative." The vehicle was appropriate, a box of biscuits. However, the message inserted cost the agency its dough: "We'll work our buns off for you."

The new client CEO was appalled by the agency's bad taste and promptly notified them of being persona non grata. And within 24 hours, the agency went from the pinnacle to the pits.

There are a couple of often overlooked lessons that need to be relearned:

◆ Never risk a gimmick with someone you hardly know.

◆ If a gimmick could be construed as cutesy, don't try it with *anyone*.

If, upon winning, you're tempted to follow through with a post-clincher, heed the astute advice of Mies Van Der Rohe: "Less is more."

In conclusion, it's during this period between presentation and purchase that you finally establish whether you are a professional or an order-taker, an initiator or an implementer. And if you are their kind of people. Thus, use this crucial period as a clincher—in an imaginative, pertinent manner. Yet, while the only risk is in playing it safe, apply mature judgement in representing your company, your product or service, and yourself as being preferable to any other.

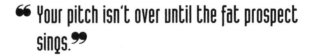

❝ Your pitch isn't over until the fat prospect sings.❞

How the Buying Process Works—
And Your Options

◆ Perspective ◆ Sum of Activity Required to Win
◆ Prospect Criteria ◆ Actual Procedure ◆ Alternative to Losing ◆
◆ Learn from Losses ◆ Stay in Touch

Perspective

This brings us to the bottom line: product/service purchase. How does this process *really* work? I am not going to give you the published scientific procedure. Usually that is just given lip service.

Instead, here is what actually happens, what to do about it—and what your options are if you don't score.

Sum of Activity Required to Win

But first, there is a deadly strain of selling myopia against which you need to be inoculated. The most frequent question I am asked about the new business operation is, "What is the best presentation?"

This question presumes that for all practical purposes supplier selection is based entirely on the presentation. But

◆ If your initial contact isn't sufficiently intriguing, and

◆ there isn't persistent follow-through, and

66 You can only be defeated if you accept defeat. 99

♦ the pre-presentation meeting isn't conducted in the most impressive manner,

there won't be any presentation. Further, if you don't prepare to win with respect to

♦ Prospect research,

♦ Presentation graphics,

♦ Buyer involvement, and

♦ Rehearsal,

you won't make the cut.

Of course, the best presentation is one that is most appropriate to the prospect and the circumstances. Even so, it still takes

♦ A compelling "leaver,"

♦ an appealing tour of your facilities, and

♦ shrewd post-presentation activity

in order to win.

So as dynamic as your presentation may be, if the other components of your solicitation activity don't measure up, your show will close on opening night—in Peoria.

Prospect Criteria

Prospect purchases are governed by a variety of buying requirements and specifications. That's no surprise. However, where they rank in influencing product/service selection may jolt you. The prospect's buying decision nets down to their gut response to these four questions—in the following order of importance:

1. "Did you believe him or her?"

2. "Is she or he our kind of people?"

3. "Does he or she know our business?"

4. "Does their company produce a better product (service) at the best value?"

This sequence may strike you as heresy. But if you don't first satisfy the prospect in regard to honesty, compatibility, and expertise, they won't *believe* your company can produce a better product or service at the best value.

Actual Procedure

After they have applied these criteria, do you know how prospects select the winning supplier? They don't. It's too tough for them to pick #1. Instead, the losers are methodically eliminated—from which the winner coincidentally emerges. That's why sometimes the winning supplier is the one whose salesperson made the fewest mistakes.

Alternative to Losing

If the worst happens, and you don't make the cut, ask for another chance. Or if you are eliminated in the finals *before* the winner is selected—again, ask for another crack at it.

Are you above this? The biggest US-based agency, Young & Rubicam, isn't. In both instances, they ask. And sometimes they get this concession—and the account. This tactic was spawned by the belief that you can only be defeated if you accept defeat.

Try it. This gutsy attitude can work as well for you, too.

Learn from Losses

If you don't score, the experience needn't be a total loss. There must be something you can learn from this experience which will make you more appealing next time.

Whenever a sale is lost, try to flush out why the winner was preferable. Here is an easy and productive tactic for doing so. Contact and congratulate the prospect—acknowledging you respect that they did what seemed to be in their best

66 The shame is not in falling down; it's in not trying to get up. 99

interest. Having established this favorable environment, inquire as to the reason for their selection. Because of pride in their judgment, they will generally reveal enough to provide the insight you need.

By contrast, *never* probe as to why you lost. This creates an adversarial situation in which they become defensive—and either refuse to answer or provide misleading information. In the follow-through, remember: your motive is not to find an excuse for losing, but to seek that key clue for winning.

Stay in Touch

You've lost the sale. You're down—but not out. Your first course of action should be: *stay in touch.*

Even though prospects prefer to believe they are infallible in supplier selection, sometimes they discover three months later that they made a bum choice. When this occurs, it is impractical and unnecessary for them to go through the entire search process again. Being unable to afford further disruption, they will move quickly and pick from the previous finalists. And since each has already given the prospect its full treatment, it now comes down to just a beauty contest.

However, by your maintaining top-of-mind awareness and interest in them during this traumatic period, the prospect will be more comfortable with you. And they will love you even more on the rebound.

By now, you've taken every conceivable action to win the business. Thus, for solicitation purposes, there isn't anything left to do.

Except if you lose. Then, as discussed, it's a matter of applying what you learned so as to increase your appeal next time.

Even more important, though, is your mental state afterwards. Granted, show me a good loser and I'll show you a loser. Yet, you still need maintain a mature attitude and, not become unglued. Instead, harness the emotional juices this experience has released—and rededicate yourself to succeeding. As is said, "The shame is not in falling down, it's in not trying to get up."

26

Summary of the Guts of a Program That Sells

There you have it: the top-of-line set of clubs. However, as I mentioned, you still have to play them. Now, in order to win, let's recap the set you need to have in your bag to go out on the selling course.

I will admit to having taken some license: I am recommending fifteen clubs and the U.S.G.A. only allows fourteen. But on your tour, you can't afford to miss a single shot. So here goes. Fore!

◆ Set goals: for dollar growth and consistent missionary presentations.

◆ Institute a total company team concept.

◆ Prepare a Marketing Plan.

◆ Survey employees for their perception of your company's strengths and weaknesses in regard to personnel and operations.

◆ Create a Unique Selling Proposition.

◆ Implement a rifle/buckshot strategy for prospecting.

◆ Institute a system for keeping informed of a prospect's susceptibility to change.

◆ Set target dates for planning your selling program, developing prospects, and exploiting leads.

◆ Prepare an introductory letter for getting an initial appointment.

◆ Establish a format for the conduct of the pre-presentation meeting.

◆ Decide on the content for the prospect factbook.

◆ Design your company look for presentation, "leaver," and agenda.

◆ Plan the tour of your facilities.

◆ Prepare an emergency kit to be taken to presentations.

◆ Develop a post-presentation critique.

If you are this organized and prepared, you won't have to default on a desirable prospect because you're too busy to make the 100 percent effort required. Having these basics on line, your work will be mostly a matter of *customizing* rather than starting from scratch. Therefore, you should never have to forfeit a game due to lack of equipment.

As I promised, you have now landed the most important customer you will ever have. Your company. Thus, this completes the revelations on selling that works.

But it is the beginning of your opportunity. If you take advantage of this input, it can be one of the best investments you can make in your future. Otherwise, this book has been an expense.

Therefore, since experience is the comb that life gives you after you've lost your hair, use these "street smarts" *before* going bald.

Specifically, for the tested ideas furnished that you can individually capitalize on: *Go for it*. When higher stakes are involved, requiring management support: *Ask for it*. Implementers get paid only what the market requires. Innovators are *rewarded*—and there is no limit.

❝ Experience is the comb that life gives you after you've lost your hair. ❞

27

How to Keep Your Customers— And Your Job

◆ Perspective ◆ Developments Profoundly Affecting You
◆ Stay Exciting ◆ Provide for the People Factor
◆ Working Knowledge Needed
◆ Consider Your Contact's Ambitions and Security
◆ Rapport Is the Supplier's Responsibility ◆ Preventative Maintenance

Perspective

Congratulations!

Having read this far—and having become sales-driven—your sales performance should increase significantly. However, it's only as good as the duration for which the business won is kept. Anyone can sell something once. It is the repeat sales that count. Whatever you can contribute to retaining customers will compound your value because you associate yourself with what your company is all about: getting business and keeping it.

This involvement furnishes you with two personal benefits. First, when the opportunity for promotion occurs, your broader experience and dedication will make you preferable. The other side of the coin is that if economic conditions dictate a cutback in personnel, your versatility makes you less dispensable.

241

Therefore, the care and feeding of customers is as much your concern as landing them is. Although an entire book could be written on this subject, here is what is most critical for you to know.

Developments Profoundly Affecting You

Have you looked at your buyers lately? They are changing for better and for worse. He no longer wears a green eyeshade, sleeve garters—and plays it the company way. Rather, he or *she* is more sophisticated, better educated, and goal-oriented.

This new breed is no longer willing to function in their present capacity indefinitely, or to play it safe so as not to jeopardize their pension. Rather, these ranks are now being populated by gung ho MBA's anxious to make their mark. And to succeed, they expect you to make them look good. Granted, they will be tougher to deal with, but there will be less need to educate them. If you fail to accept that the buyer has come out of his or her cocoon, it will take more than a butterfly net to keep them.

As a result of these changes in buyer characteristics, a dramatic evolution is occurring in your relationship with them. There was a time when it was assumed buyers could be best dealt with by *satisfying* them. This consisted of fulfilling whatever their desires in respect to performance and relationship: faithfully implementing their direction on product or service requirements—and entertaining them as appropriate. Supposedly, this combined method of operation would result in a happy buyer—and thereby a safe one.

Then, with companies becoming increasingly confronted with rugged competitive conditions, buyers began to demand more involvement from their suppliers. And with the suppliers, the buzz word became *service*.

But now with the marketing function becoming so complex, your diligence in satisfying and servicing accounts is no longer enough. In addition, they want to be *challenged*. They want waves made—beyond what is strictly your job. Specifically, they want ideas and solutions from *your* perspective that will increase their product's appeal and sales. Because customers admittedly can't be objective, they are now expecting intriguing options and alternatives from you. Since it is such a jungle out there, this initiative has become a key requisite for customer retention.

❝ Always treat the customer like they are brand new. ❞

In the event you may mistake what I'm saying for rhetoric, here are a couple of substantiating examples. The first involves an agency making a new business missionary call on an account with one of the top ten agencies. They felt their chances were remote because the incumbent had a reputation for servicing their clients so intensively. However, the prospect was so appealing as to be worth trying to cultivate over an extended period.

Much to the soliciting agency's surprise, the prospect was quite receptive. This agency guessed out loud that it couldn't be due to inadequate service. And the advertiser said, "No way. Whatever we want, we get the previous day." Then the soliciting agency asked if the incumbent's vulnerability was caused by dissatisfaction with any of their functions (i.e., creative, media, research) And again the prospect said no, they were pleased with the incumbent's performance.

With some amount of exasperation, the soliciting agency asked, "Then why are you interested in leaving them?" And the prospect answered, "Because our present agency doesn't challenge us. They never ask, "How come you've always done it that way? Why don't you try it this way?"

Regardless of how great a job an incumbent is doing, they risk losing the client if they do not also *inspire* them. (This would be a good time to become introspective and determine the extent to which you are firing up *your* customers.)

The head of communications for a major oil company told me, "We've been with the same agency for over twenty years. And for all practical purposes, they are locked in." And he mused, "But I sure wish they would kick us in the ass now and then." Taking this into account, do you have the guts to rattle your customers' cages? Consider this. The Chinese use the same word for *challenge* and *opportunity*. Clever these Chinese.

Stay Exciting

A key reason your company was selected was because the account sensed an aura of dynamism about your operation—and about you individually. You must continuously work at maintaining this impression. How? Go back to when you first attempted to sell them. At that time you exuded success, confidence, enthusiasm—and promise. If any of these attributes begin to diminish, doubt arises. So stay exciting, certainly as much as you were in the presentation. That's what helped you get the account, and can be instrumental in keeping it for you.

I am making this point because of numerous customer references to the supplier's post-honeymoon letdown. They are extremely sensitive to any onset of this condition—and very cynical about expecting it to occur.

To minimize their suspicion, continuously conduct yourself as if you had just landed the account. Always treat the customer like they are brand new—staying ahead in challenging and servicing them—or they will become new for your competitor.

Provide for the People Factor

Your customer relations begin with the human equation. When your account was a prospect, your pledge to assemble the best team for their needs was a strong inducement for selecting your company.

Your intentions were honorable. Now your promise has to be tempered by what you can afford. Obviously, the income you receive from the account will determine the amount of employee salary you can allocate to it. Thus, the team assigned to the account is actually the best you can provide—under the circumstances.

But your competitors pitching this customer have put their top heavyweights on the soliciting team—irrespective of the cost of their actually being put on the account. Unfortunately, your customer takes this come-on literally. And your reality-based team may suffer by comparison. For this reason, your team has to perform over their heads to continuously give the impression of being better than whomever any other company has to offer.

Your company must also have the built-in flexibility of a professional sports team, knowing which of your players are best against theirs. This matter of compatibility can't be stressed strongly enough. Its importance is confirmed by one of the highest compliments paid by a customer: "Our supplier is willing to assemble the best team for our needs." Implicit in this statement is that exceptional performance is a given. In addition, as mentioned earlier in this book, they must be the customer's kind of people.

To what extent are you satisfying this up-front requirement for each customer? Your security begins with—and will last only as long as—the appeal of the team assigned to them.

Working Knowledge Needed

Can you adequately discuss the customer's business with them? Possibly not to the extent they would prefer. Having visited the factory several years ago is not good enough anymore. They now expect you to have a working knowledge of their company, industry, and market—in essence, whatever would affect their marketing activity. Your familiarity with these matters forms their primary basis of respect for you. This is because the customer believes that the quality of service received is in direct relation to your expertise in these areas.

So do your homework. Osmosis isn't enough. From the customer's standpoint, being a pro is knowing more than is expected of you. Developing this familiarity will enable you to anticipate changing conditions, and the customer's response to them—and be ready to contribute as appropriate. From a survival standpoint, it will reduce the number of bombshells dropped in your lap—and the danger of trying to defuse them.

Such being the case, have you stayed up to speed? Think back. In preparing for your solicitation, you explored their buying needs and objectives, and you probed as to their operating procedures and service expectations. It is now several years later. Hopefully you've been sensitive to the insidious onset of any post-honeymoon letdown. Even so, there have been some changes in the cast of characters—both at your place and theirs. Further, the customer's purchasing and service needs have also changed to some degree.

Do you have the same top-of-mind awareness of these vital matters as when you first pitched this business? To whatever extent their requirements have receded into your subconscious, you have become that much less effective—and less valuable.

You need to be continuously current on your customer's circumstances and desires—as much as when you first tried to make the most favorable impression. To guarantee more than a lip-service commitment, prepare a quarterly update on customer developments. Furnish a copy of this report to all personnel involved with the account. This will provide them with an ongoing familiarity with the customer's current mindset. In addition, it furnishes the discipline for you to operate in a present and projected environment—instead of reacting to outdated ones.

Stay as knowledgeable about each account as when you made your grand entrance. Otherwise, your obsolescence will hasten their exit.

Consider Your Contact's Ambitions and Security

Any treatment of the subject of customer retention needs to begin with their perspective. While your contact won't tell you what he or she *personally* expects of you, I can reveal this information from the most authoritative source, as a result of a jolting experience I had.

It happened at D'Arcy MacManus Masius in Bloomfield Hills, Michigan. They scheduled my shirt-sleeve session on "New Business"—after which I was invited back to conduct the follow-through session on "Client Retention." As their president, Jim Doyle, was walking me to the meeting room, he said "We don't have to go through the introductions again. You've already met the 35 people who are attending. Then, as we entered, he continued with, "all except one. Jack, shake hands with Gale Smith."

Being fairly impressionable, I was somewhat awed meeting this legend. Heading up advertising for Procter & Gamble and then General Motors during his 42-year career had earned him the title "Mr. Client."

After exchanging pleasantries, Gale asked, "What are you going to talk about?" I said, "Client Retention." He then asked, "How long will it take?" I told him, "Four hours." And he replied, "I can do it in four words."

At this point, I needed that zinger like Custer needed another Indian. Nevertheless, I chuckled through gritted teeth and headed to the podium. Undaunted,

Gale followed, grabbed my sleeve, and insisted, "I told you I can do it in four words." Not wanting to risk being sniped at in the session, I figured I'd better let him get it over with. So I begrudgingly asked, "Okay Gale, how would you cover the subject of client retention in four words?" And he said, "Make 'em look good."

It struck me: he is so right! Because you're not dealing with a corporate logo, or bricks and mortar, but with a person's ambitions and security.

In any business there is still the naive belief among some purists that keeping customers is the by-product of a job well done. But regardless of the quality of your product or service, keeping customers is a separate function that requires a steady effort as much as your tangible output.

Your sensitivity to your contact's career aspirations is where account longevity begins. So without minimizing your contribution, acknowledge the value of your customer contacts. Their jobs also depend on recognition, and this altruism can build the loyalty to extend account retention.

This attention particularly applies to their second echelon of "comers." Don't ignore them by concentrating entirely on cultivating those presently in authority. The line-ups are changing much more rapidly now. And it's taking much less time to go from rookie to star. So make sure to pay reasonable attention to those on their way up. For instance, when appropriate

◆ Send them copies of correspondence.

◆ Suggest they be included in meetings.

◆ While there, drop in to pay your respects.

◆ Compliment these "comers" to their superiors—and let them know.

Otherwise, when they get up to bat, you may find yourself out in left field without a glove.

Rapport Is the Supplier's Responsibility

Manufacturers ask me what it takes to achieve an acceptable relationship with their suppliers. Rather than offering any magic manipulative devices, I will surprise them by advising that they resolve any grievances before they become insurmountable. The usual response is, "If we're unhappy about anything, we're not bashful about making it known to our suppliers."

What was intended to pertain to *both* parties they interpreted in respect to themselves only. It has become apparent that few companies are concerned with rapport being a two-way street. The bright spot, though, is that they are receptive to another lane—if you build it. This involves determining what it will take to establish a compatible relationship—acceptable to both—and then taking whatever action necessary to consistently adhere to it.

66 Salespeople generally do a lousy job of justifying their worth to customers. 99

As a supplier, you can't afford not to. This was driven home by an experience at a very large drug firm, possibly one of the largest—using thirteen ad agencies. Their director of marketing services said to me, "We sure have a can of worms situation with our agencies. The account executives are bitter because they never get to see anybody above the brand manager level. And the brand managers have their noses out of joint because they aren't contacted by anyone beyond the AEs."

So I asked the obvious question, "What are you going to do about it?" And he indignantly replied, "What are *we* going to do about it? Our products have a home here. The agencies don't."

Was he behaving like a child? Maybe. But remember, he has the candy.

Like it or not, in your business, too, the supplier is considered responsible for establishing and maintaining the relationship. Since that is the way the game is played, determine whether the account is worth the ante—and whether you would be better off raising or folding.

Preventative Maintenance

The best strategy for keeping customers is the attitude expressed by the hard-nosed president of an Atlanta agency who has a remarkable record in this respect. As he put it, "If anyone can take an account from us, we deserve to lose it."

Granted, there can be situations beyond their control. Nevertheless, this concept of placing full responsibility on the agency keeps them constantly sensitive to the fragility of client tenure, and of the risk of complacency occurring, even insidiously. So if there is any deterioration in satisfaction with the agency, it isn't sloughed off as being the client's fault. As remote as this industry may be to yours, this strategy is directly relevant, and can work just as well for you, too.

Therefore, rather than being fatalistic, remember: the bottom line is keeping desirable accounts. Thus, it is worth the disciplined conduct this attitude requires—as opposed to reacting to conditions.

So *control* your destiny on accounts so they will last longer. Perpetuate whatever you are doing right. And continuously anticipate anything that can go wrong—promptly taking whatever corrective action is necessary. Then compound your defensive measures with the follow-through offense required to complete the job.

Salespeople generally do a lousy job of justifying their worth to customers. This activity usually ranges from insignificant to boring.

Inertia in this respect is the result of assuming that the customer can't help but be aware of and grateful for your outstanding performance. However, this presumes that you are the customer's only concern. The upshot is that those at the account have only varying degrees of indication of the amount of your effort on their behalf. To whatever extent you relax in promoting your operation to customers you increase the transient nature of this affiliation.

Therefore, even if you are too busy working for them to work on them, it takes *both* functions to keep customers: performance and protection. Which comes first? Your justification to accounts must begin with yourself. Because they first have to buy you before they will buy your product or service.

For this purpose, here is an idea for extending account longevity. One whose time has come.

Conduct an annual presentation to each customer, setting forth how the value of what you have to offer—corporately and personally—has been increased. In effect, this is *your* annual report.

Here is its content—and how it would benefit you:

◆ Cover how much more you have to offer them due to action taken to strengthen your company in respect to personnel, operations, new products and services. And from an individual standpoint, include whatever improvement due to further education and experience.

◆ Remind customers of the breadth of your product line or extent of your services—and why it would be to their advantage to purchase more of them. Yet remember, the customer, as with the prospect, is sold by the benefits, not the availability of what you can offer.

◆ Cite achievements for other accounts—particularly those whose application could also be of value to them.

You say nobody in sales does this sort of thing? Then going this extra mile offers a great opportunity to distinguish yourself from your multitude of competitors. Keeping customers is what your business is all about. And it is what makes the difference between being a peddler and being a star salesperson.

P.S.: You've just learned the easy way what all those mentioned learned the hard way. So now you can sell smarter rather than harder. Do so to increase *your* job longevity and income.

Index

About the Author

Jack L. Matthews got his hands dirty in the toughest- and most creative-selling league: Ad Agencies.

He was a quarter-century heavyweight at major agencies, managing multi-million dollar accounts. He also had key responsibility for the development and conduct of over 150 full-scale new business presentations.

Then, 20 years ago, he parlayed the success of this experience into forming a firm to pioneer in consulting on advertiser/agency relations. During this time he has been retained by 396 Agencies to conduct shirtsleeve sessions and counsel them on how to land the right new business, faster.

The tested ideas and solutions flushed out from this unique perspective can make the difference between the reader winning and coming in second.